THE HIDDEN ART

OF INTERVIEWING

PEOPLE

THE HIDDEN ART

OF INTERVIEWING

PEOPLE

How to get them to tell you the truth

Neil McPhee

and

Roger Terry

John Wiley & Sons, Ltd

Other Wiley Editorial Offices

John Wiley & Sons Inc., 111 River Street, Hoboken, NJ 07030, USA

Jossey-Bass, 989 Market Street, San Francisco, CA 94103-1741, USA

Wiley-VCH Verlag GmbH, Boschstr. 12, D-69469 Weinheim, Germany

John Wiley & Sons Australia Ltd, 42 McDougall Street, Milton, Queensland 4064,
Australia

John Wiley & Sons (Asia) Pte Ltd, 2 Clementi Loop #02-01, Jin Xing Distripark,
Singapore 129809

John Wiley & Sons Canada Ltd, 6045 Freemont Blvd, Mississauga, ONT, L5R 4J3,
Canada

Wiley also publishes its books in a variety of electronic formats. Some content that
appears in print may not be available in electronic books.

Anniversary Logo Design: Richard J. Pacifico

British Library Cataloguing in Publication Data

A catalogue record for this book is available from the British Library

ISBN 978-0-470-06079-7 (HB)

Typeset in 11.5/15pt Bembo by SNP Best-set Typesetter Ltd., Hong Kong
Printed and bound in Great Britain by TJ International Ltd, Padstow, Cornwall
This book is printed on acid-free paper responsibly manufactured from sustainable
forestry in which at least two trees are planted for each one used for paper production.

CONTENTS

FOREWORD

Resources for the education of qualitative market researchers have grown dramatically as my own career has progressed over the last twenty-five years. As this field continues to move from a craft to a profession, more and better guides for practitioners will continue to change the manner in which newcomers are recruited, socialized and professionalized. McPhee and Terry's *The Hidden Art of Interviewing People* is an important milestone in this progression.

When I faced the field as a novice, a major barrier was the nearly complete absence of published resources specific to the applied practice of qualitative research. By the early 1980s, a considerable academic literature had grown around the qualitative orientation in the social sciences. Unfortunately, this outburst of creative energy tended to be rather sectarian in its tendentious argumentation about what constituted proper qualitative research.

The field's intolerant denominationalism kept it bottled up in academia. Advocates of Erving Goffman's dramaturgical perspective contended against proponents of Harold Garfinkel's Ethnomethodology who sneered at the older Symbolic Interactionists and Neo-Freudian schools. Anthropologists steeped in the guidance of Clifford Geertz scoffed at scions of the Chicago School's second generation, such as Howard Becker and Anselm Strauss. Structuralists vied against Semioticians and neo-Marxians hated everybody! Let's not forget the tribalism that grew around feminist, African-American and queer critiques of social research.

Given this contentious state of affairs, it is astonishing that good work continued to be conducted, both inside and outside of universities. Graduate study in qualitative research was and, in many respects continues to be, a series of tripwires designed to reward doctrinal purity and confront dogmatic drift.

While this was going on, virtually invisibly to the academicians, a countervailing movement was taking the qualitative approach away from the ivy-covered halls and into America's boardrooms. A corps of practitioners – most completely oblivious to the academic debates – was redirecting qualitative concepts and approaches toward something more practical and useful.

A new practice modality had come to life in the wake of Robert Merton's and Paul Lazarsfeld's World War II experiments with communication effectiveness. At Columbia University's Bureau of Applied Social Research, a form of 'non-directed' interviewing, called 'focused interviewing' was developed and used with individuals and groups to maximize the influence of promotional messages.

When this field of practice became augmented by Carl Rogers's humanistic group psychology in the 1970s, a self-conscious profession of qualitative research practitioners was born. Their métier came to be the conduct of competent, effective and influential 'focus groups' – as this method of research came to be known – on behalf of a growing clientele of corporations and politicians. The heyday of focus groups was bracketed by the disastrous release of New Coke in 1985 through the elections that brought Bill Clinton and Tony Blair to power in the 1990s.

The Coca-Cola Company backed into a lesson about the significance of the symbolic and iconic meanings attached to brands when it used consumer information based solely on the metrics of sweetness to refashion its flagship product. The essence of this lesson was that people's typically emotional ideas about a person or brand were a major force influencing them to buy a product or vote for a candidate – or, as in Coke's case, complain vociferously when a brand owning a unique heritage, impeccable image and loyal customers was changed.

Plunging into the source of those feelings through focus groups would continue to provide most marketers and planners the necessary clues to create convincing messages and enticing goods and services. Politicians were able to use this technique to craft cunningly effective messages and win elections. All they had to do was use terms like 'congestion charges' or 'usage fees' instead of indelicately calling them 'taxes'.

Qualitative market research has traveled a long journey since then, expanding its toolbox well beyond group interviews. Regularly purloining its academic heritage for methodological devices and conceptual insights, the profession has vigorously adopted tools from ethnography, semiotics, socio-linguistics and neuro-psychology to enhance its powers of insight production. In some cases, however, these borrowings have been methodological 'tricks' employed to dazzle and beguile clients exhausted from watching too many focus groups, rather than to produce novel solutions.

Correspondingly, focus groups have become the targets of frequent criticism, as the media has debated their substantive adequacy relative to the degree of reliance being placed in qualitative market research. The rhetoric of 'not listening to focus groups' has come to stand for a certain kind of macho confidence among marketing managers or, in the case of George W. Bush, a way of projecting resoluteness and steadfastness impervious to any countervailing arguments.

We've come full circle, then, back to our academic heritage because we need to place qualitative research on a sturdier foundation. It is here that McPhee and Terry's work makes its mark. I enthusiastically agree with their insistence that placing qualitative research on stronger theoretical and empirical grounds is necessary to restore the credibility that our enterprise is losing.

A firmer foundation is required to add weight to this fallible category of human interaction that we call 'interviewing'. Right now, we have few behavioral models to distinguish the uniquely celebrated from the adequately competent moderator/interviewer. Until we recognize these distinctions, we have few grounds to differentiate performance and grant proportionately greater rewards to those that deliver exceptional service. Many discerning clients recognize the value of highly skilled moderation but, as McPhee and Terry complain, their choices can be overruled by miserly bean counters in purchasing departments.

Better theoretical tools are also needed to help explain the meanings, significance and likely human impacts of our substantive findings. Qualitative research has little value if it limits reporting to what respondents merely say in a focus group. We need to start linking what we are hearing and seeing among respondents to deeper truths about human nature and culture, and then directing this understanding toward predictive and prescriptive ideas that educate marketing strategy. If we do not advance our clients' interests through the application of theoretical and empirically validated insights about motivation, choice, cultural dynamics and historical change, then our product will diminish to insignificance.

McPhee and Terry place their reliance upon a field known as Neuro-Linguistic Programming (NLP) to establish a foundation for interviewing. Rather than thinking of NLP as a coherent theoretical model, it is best to describe the field as an amalgam of ideas and principles, drawn from diverse social psychological schools, that distinguish highly competent from merely adequate performance across a variety of occupational fields.

I hasten to admit that my earliest encounters with NLP in the early 1980s were not very favorable. NLP's ideas and practitioners seemed too reminiscent of the sly behaviorism practiced by sophomore psychology students convinced that they can close any sale and coax any co-ed into the sack through some kind of verbal artifice. I found NLP's fixation upon credentialing and numerous levels of competence redolent of Freemasonry run amuck.

Happily, McPhee and Terry report that NLP has overcome its Watsonian and Skinnerian roots to become a more humanistic practice respectful of cognitive processing and human volition. Moreover, the authors bring us many important messages from the world of NLP about establishing rapport and reading body language that deserve serious attention, despite any behaviorist inhibitions.

Interviewers need to understand the impact of their own words and gestures upon respondents. Conducting qualitative research is a complex human process in which living, breathing people are sending signals to each other well beyond the transcript produced at the end of an interview. It takes a high level of skill to listen attentively through multiple channels while carefully managing your own presentation of self. The charmingly seductive interviewer/moderator can be producing as much invalidity as one who is aloof or overbearing. McPhee and Terry offer many insights that will help beginning to experienced qualitative researchers carefully calibrate and modulate the messages they are sending to respondents during interviews, while they better assess and appraise the signals they are picking up in return.

Qualitative analysis, too, is in major need of reformation. Refreshingly, McPhee and Terry resolutely insist that the process of drawing conclusions needs to be rescued from client-side boobs who refuse to listen to anything beyond the transcript. Indeed, qualitative analysts need to consider the ways things are phrased and the subtext or implicit communication in a dialogue. What is left unsaid often has equal significance to what gets said in a focus group, and the rules of NLP combined with the authors' many years of experience offer many guidelines for taking analysis deeper than transcript fixation.

The Hidden Art of Interviewing People is foreshadowing developments likely to grow as our field continues to develop in the years ahead. We will continue borrowing from those contending schools we left behind in our drive to become practical. In fact, I envision a continuing effort to improve the theoretical foundations of qualitative market research – not only to improve researchers' interviewing skills but also to make our findings more predictive and better grounded in substantive truths about how humans operate.

A case example drawn from a recent assignment on behalf of a multinational appliances manufacturer may help to elucidate this point. In contemporary American homes, the kitchen is becoming center stage, a showplace, out in the open, where cooking becomes part of home entertainment in much the same way that a high-end stereo system located in the center of the living room may have captured guests' attentive admiration a generation ago.

It was in this context that an insight drawn from the work of Erving Goffman helped our team with recommendations for the client. Goffman's 'dramaturgical perspective' postulates that much social life is lived as a kind of performance for others. In this context, we operate on several levels of exposure. Much like a theater, there are two regions in which we perform. The first is the 'front region', where showmanship happens. Our activities within this region embody high standards, politeness and decorum. Contrastingly, there is also 'backstage' or the 'back region', where impressions are not as well managed, where the staging is processed, where things are not perfect. Using Goffman's ideas as a guide, though cautiously not citing him in our conclusions, we were able to show how these two regions have evolved in the kitchens of contemporary households. We were also able to recommend separate product lines with features and benefits customized to each region, appropriate to emerging lifestyle expectations.

This is a brief, quick example but I believe that it points to a future in which qualitative researchers will be paying greater attention to ideas drawn from the social and behavioral sciences, from 'grand theories' to 'grounded theories' and 'theories of the middle-range'. We will be paying more attention to emerging theories of consumption and consumerism − to basic ideas about why we shop and why we buy. All this will be done to gain deeper insights and drive better recommendations to our clients − not merely to take sides among competing schools of thought. Ideas drawn from NLP, Phenomenology, Symbolic Interactionism, Structuralism and other perspectives, will continue to become unbottled from academia − not to confound us with extra verbiage but to better unlock the human experience. Qualitative researchers able to harness explanatory concepts to deliver enhanced client value will be the winners in this next development of our discipline.

Hy Mariampolski, PhD
Managing Director of QualiData Research Inc., New York

ACKNOWLEDGEMENTS

For Isabel, Alyson and Iain, for tolerance and support during this book's progress. Also, huge thanks to Emily Terry for her assistance and for our chance meeting many years back.

Neil McPhee

In writing this book I would like to acknowledge and thank those who supported me in the endeavour. First, my wife Emily for her patience, encouragement and help in all aspects of the project. Second, Ali Mobbs for the wonderful cartoons and Tony Mobbs for being a willing model for the eye-accessing cues photo. Third, everyone at Evolution for easing my workload so I could write, and fourth, our clients for all their encouraging words.

Roger Terry

ABOUT THE AUTHORS

NEIL McPHEE

Neil is a long-time qualitative researcher, who began his career in 1972. Having been told by his boss, in his first week's employment in research, to go and help out with some interviewing (of retired people, applying for old-age bus concession passes), he discovered his probable incompatibility with structure by omitting to fill out any questionnaires at all. Instead, he spent a day with a retired bus driver (not the 20 plus interview sample he was expected to complete), and proudly came back to the office the next day with a long list of what would now be termed 'ethnographic findings and anecdotes', including the fact that, in the 1920s, a bus driver was expected to be responsible for his own bus's care, and would be expected to polish scratches out himself.

Some 25 years ago, Neil was introduced to new thinking by Allan Pease, the international speaker/writer/trainer in body language, who he met at a presentation on Nonverbal Communication and Body Language. He became sold on the possible applications and the subject in general. Soon after that, Neil discovered NLP.

There was little turning back after that. You cannot unlearn something so potent and pretend that none of it existed.

Since then, Neil has variously bought, run and sold his own full-service agency and worked as Qualitative Research Director for an American-owned agency. He now offers his services as a Qualitative/Ethnography Practitioner and Consultant, both in the UK and internationally.

Neil trained in NLP/Hypnotherapy with Roger Terry.

ROGER TERRY CBIOL, MIBIOL, INLPT MASTER NLP TRAINER, ABHI, MANLP

Roger is a scientist with over 25 years' experience in running and building successful businesses. Ten years ago, he founded

Evolution Training with his partner Emily, and he now works with businesses and individuals, guiding them to evolve to their full potential. Previously, his career was within the utility sector, where he was responsible for new business creation and innovative business development.

An international NLP Master Trainer, hypnosis instructor and expert on human value systems, Roger leads seminars and consults with companies on executive teams in the UK, USA, Europe and the Middle East. His expertise in cultural change has helped businesses revitalise their organisations and people, bringing their cultures in line with the business strategy required to produce profit and growth.

He has been involved designing and running qualitative research projects to discover the levels of knowledge of disease transmission in drug addicts in the community and the prison population. His analysis of the hidden messages in advertising copy helped hone and target communication to drug and prison populations in the UK.

With a talent for using Neuro-Linguistic Programming and personal development techniques, Roger has a pragmatic and practical style. His enthusiastic and forthright approach to coaching, with a focused Neuro-Linguistic Programming methodology, provides a unique intervention approach that allows a client to achieve the maximum movement in their chosen direction for minimum effort.

INTRODUCTION

WHY THIS BOOK?

This book is written for all those involved in interviewing other people, whether in (qualitative) market research or elsewhere. The nature of human interchange is a complex one, and the tools offered by Neuro-Linguistic Programming (NLP) provide you with a powerful and ecological framework to enhance your communications with others, and to achieve your own goals. This book is not a self-improvement book, though many of the lessons will help you achieve this: it is designed as a practical tool for undertaking better (interview) communications with other people.

I (Neil) was recently told by a client that market research is now seen as "one of the marketing or administrative services: it's pretty much a commodity which we have to buy". The distinction between qualities in researchers was largely ignored in place was a simple cost equation, linked with a simple 'these are the questions we want you to ask' (i.e. read out). It is hardly surprising that clients are frequently disappointed with results, if this is the way it is commissioned.

After 35 years of active qualitative research as a practitioner, I feel strongly that the buying and selling of qualitative research has become far too often a commodity and process, where the offering is essentially one of straight question and answer, interspersed with the superficial use of 'projective' techniques, which are, in turn, not analysed, but whose output is simply reported, verbatim, and assumed to be a simple matter of respondents 'meaning exactly what they say'. We have over 60 years' experience between us, and are able to guarantee that few people are able or willing to say exactly what they mean, or mean exactly what they say.

So, how can we penetrate this apparent impasse? Well, there are several routes into the 'mindfield', and this book covers just one of the ways — NLP — of understanding more about the ways in which people communicate with each other. It gives practical tips as to how to apply the learnings in a day-to-day qualitative research framework.

WHO IS IT FOR?

Some of you will be experienced interviewers, others will be relatively new to it and some will be just starting out on a career. Some, too, will be clients/research buyers or users, others will be research suppliers or practitioners. Some, too, will not be qualitative market researchers, but instead will be reading this book for another reason, perhaps to enhance skills at work or at home, perhaps in other marketing-related business contexts or in a more social setting.

We welcome you all, and know that you will learn much and feel more confident about your skills and approaches to qualitative research.

HISTORICAL ROUTES AND CURRENT TOOLS

Qualitative research began its current identity sometime in the early to mid 20th century (1920–1960), standing on the foundations of psychology and psychotherapy, and academic studies of various forms of therapy. It inherited a number of techniques which are still in use today, but too often either are only partially applied or understood, or are used by those with little or no real training or experience. This results in a superficially similar appearance, but a fundamentally different product.

Additionally, in the last 20 years we have seen a huge upsurge in understanding about exactly how and why we make decisions regarding brands, marketing communications, products, and so on. Neuroscience is beginning to gain ground and availability but has yet to confirm its full potential. However, it has proved that the brain is complex and gives proof to the notion that the words a respondent uses are often different to the feelings/ emotions that are really at work. We also know from now well-established studies and scientific work, that most of the really important 'tells' about how someone really is feeling are nonverbal.

Learning Point: Neil says . . .

In 1996, after giving a paper to a conference on the use of videoing interviews to enhance analysis of NVC, I met a client afterwards. 'Very interesting', he said, 'the only thing is, you can't tell anything by body language.'

How wrong he was . . .

However, in far too many cases, much or most of the available evidence, before your eyes as an interviewer, is ignored, or at best is incompletely used. Why is this?

PROBLEMS FACED

In the speed and cost-driven environment of most qualitative research in the 21st century, we are faced with a situation of needing more and more from our respondents, while at the same time having less and less time to spend with them, and on the analysis of what they have told us. At the same time, equally, we are being driven by clients and corporate owners of market research businesses to produce more at the lowest cost – to act as a factory and to break production targets; to bring down unit costs.

Too often this means treating the qualitative experience as a process, as a group discussion or a depth interview to be completed as fast/economically as possible, and for results to be in a simple, reportage format: not fully analysed. All this to meet the current standards of media output for simple sound-bites, to match the structure of corporate clients' wishes for 15–30 minute debriefs, such that they can dip into and out of the information.

It's a little like the patient saying to the psychotherapist, 'Cure me in the next 30 minutes: I don't have time for the full 1½ hour session and I can only attend once, so a course of six visits is impossible. Just do it.'

PRACTITIONERS

Qualitative research is also often very much a younger person's arena. Perhaps because of the anti-social hours, the nature of the work (pressured, physically and mentally challenging, etc.) or the lower costs of more junior staff, we frequently find our practitioners to be in their early 20s to early 30s, and those risking day-to-day fieldwork after that age find that burn-out, or promotion to a supervisory role, are very real possibilities. Many, too, leave the industry for different careers or to pursue management positions.

This means that, in practice, many of those entrusted with the *crucial role of the actual interface with respondents* are relatively junior, with limited training or more general life experience. This is not to say that they are not well educated: quite the reverse, often. Simply that what training has been given is relatively limited (often to a couple of industry/in-house courses) coupled with some basic interest in people. Few have any more than an academic knowledge, at best, of human functioning/decision-making. Equally, many are very nervous of being the focus of attention in a viewing studio, with many clients watching, so stick religiously to the prepared script (topic guide) and thus lose many opportunities to explore the respondents' responses. It is a bit like the early stages of driving, where the knowledge is not fully embedded and automatic, so the driver focuses on the process and not on the road. Using the Learning Ladder concept in NLP, too many practitioners who do the face-to-face work with respondents are still at the early stages of unconscious non-competence or conscious non-competence.

Stage 1: Unconscious Non-Competence   Learner

Stage 2: Conscious Non-Competence

Stage 3: Conscious Competence

Stage 4: Unconscious Competence   Expert

If you were a client, at which level would you want your Moderator to be?

RATIONAL SOLUTIONS AND NONLINEAR THINKING

Increasingly, too, clients, media and, ultimately, public perception sees solutions in the rational arena, because it makes them feel in control, perhaps, or because marketing and research have been presented as Science, not Art. It is a truism in psychology and anthropology that things are seldom what they appear to be, and many a complex explanation is required.

This seems not to inhabit the market research or marketing worlds, where literality and 'left-brain' responses rule. This is probably true of most of the Western countries in the world, in many fields including marketing, politics, media, sport, etc.

We, the authors, see people and those activities engaged in by people, including decision-making and marketing-related choices, as inherently right-brain, complex and often hidden.

NEURO-LINGUISTIC PROGRAMMING: NLP

Despite its rather off-putting and jargon-like name, Neuro-Linguistic Programming, NLP, is simply one of the finest tools for developing yourself. NLP helps us find out how we communicate with others and ourselves, and how to change the things we don't like. Whether you want to excel at work, develop your sporting capabilities or find out what makes people tick to improve your relationships, NLP provides the tools.

The fundamental building blocks that the models of NLP provide, allow you to rediscover and update the natural communication skills all humans are born with. We start by learning how to gain and enhance rapport with anyone we meet, how to read the signs which humans give out through their facial expressions and body language, and to hear the hidden language behind what we say.

As you progress in your understanding of NLP, you will learn how to develop powerful outcomes. By utilising your natural stimulus–response mechanism, you can be the way you choose in any situation. Discovering the way we hold and process our perceptions can become a pathway to excellence.

There is now almost 30 years of experience and discoveries that make NLP one of the most comprehensive development tools available. Indeed, once you know some NLP, you will start to recognise its imprint on the majority of high-profile self-development gurus.

The tools of NLP can be applied to almost every field where communication and interaction with people is essential to success.

If you have a speciality then the application of some of the NLP models may lead you to excel in ways that were beyond your dreams. Research, especially qualitative research and interviewing, has these requirements at its core.

Neuro-Linguistic Programming originated in the early 1970s, and is dynamic: it is not a fixed, academic learning. It is essentially a framework of 'what works': if it isn't working, do it differently.

Neither is it inventing or promoting completely new concepts. It is, rather, a collation of how we best communicate with ourselves and others. So, you will find elements of nonverbal communication in here. So, too, will you find echoes of psychology, voice use, etc. It does not seek to reinvent any wheels, rather it seeks to codify what has been found to be most effective in qualitative research, and to apply learnings from the wider field of NLP.

History

NLP was born in the seventies in California, when a linguist, John Grinder, and a mathematician, Richard Bandler, set out to identify the difference between the behaviour of people who are competent at a particular skill and those who excel. By careful and detailed observation, they modelled the behaviour of top psychotherapists, Virginia Satir and Fritz Perls, together with Milton Erickson, the world-famous hypnotherapist. Although these individuals had very different styles, they used surprisingly similar underlying patterns.

From this original exercise and studying other excellent performers, Grinder and Bandler designed an elegant model for others to use, in order to improve their own performance, become excellent communicators and learn how to access and change their own patterns, leading to personal evolution and growth.

This class of activity, called *modelling* in NLP, has remained central to developments in the field of NLP, in business, teaching,

personal development and therapy contexts. Top teachers, sales-
men, financial dealers, motivational speakers and therapists have
been modelled so that their skills can be passed on to others.

Many other individuals have contributed to the development
of NLP. Whilst much of the original work could be described as
having a 'behaviourist' approach, more recently, importance has
been placed on the person's identity, beliefs and values that underpin his or her behaviour. The understanding of the relationship
and balance of the conscious and unconscious minds is central to
most current NLP training.

THE GOAL/MISSION OF THIS BOOK

The purpose of this book is to offer a practical guide for qualitative market researchers, and all others who are involved in interviewing other people.

This book is NOT about self-help or self-development, though
if you take on board the lessons here, we are not sure when you
will notice, but they will follow in your day-to-day life.

The reason behind the writing is to increase your awareness
of how you and your respondents are when you interview/analyse
qualitative research.

Some of you will already be using some of these learnings,
others will need to increase your awareness of yourself and your
respondents to get full benefit and some of you will be very sceptical. We have written this with you all in mind.

THE FORMAT OF THE BOOK

We have tried to make it easy to relate to a researcher's day-to-
day life, so you will find chapters on each of the main stages in
the research process. This starts with meetings, moves onto taking

the brief, and so on through to the presentation. Some chapters are longer and more detailed than others: so the chapter on interviewing is the longest (most important) and also contains much stuff that can be applied/is apparent in other chapters, too. Dip in and out of it, re-read chapters, do the exercises. You will find that they work.

CHAPTER 1

TAKING THE BRIEF

WHAT'S IN THIS CHAPTER?

- The importance of the first steps
- Being at your best
- Anchoring: create the state you want
- The dance of communication
- What is rapport?
- Reading the signposts
- True listening
- Quality questions
- Eliciting values
- Setting the scene
- Checklist for taking the brief

THE IMPORTANCE OF THE FIRST STEPS

In many sales environments, much time is spent training personnel in specific techniques to enhance sales potential. We train our researchers (to an extent) in the skills for the research task, but we seldom train them in these early stages of the sale. However, with an increasing number of agencies being owned or controlled by larger corporate bodies, to whom research is simply a route to profitable investment, does it not make sense to maximise the sales stage? Is it not realistic to see many research managers as the conduits between their internal staff and the clients' budgets?

Even if we train them in sales, we would seldom recognise the need for sales writing, and while the research proposal is a method document, in part it is also a core sales tool. Let's at least get it as good as we can get it.

Most market research begins with the briefing stage, either taking a brief from a new or existing client, or simply responding to an email or, very occasionally nowadays, a posted brief. Getting this stage 'right' is crucial to the long-term commercial health of any research agency or consultant. In short, we need work.

It is very satisfying to be 'right', but without the consequent stage of fee-paying projects, the whole thing becomes rather academic and short-lived! Indeed, the whole of this book is directed towards the basic aim of making you more effective. It is not intended that it teach you research skills, though there are several pointers along the way, rather it is intended to ensure that you are in possession of the basic communication skills to enable your research skills to show through.

In specific terms, this first stage seeks to ensure that when you take this brief, you are 'ready'. This means being ready to listen, respond and create rapport with the client (and colleagues).

Many of these skills and learnings can and will be reapplied later in the book and in later stages of the research process, so don't be surprised to find them mentioned again.

Every successful project begins by taking an accurate brief, and our ability to be our best, create rapport, listen and ask quality questions will determine our success in the end. In this chapter we will guide you through the NLP methods and concepts that will enable you to be at your best when in front of a client. You will begin to have new understanding of how we humans tick and start to hear the hidden signals that tell us how someone is thinking. We, in turn, can ask questions that match our clients' thinking patterns to access their values for the project and so go away with an accurate and clear brief.

For many of us, the work starts with a call or email from a client, which is followed up with a written (often very short) brief. A meeting may be called to take further details or to discuss the problem, and at this stage, the NLP-trained researcher will have the opportunity to gather lots of additional information and feedback, to prepare the response that accurately reflects what the client wants.

BEING AT YOUR BEST

Imagine it's 9 am on a rainy Monday and you get a call from a new client who needs a research project quickly for a new product; you're the only one who can go. You have been to meetings to take briefs before, but usually with a senior from your firm. So, you take a breath and get ready for your first solo mission. What if you could really excel and show just what you can do. Is this your opportunity to shine?

In this section, we will explain some NLP tools that help you to be at your best when taking briefs, so that you can produce an excellent project proposal.

Controlling your state

In NLP, your state refers to the collection of thoughts, emotions and physiology at any one time, and the state we are in determines our capabilities. If you are in an unresourceful state, the chances are you are not at your best – your performance and access to your resources become lowered, and your meeting will not go so well.

Spend a few moments thinking back to a time when you were not on form at a meeting, and as you do that, become aware of how those capabilities that you know you can call on in other times just seemed to melt away. Maybe you lost the ability to think quickly on your feet or you felt extra nervous and your mouth dried up at the first question.

Now imagine a time when you were feeling on top form, bright and breezy, you had everything at your fingertips.

What are the differences between these two memories? Would questions throw you? Would you be more flexible? Just imagine if you could call up one of these states at will. NLP enables you to choose whatever state you want, whenever and wherever you need it.

Getting your mind and body in the right space, i.e. taking control of your state, before the meeting starts will get you great results. There are some extremely easy wins here.

Sometimes we forget ourselves in the rush to get to the appointment and when we arrive, realise just how nervous and mentally unprepared we are for the meeting. We may have had a frustrating journey by car or public transport, the weather may have been unkind or we have had an altercation with someone before we set off. We will tend to carry these states through with us into the next event. The 'I got out of bed on the wrong side syndrome'. How many times have you had a frustrating day and found that you have taken these feelings home with you, or something great has happened to you and the rest of the day has been wonderful? Our states of mind will strongly influence our performance.

Everyone remembers the work of Pavlov. He experimented with stimulus–response mechanisms in dogs using food and tuning forks; he was eventually able to make the dogs salivate on the sound of the tuning fork with no food present. Well, with dogs it can take some time, but for us, fortunately, our brains work fast and we can quickly set up and utilise a stimulus–response mechanism of our choice (called an *anchor* in NLP) to get us in the best state possible for what we are doing. This is the first step towards excellence.

Anchors are natural mechanisms; you already have anchors or stimuli in your lives that create states of being. For example, the smell of newly baked bread may bring back the whole experience of being in your mother's kitchen. A couple's favourite song brings back memories of the romance of when they first heard it. Many car advertisements on TV give little technical information about the model. What they do is to set a scene, which shows a desirable state like being free, successful or attractive to the opposite sex. They anchor the stimulus of the car to the state that people are likely to be attracted to. Such experiences can bring about powerful changes in our state. Think for a moment about the different ways people speak your name and how one way may make you feel instantly that you are in trouble (often the way our parents say our name), and another way may make you feel that you are loved and appreciated. The stimulus is the unique combination of tone, volume, pitch and speed of the sound, and this generates a particular state in you.

Thought Experiment

It is useful to get to know our personal anchors. Some will be resourceful – perhaps walking through your own front door, being touched by your children, putting on golfing shoes. Some will put you into an unresourceful state – perhaps meeting a certain person, going into a particular office, hearing a particular phrase. Once you know them, you can decide whether to respond or not.

Spend a few moments and identify some of the stimuli in your life that create either positive or negative states in you.

Anchoring: create the state you want

The NLP method called *anchoring* is used to create and access positive states. Every experience that we have had includes some or all of the five senses – visual, auditory, kinaesthetic, olfactory and gustatory. Anchoring refers to the tendency for the repetition of any one of these elements to bring back the whole of the experience. When we show our holiday snaps to friends, we re-experience the holiday – it's almost like we can take ourselves back there. To our friends, however, it's a secondary experience as they try to imagine what it might be like.

It is this normal human process that allows us to have access to any state we have had in the past or any state we can imagine.

The strange thing about our brain is that it does not know imagination from reality as far as producing physical and emotional responses to situations is concerned. Think about our reactions to movies, where we feel excitement, sadness, fear and even have adrenalin rushes. The states are real and palpable even though we are experiencing a fictional event sitting in a cinema with others. Our minds are capable of delivering any state we want instantly, we just need to know how to retrieve the state and programme it.

The brain reacts to both real and imagined experiences in exactly the same way, by producing the same chemicals.

Spend a moment just thinking of the sort of states that would be useful when taking a brief. These are some of the states that Neil uses when taking a brief:

- energised
- confident
- eloquent
- humorous
- attentive

- calm
- creative
- organised
- focused

Why should you use anchors?

Key states used in taking a brief, dependent on whether the researcher knows the client people, what type of client company ethos is present, and how the agency wishes to be 'seen', for instance, creative & quirky, solid & reliable, fun & imaginative, sober & reliable, etc.

Researchers are human. We have our good and bad days. We are prone to be better at some stages of the process than others, but at the same time, we need to be 'on form' for the client meetings, the interviews and the debriefs. We do not have the luxury of underperforming. We usually only get a single chance at these stages, so here is where the use of states and anchors comes in: when we are NOT on form, or cannot change how we feel easily, NLP comes to our rescue and allows us to learn a reliable way of 'acting', and then becoming, the presentation of ourselves that is most useful.

The best thing about an anchor is that once you have set it and used it many times in a particular context, you suddenly recognise that you are not firing the anchor any more and you still have the state you want. This is because our brains learn that this is how we want to be in that particular context, and they automatically produce the state for us.

How to create a resource anchor

An anchor is some specific stimulus that we can use to invoke a desired emotional state. We can use an anchor, for example, to maintain confidence, become relaxed or alert.

Creating an anchor is quite easy. Suppose that you remember a time when you felt especially confident, a time when something had worked really well. Go back to that scene and replay it as if you

Learning Point: Anchoring a State

'Think of a time when you were feeling completely in control, you were feeling calm and ready for anything . . .'

are there again, and as you mentally replay it, make sure that you are seeing through your own eyes, hearing and feeling what happened (in NLP this is called being *associated*, if you see yourself in the picture then you are not associated and this is less effective). Now notice the colours and make them brighter, listen to the sounds and make them louder. Have your image come closer and make it bigger. Does it have a frame or border to it? If it does, make it panoramic (so you can see all around you in every direction in the same way as you would on a hill top). As you play with these aspects of your event, notice what happens to the way you feel – some of the changes will make the feelings stronger. When you have found out which changes give the very best feelings, run through the memory again (with the changes) and just before the feelings reach their peak, press the thumb and finger of one hand together.

Do this sequence FIVE times using the same thumb and finger. You will find that you have created a stimulus–response mechanism that has attached the stimulus of pressing your finger and thumb together to the enhanced feelings of the event. You have just *anchored* those feelings, which means that whenever you want the feelings back, pressing your finger and thumb together will give them to you.

You can also add other states to this anchor point. Suppose in a meeting you want to be calm and confident but don't have a memory that includes them both. Find memories for each state and then just repeat the process with each additional state. The thing is to experiment until you have it just the way you want it.

This business of mentally manipulating the colours, sounds, size and shape of your picture is called *changing the submodalities*, and is a really powerful way of changing the way you react to things. These are the building blocks of anchoring, although more advanced methods exist for building, combining and merging anchors to create different effects.

What we have been through here is the simplest form of anchoring; it is easy to do and can be incredibly effective – practise, practise, practise! Experiment using a combination of states to create anchors for different purposes.

Another way of using anchoring is the *spotlight technique*, also referred to as *circles of excellence* or *spatial anchoring*. In this technique, an imaginary space is used to hold the states or resources. Our mind is then able to access these in particular spots in a room, or even transfer the spotlights to other environments. This is especially useful in presentations where you want to access different resources in different places.

Creating spotlight states

1. In your mind draw an imaginary circle on the floor in front of you.
2. Remember experiences where you felt powerful, creative, composed, or any other resourceful state where you were balanced and centred.
3. Step into the circle only as quickly or slowly as you need to. Remember and reaccess the resourceful state through your inner senses. In other words, see what you saw through your own eyes, within the actual experience . . . hear the sounds and language used and get in touch with your posture, breathing and emotions when inside the desirable resourceful

Figure 1.1 Spotlight states.

memory. *Note: an observer would see changes in your physiology, such as changed posture, deeper breathing and skin colour changes. If there is no noticeable change in your physiology, the resource state is either poorly accessed or low intensity. If it is low intensity, choose another resourceful state that is more powerful.*

4. You can continue to repeat step 3, adding other different resourceful states if you like. When you step back into the space you will be able to reaccess the positive feelings and states of being that you anchored there.

5. You can take this imaginary spotlight and use it whenever you need to, or you can set up spotlights in specific places in your presentation room. Remember, you can choose to build spotlights with any number of different internal states and for any positive purpose!

THE DANCE OF COMMUNICATION

So, you have arrived in good time and your preparation is done, you are wearing the right clothes to match the client and their business. You have fired your resource anchor and are ready to take the brief. Your next task is to begin to create a relationship with this new client in order to take an accurate brief. The question is, how can NLP help with this? Let's take our first steps towards a simple model that lets us understand how people tick, and that we can use to guide our communication and relationship building, assisting us to ask the most useful questions.

What does the client actually want (as opposed to actually need)? Chances are, he/she is giving you clues as to their preferred approach, solution and framework. These will come in the words used and nonverbal clues as to what is required, and as to what the company value system is. A client whose company leans towards structure, process and financial performance (to the diminution of other measures) will be unlikely to appreciate a full ethnographic study lasting several months and costing lots of money. They may, though, be able to appreciate a 'quick and cheap' telephone count.

What is communication?

'Communication' is a word used to describe any interaction with self or others – casual conversation, persuading, teaching and negotiating. It is a dynamic process, the internal and external dance we engage in that imparts the passing of understanding from one person to another, or indeed internally within ourselves.

Although we interact with others a great deal, we take for granted how it actually happens and when it works – words flow and 'understanding' occurs within the listener. However, it's not always that easy: how often have you told somebody something and found that they remember a very different version to you?

Often, what we truly mean is not what the other person understands. Within NLP, this phenomenon is called *the meaning of your communication is the response you get*. This is useful to hold in your mind, as it allows you to be responsible for communicating clearly exactly what you mean.

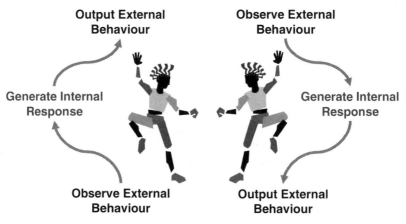

Figure 1.2   The dance of communication.

So, what happens when we communicate? When one person pays attention to another, they take in what the other person is saying and doing. They then get in touch with their own internal thoughts and feelings and respond in their individual way. The other person pays attention to them . . . and so a communication loop is formed.

Communication is much more than the words we say. Even saying nothing at all is a method of communicating. Research by Mehrabian in 1970 showed that in communicating to a group of people where there was no opportunity to ask questions of the speaker, 55% of the impact was determined by body language – posture, gestures and eye contact, 38% by tone of voice, and only 7% by the actual words spoken. Clearly, these percentages may change in certain circumstances. However, it does seem that in getting across your message, it is not what you say so much as how you say it that makes the difference.

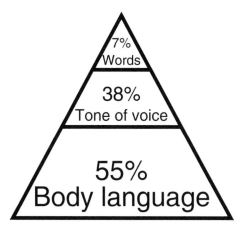

Figure 1.3 The impact of communication.

Think of a simple sentence – 'I love walking the dog'. Say it six times, with the emphasis on different words. Notice how, by changing tone of voice, loudness and timbre, you can change the meaning. Then add gestures: look up or down, be still or active, breathe fast or slow. Get the message? To change your communication, consider your body language, hand and feet gestures, tone, pitch, rhythm and volume of your voice and the words that you use.

What is rapport?

When communication is flowing, we sometimes have a comfortable or easy feeling; this is often a sign of *rapport*. We often just wait until this 'happens', although this is a skill that can be learned, and to communicate in the most effective way it is necessary to have rapport. This doesn't mean that you have to agree with someone. It does mean that you respond to them and give them the experience of *feeling understood*.

You might ask why this works. We are bombarded by an enormous amount of information every second – the light levels in the room, our heartbeat, the look on someone's face, the *'We like people who are like us'* feeling of our foot in our left shoe and everything in-between. Our minds filter out most of this information, which is just as well or we would go into overload. However, as humans, one of our basic needs is for relationships, so our minds have a way of searching out those people with whom we might build one. In order to do this, the brain must match incoming data against a pattern. The pattern it uses is the only one it knows intimately – our own – so we scan the outside world constantly for people who are like us. To build rapport easily, we don't need to do any interpretation in the classic sense of body language, all we need to do is to engage in the art of rapport and enter the dance of communication. This creates a bridge between our world and theirs; it builds trust, and is the basis of effective communication.

Creating rapport

People Respond Better To People Like Themselves

Rapport is being in harmony with someone, to improve (or create) a useful and effective relationship with an interviewee or a client, or a colleague, so that we get the best out of the situation as researchers. It is based on managing and recognising language, posture, space and tone.

By using people's natural response of liking those who are similar to themselves, we can create rapport in several ways: body postures, verbal patterns of speech and sound, words and phrases and movements. There are two basic patterns that we can use: *matching* and *mirroring*. Look at Figure 1.4 and you can see that the matched pair are both in exactly the same posture; they are both scratching their heads with their right arms and have their left arms balanced on their left hips. In the mirrored pair, they are in the same posture but are a mirrored reflection of each other – one has their right arm up and the other has their left arm up. The aim is definitely not mimicking, but just to adopt a similar posture or use similar words. You can use either pattern, which gives plenty of room for variation. The aim is not to be identical but to be similar; all we want to do is have the other person's unconscious mind recognise that you are someone like them.

Some examples of things that you can match are shown in Table 1.1.

Figure 1.4 Matching and mirroring.

Table 1.1 Matching and mirroring.

Body	Voice
Posture★	Volume
Facial expressions	Tone
Hand movements★	Pitch
Eye movements	Tempo
Breathing	Descriptive words
Movement of feet★	Repetitive phrasing
Body shifts★	Using their words exactly
Spine angle★	
Head angle★	

★Things that you can also mirror.

To create rapport in this way is called 'pacing', in the sense that you are using your own physiology to get closer to the other person's experience. The art of communication is to pace, then gradually begin to lead into what you wish to communicate. This will also be important when it comes to the interviewing stage, when the ability to get respondents to perform certain tasks, projective and enabling techniques, etc., will be essential.

In all this, remember to be subtle; you are not mimicking the other person, so similarity and timing are important. Once you have become accustomed to doing this, experiment and move on to the next level by moving your posture a little and see if the other person also moves in a similar way. This is called *pacing and leading*. The trick for success is: pace, pace, pace, pace then lead. If the other person does not move with you, then go back to pacing. Eventually, you will learn how to pace not only the physical gestures but also the tone and language.

Experiment

Before you use rapport in an important meeting, get some practice. Experiment with matching and mirroring in various circumstances. For example, when at a party or social engagement you could match or mirror someone new and notice how quickly you can build a relationship. Alternatively, use rapport when you are having a disagreement and notice how quickly common ground appears.

One more thought from NLP: 'There is no such thing as a resistant client, only a lack of rapport'; by taking responsibility to be as flexible as possible, you can get anyone into rapport.

READING THE SIGNPOSTS

NLP is all about making distinctions and relying on the information that is available to your senses, rather than sending yourself off track by mind-reading (believing what you assume to be true rather than what you actually pick up from what the other person says or does). Being able not only to notice differences from sensory information but also know what to do with that information is the gift that NLP brings to the world of human communication. This gives us the ability to track people's internal shifts, allowing us to know if we are in rapport, when the other person is feeling comfortable and open (and we can proceed) or when they are uncomfortable and we need to adjust our own behaviour to get back into rapport.

Being observant in the context of communication and taking note of what we are seeing and hearing from the other person can pay dividends, taking competence towards excellence. If you are going to be aware of human beings, you must first observe their external behaviour. For example, a shift in internal state from 'I'm unsure of this process' to 'I'm ready to proceed' will be mirrored in a change in thinking and in external behaviour. In NLP we treat 'external behaviour' as any change that you can see or hear in the other person. This may be as gross as getting up and moving or as subtle as a change in skin colour.

Sensory acuity

Being able to notice these behavioural changes is called *sensory acuity*. This is a skill we learned as children – reading our parents' faces for signs of danger, etc. – and NLP training allows us to enhance this ability and put it to good use when we are talking to others.

To do this, we observe closely the signs, signals and information conveyed to us along the nonverbal, as well as the verbal, channels. With practice, we are able to make finer distinctions and comparisons, which ultimately track the success of our communication; we can then stay on track and in accord with the other person. It is interesting that many business environments, writers, trainers and the like, seem to forget about these dimensions when in a business context, but often recognise their role in a social setting. Frequently, we meet partners in this way. Poets often write about 'the looks across a room' or, more contemporarily, in a bar or supermarket. Here, such exchanged signals are often our first introduction to someone. How come we assume that they do not play a role while at work?

Calibration

Noticing how people shift is one thing, understanding what that might mean is another, and to make accurate assumptions for an individual person, we have to match a 'snapshot' of when we know what is happening inside. For example, the person says, 'I'd like some more information on that' and they move their head slightly down to one side and lean towards you whilst raising their eyebrows. The next time they do those exact same movements, you can assume that inside they want more detail and to know more. This is called *calibration*.

The first step is to learn how to calibrate. You can think of yourself as a camera that can take sequential shots, rather like those of plants growing, which show you the changes that you cannot normally see. Your unconscious mind is very capable of doing this, and indeed already does. What we learn to do is aim our camera and focus this ability on communication. With some conscious practice, just like taking an advanced driving test, our unconscious mind learns to do this in the context of communication, and so you have access to a stream of useful feedback information related to how you are communicating with others.

So, how do we train ourselves to do this? Here are a few examples of what you can do to learn to calibrate and to enhance your sensory acuity.

Play this game with a colleague or your family (children especially like this). One person adops a pose and another takes a mental snapshot, then closes their eyes. The first person then moves and the other person opens their eyes and notices what has changed. It is surprising how subtle the changes that can be detected; very quickly, you will be able to detect a minute movement of a finger or slight turning of a head. The purpose is to teach your brain the strategy of taking snapshots in human-to-human interactions. After practice, this becomes an unconscious process and you will begin to notice changes and subtle differences in physiology as people communicate.

Become the observer; listen closely to what someone is saying and notice the minute changes in their expression without making any judgement of what this means. Notice if you can recognise when someone likes or dislikes something by the changes in their expression. You can facilitate this by asking questions so that you can see them access the thought. People, food or animals are usually good topics to choose.

Reading facial clues

There are 269 muscles in the face and many of them are impossible to control consciously. This means that our faces are treasure troves of available information and are well worth a more detailed look. Have you ever noticed how parents look at their children with love? It's great to get a child to take photographs because of the relaxed poses their models take; their muscles take on an extra softness and their eyes sparkle. Compare this to how they look when their mother spots them coming in muddy from the garden just as they are about to leave to go out. Although we don't make a conscious decision to tense or relax a particular muscle, we all have our own patterns that are made up by a particular set of muscle configurations.

Figure 1.5 Old Chinese proverb.

Under normal circumstances we ignore this valuable information. In NLP, we can use this information to begin to understand the reactions of others to our communication.

Imagine you are on a hillside, it's a bright summer's day, the sun is shining and light fluffy clouds are gently moving across the sky. You notice what's around you, the grass beneath you and the calls of birds as they sing to each other. Look across to the opposite hillside and you can see the clouds moving as the sun creates their shadows on the surface. Then the wind picks up and the shadows move quicker and become bigger, the light levels fall and the hillside is now completely covered. As you continue concentrating, the thought occurs, 'I think it's going to rain,' so you pack up and quickly get back to the car just before the rain starts. This is how sensory acuity works. By reading the signs and paying conscious attention, we can make accurate assumptions.

Table 1.2 shows some of the physical changes that you can notice as a person changes from one state to another. Spend a little time just becoming aware of these changes. Again, we are moving away from traditional 'people watching' to what we can actually see in terms of physical shifts.

Although we cannot recreate these clues consciously as a way of creating rapport, they are invaluable signposts allowing us to follow state changes and to give us feedback on our communication.

Initially, we need to pay conscious attention but after a while, once we have practised calibration, our unconscious mind will begin to read the signals and use them to assist us in gaining and maintaining rapport, which has the effect of keeping the communications on track. Once we learn to notice how a person 'looks' when they are 'not sure' or 'are completely convinced', this skill becomes second nature and it is hard to understand how we did without it before.

With practice, we begin to be able to built rapport, read the signs of state changes, become aware of voice tone changes and utilise this information to enhance our ability to build relationships and communicate in the most effective way.

Listening to language

Now we move from facial signals to exploring some of the information revealed in the words people use in conversation. One of the easiest places to start is with our senses. We process the world and the incoming information through our five senses and this sensory processing is revealed in our language. In NLP, we call

Table 1.2   Changes to tune into.

Watch for changes in	Range	What is happening?
Skin colour	Light to dark	The amount of blood supplied will affect the colour. This is most easily seen on the top of the cheek bone.
Skin tone	Soft to hard	The contraction and relaxation of muscles will affect their size and shape, and hence the tension in the skin. Look at the muscles at the outside of the eyes and mouth. The eyebrows also give great clues.
Skin texture	Shiny to matt	The amount of perspiration being produced will affect the appearance of the skin.
Breathing rate	Fast to slow	The amount of oxygen required by the body will affect the breathing rate. Watch the upper chest to lower abdominal area.
Lower lip size (Tumescence)	Thick to thin (lines or no lines)	The amount of blood supplied will affect the size of the lips.
Eyes	Focused to defocused	The focal point will change the muscles around the eyes, the iris and the general 'look'.
	Dull to shiny	The tear production level will affect how sparkly the eyes look.
	Small to large pupil size	The iris reacts to both light levels and internal processing.

this our *primary sense* or *primary representational system*. It is called a representation because it is how we internally store our memories and what we have recorded; our language is then chosen to best describe what is reaccessed and delivered back out into the world. You can think of this as the sense that you use most often in order to access the world; the sense that is most often in consciousness and our natural bias.

The experiences we take in through our senses are stored and we have the amazing ability to use our thought processes to recreate these sensory experiences internally. For example, remembering a pleasant memory will make us smile, an unpleasant one will kindle painful emotions, the thought of a favourite food or drink will make us salivate.

We use notation in NLP to show these senses:

Sight	Visual	V
Hearing	Auditory	A
Feeling	Kinaesthetic	K
Smell	Olfactory	O
Taste	Gustatory	G

There are subdivisions within the systems. Auditory includes both imaginary hearing of words and sounds and talking to oneself. Kinaesthetic includes bodily feelings, touch and emotions. The most common systems used are V, A and K.

Each sense system is part of a network:

1. *Input* – the gathering of information internally and externally through our five senses.
2. *Thinking/Processing* – mapping, learning, decision-making, motivation strategy, storage of information, memory, visualisation of the future.
3. *Output* – how we express ourselves to others: language, voice, physiology.

As individuals, we have very different preferences with regard to how our representational systems are used. If you ask someone to describe a recent holiday, one person might talk about the view from their hotel and the glorious sunsets (V), a second may talk about the sounds of the birds and repeat the stories told by fellow travellers (A), a third may express how they felt with the sun on their body and the sand between their toes (K), whilst another may describe the smells or even the tastes that they experienced.

Thought Experiment

Just sit back right now, and as you do, recall a pleasant memory. Notice what sense you were first aware of – a picture, sound or feeling – and as you do that, notice how your mind can build a full representation of that time with each of the other senses. For example, if you are first aware of seeing a picture, notice what sounds you can hear.

Understanding how we, and others, use our representational systems is the key to self-knowledge, and the starting point for good research projects. It helps us to recognise our own strengths and the preferences of others. We can use this information to significantly improve all our communications, written or face-to-face.

Sensory preferences in language

The language that we use is an indication of the way we think. Most of us have a preference for one, or possibly two, representational systems. If you listen to your own, and other people's, language, you will begin to notice what their preferences are. Matching a person's language is an excellent way of increasing rapport.

To be able to use all our representational systems enriches both our language and our experience of life. Table 1.3 shows some examples for you to explore.

Table 1.3 Sensory words and phrases.

Visual	Auditory	Kinaesthetic	Olfactory and Gustatory
see	hear	feel	smell
look	listen	touch	taste
view	sound(s)	grasp	yummy
appear	make music	get hold of	tasty
show	harmonise	slip through	sweet
dawn	tune in/out	catch on	sour puss
reveal	be all ears	tap into	it's a matter
envision	rings a bell	make contact	of taste
illuminate	silence	throw out	let's chew it
imagine	be heard	turn around	over
clear	resonate	hard	I smell a rat
foggy	deaf	unfeeling	it's a bitter
focused	mellifluous	concrete	pill
hazy	dissonance	scrape	that's an acid
crystal	question	get a handle	comment
picture	unhearing	solid	that leaves
an eyeful	after-thought	he's thick-skinned	a bad taste
appears to me	blabber-mouth	a cool customer	in the back
beyond a shadow	clear as a bell	I grasp the meaning	of my
of doubt	clearly expressed	heated argument	mouth
bird's eye view	call on	I will be in touch	it was so
catch a glimpse of	describe in detail	I can't put my	close I
clear cut	earful	finger on it	could taste
dim view	express yourself	she's a cold fish	it
eye to eye	give an account	a warm-hearted	it's a bit fishy
flashed on	of	person	it leaves a
get a perspective	give me your ear	we are scratching	bad taste
on	grant an audience	the surface,	
get a scope on	heard voices	let's dig deeper	
hazy idea	hidden message	hit the nail on the	
horse of a different	hold your tongue	head	
colour	idle talk	you'll get shot	
in light of	inquire into`	a lukewarm attitude	

Table 1.3 *Continued*

Visual	Auditory	Kinaesthetic	Olfactory and Gustatory
in person	keynote speaker	I feel it in my bones	
in view of	loud and clear	boils down to	
looks like	manner of	chip off the old	
make a scene	speaking	block	
mental image	pay attention to	come to grips with	
mental picture	power of speech	control yourself	
mind's eye	purrs like a kitten	cool/calm/collected	
naked eye	outspoken	firm foundations	
paint a picture	state your purpose	floating on thin air	
photographic	tattle-tale	get a handle on	
memory	to tell the truth	get a load of this	
plainly see	tongue-tied	get in touch with	
pretty as a picture	unheard of	get the drift of	
see to it	utterly	get your goat	
short-sighted	voiced an opinion	hand-in-hand	
showing off	well-informed	hang in there	
sight for sore eyes	within hearing	heated argument	
staring off into	that rings a bell,	hold it!	
space	we're on the	hold on!	
take a peak	same	hot-head	
tunnel vision	wavelength	keep your shirt on	
up front	let's talk about it	know-how	
I get the picture	who calls the	lay cards on table	
I see what you	tune?	light-headed	
mean	within earshot	moment of panic	
let's get this in	let's discuss things	not following you	
perspective	I'm speechless	pain in the neck	
it appears that	shout from the	pull some strings	
show me	hilltops	sharp as a tack	
the focus of	people will hear	slipped my mind	
attention	you	smooth operator	
looking closely	this silence is	start from scratch	
a blind spot	deafening	stiff upper lip	

Table 1.3 *Continued*

Visual	Auditory	Kinaesthetic	Olfactory and Gustatory
it's clear to me	it's music to my	stuffed shirt	
a different angle	ears	too much of a hassle	
he's a dark one	word for word		
there's a cloud on the horizon	turn a deaf ear		
this is the outlook			
with hindsight			
she's short-sighted			
you'll look back on this			

It is useful to understand your own preference, as this will be the mode in which you do most of your communicating. Building your own flexibility by learning sensory language that is not your preference will help you broaden your scope of rapport-building using language. In any situation where you are dealing with groups, the most useful strategy is to be able to illustrate your arguments using sensory language drawn from each system – visual, auditory and kinaesthetic. If you are operating in the food or perfume industries, you may also want to add olfactory and gustatory words as well.

Often, when we are talking about a process, we do not use sensory language. Words such as sense, experience, understand, think, learn, process, decide, motivate, consider, change, perceive, insensitive, distinct, conceive, know and aware do not convey the senses. If someone does not seem to be using sense words, then consider asking appropriate questions, such as, 'When you remember *x*, what is the first thing that comes to mind?'

For example, at a presentation . . .

'in this slide *you can see* . . .' (or you will note . . . or you will sense . . .)

In a group . . .

'how *do you feel* about this idea? . . .' (or how do you see this? . . . or how does it strike you?)

Whilst it is possible to tailor language to an individual in a depth or small group situation, in a larger group situation it is more beneficial to use a mix of sensory preferences. In this situation, the moderator should adopt the neutral stance (e.g. 'I know what you mean', 'what do you think?'), and play down their own natural preferences. Just as good moderators do not ask leading questions, they also need to be able to ask neutral questions when this is the appropriate thing to do.

Speaking in the same tongue

Now that we can listen for words and phrases, the next step is to hear and use tonality. Again, this is not mimicking but the gentle use of the same tone, pitch, volume and speed. This skill is especially useful on the phone.

Practise repeating sentences concentrating on speed and volume. Then move on to tonality. Find a willing guinea pig, preferably two, and then you can ask one to coach you. What you want to aim for is to have the same 'structure'; the timing, speed and volume are the most important. Avoid at all costs copying local dialects, it just does not work!

Concentrate on increasing your range to be more flexible. These subtle patterns added to the sensory language create a powerful tool for your rapport-building toolkit.

TRUE LISTENING

The meeting has begun, you have put yourself in a resourceful state and now your challenge is to understand exactly what the client wants. In this section we will examine the various NLP tools that can help us think about the question that all of us interested in human reactions and relations have: How can we be sure that we have interpreted the client's wishes correctly?

There should never be a time when you are not listening. The time spent listening is an investment in relationship building. When you want people to respect you and believe in you, when you want them to follow your example, when you want them to be confident in their work, *listen to them*, take an interest in what they do and say and show that you care about them and the problems they are dealing with.

> *'I know that you believe you understand what you think I said, but I'm not sure you realise that what you heard is not what I meant.'*
>
> *anon*

The only time you speak when you are listening is to ask questions to allow you to understand their model of the world. Be constantly aware of

> *'Many attempts to communicate are nullified by saying too much.'*
> *Robert Greenleaf*

what they are saying and what they are not saying. This will give you clues to questions you are likely to need to ask later. Let the whole story unfold and avoid interrupting their flow while they are speaking. So, during the taking of a brief (or any meeting), spend less time reading and writing and more time watching and listening. If you have a problem with this, buy a digital recorder, so that you do not have to write too much down. The evidence is in front of you, not on paper.

It is important that you demonstrate constantly to the other person that you are listening. Smile, nod and keep an open body posture (legs and arms unfolded). In addition, of course, if you have built rapport with the other person, they will be smiling, nodding and keeping an open body posture while giving you all the information you need.

Mirroring

Sometimes it is not easy to keep silent when the other person pauses to think. You need to be able to stay silent during the pause. This can be particularly difficult for someone who is extrovert in nature. If you absolutely must talk, repeat back the last thing the other person said. This is a form of mirroring, which indicates that you are listening and invites the other person to continue speaking.

Undivided attention

In a given time, we can absorb far more information than the other person can deliver. When the person pauses between words to think, we should concentrate on body language, facial expression and other involuntary muscular signals that they are transmitting. Use 'quiet' time to make notes. Give the person your undivided attention with both body and eyes. Use direct eye contact and, as much as possible (given seating arrangements), place your body directly adjacent to the respondent. Make it clear that he/she is the ONLY person to whom you are giving your attention.

Separate messenger from message

Remember, it is the message you are interested in. Sometimes there is a temptation to merge the message and the messenger.

We can be angry about the message, but we do not need to be tough on the messenger. For example, the other person might say, 'Our department won't do that.' You could say, 'Typical. I expected more of you. You said you'd do it and you haven't.' You might be unhappy with the fact that their department is not cooperating but you are not necessarily unhappy with the person. So, you can be tough on the message without being tough on the messenger. A better response, which would preserve the rapport with the individual, would be, 'I have to say that I'm very unhappy with your department for letting me down. I was led to understand that they would do it.' In this way you are taking the pressure off the person and putting it on the organisation, where it rightfully belongs.

Listening is a critical success factor in relationships, whether they are personal or business relationships, and while most people understand the theory, too few take the time to practise active listening. Remember to do so, and you will find the results more than repay the effort.

QUALITY QUESTIONS

Once you have listened attentively, you are ready to enter the first phase of questioning. This will make sure your understanding of what the other person has said is the same as their understanding of what they have said. A process of clarifying, checking understanding and reflecting back does this.

Clarify

Make sure you have heard clearly. Ask questions like:

'Would you mind repeating that?'
'Can you clarify that for me so that I can grasp it clearly?'

Check understanding

Here you repeat and paraphrase what the person has said:

'So, what you're saying is . . .'
'As I understand it, what you've said you would like is . . .'

Reflect back

When we reflect back what the other person has said, we seek to understand the logic and the emotion attached to it:

'Do I understand that you're really excited about these concepts?'
'From what you've said, does that mean you're happy with the proposal?'

The art of asking good questions requires some thought about the nature of the question and what is inherent in any question you ask. What follows is a brief review of the art of good questions designed to help you be clearer and more precise when taking a brief.

'There is no such thing as a worthless conversation, provided you know what to listen for. And questions are the breath of life for a conversation.'
James Nathan Miller

The function of questions

Questions are great for eliciting answers, but they have other functions, too:

- to build rapport with the client;
- to uncover a client's needs;

- to explore values and concerns round the project;
- to build on existing relationships.

Remember the need to engage with clients (and, again, colleagues), and the implicit exchanges that require questions as part of the glue that binds people together.

Good questions

Good questions also do more than eliciting: they leave impressions about you with your subject, and they act positively on both parties. They:

- make you think;
- get you good information;
- create space to consider other possibilities.

Using good questions, as opposed to bad ones, is part of the exchange procedure and is an essential skill in building rapport.

Closed vs open questions

You will probably have heard about open and closed questions in research (see Table 1.4 for a recap). These are usually taught at the beginning of a qualitative training course (and in other course content, too). Remember, open and closed questions have a secondary dimension, too.

Types of manipulative questions

We have included these so you can recognise them, not because you should use them! That said, researchers are often asked, by certain

Table 1.4 Open and closed questions.

Closed	Open
Framed for a yes or no answer	Build rapport
Used for checking information	Are exploratory
Used to check understanding, e.g. 'Do I understand that . . . ?'	Open possibilities
	Used when you have little information
Used for focusing down on information	Used when you need to be general, e.g. 'How is business generally?'
Those that begin with is, isn't, does, doesn't ARE REFLECTIVE	

Table 1.5 Direct and manipulative questions.

Direct	Manipulative
Get the truth	Get client to say what *you* want
Make it easy for the client to say what *they* want	Route answers down the determined path
Save time	Reduce choice for customer, e.g. 'You do want this don't you?'
Save reputation	Lose business eventually

clients, to 'get the answers' they want to hear. This is a travesty of what qualitative research should be about, but it happens.

Front-loading or framing

Front-loading or framing is the art of phrasing a question to obtain a specific answer. Even if you never use it purposely, it is as well to know what it is, so you can avoid it!

e.g.   'In a recent survey, it was shown that 90% of people are dissatisfied with their present furniture. Do you share this view?'

Weight of numbers does not generally tip the scales with many people.

Polarising

This involves asking a closed question, which directs someone to say yes or no. To the example below, it's hard to say 'No'.

e.g.   'Are you concerned about your children's future?'

Negative questions

e.g.   'Would you not agree to this point?'

Here, to disagree makes you look foolish.

Statements as questions

Misusing question construction to achieve a particular answer is not just a market research issue. It is used frequently in many other situations, not least of all in politics (for evidence, just listen to any parliamentary questions), but this does not make it right.

e.g.   'Obviously, you'll be wanting to take two of these.'

These questions presuppose an answer and are expressed in a judgemental way.

Offering the answer

These are used when the questioner wants a specific answer.

e.g.   'What's important to you when you buy a car, safety I expect?'

This, in many respects, is how topic guides are written. By raising the issues with prompts, respondents have already been given the parameters to respond to, and have little chance to get their own ideas and opinions onto an agenda.

Hidden assumptions

e.g. 'Which statement best describes how you feel about the new concept?'

Under these conditions, the respondent is covertly encouraged to accept a hidden condition, i.e. that one of the statements actually does reflect their view.

Asking key questions

Poor communication and misunderstandings are often the result of the same word meaning different things to different people.

Why?

How often is this used in market research? Why is often the *least* useful question to ask. It gives you either the sequence of actions leading to the event or the reason for the action. It presupposes that there is a rational (and socially acceptable) response to give. It is frequently also approaching an aggressive question, implying some form of possibility of misbehaviour: 'Why did you buy this car (implicitly, why not the other one)?'

Why questions give justifications and very little information. This puts you in a position of being unable to refute the opinion without losing rapport or causing offence.

Rules

Use How, What, Where, When and Who to:

1. *Clarify* client needs (leave Why to the philosophers, strategic planners and the board).
2. Be specific – focus on client need.
3. Compare what the client wants to what you can provide. For example, 'I want more consumer interviews than last year.'

   Question: 'How many did you have, how many would you like?'
4. Resolve *absolutes* – always, never, everyone. For example, 'I always use XYZ research company.'

   Question: 'What is it about XYZ that you find satisfactory?'

   This will get you important information. Question absolutes by asking for an exception and building on that.
5. Open up more projects from existing clients.

   'How exactly can I serve your needs in the future?'
   'How else can I help you?'
   'What exactly can I and my company do to earn more of your business?'

Some words point to the rules Should, Must, Have To and their opposites Shouldn't, Mustn't. Comply with organisational rules. Argue only if it is important to you and will impact the project negatively. Remember, the more nonsensical a rule, the more a customer may need to justify it. You can question rules by asking, 'What would happen if it did not?'

Can't is a much stronger rule word. The question 'Why not?' is too blunt 'What stops you?' is more elegant and will get more information.

How and how not to ask questions

In some research techniques, like laddering questioning, using a repetitive style of questions can be prone to overuse and negative response generation. It is important to know (and often, just to sense) when to quit. Remember to:

- determine how much detail you need;
- know when you have enough information;
- ask more specific questions if you find you need to backtrack continually (see also the techniques surrounding chunking in Chapter 2).

Continuous questioning can be seen as aggressive and may trigger a defensive response, so be careful.

How to soften questions

Language is very much tied in with tone. We return to this subject later on, in the interviewing section, but for now, be aware that the use of voice tone and timbre can and does have a major contributory value. In colloquial terms, 'you can get away with murder if you smile'.

1. Use voice tone – soft not harsh. Use the natural tonality of a question to help you:

   'You can do that.'   (even emphasis – statement)
   'You can do *that*?'   (rising inflection – question)
   'You can do *that*!'   (falling inflection – command)

2. Precede your questions with soft frames:

   'I'm interested to know if . . .'
   'Maybe you could tell me . . .'
   'Perhaps you can let me know if . . .'
   'I wonder . . .'
   'You may . . .'
   'I'm not sure how much . . .'
   'Would you mind telling me . . .'

We can use words to soften the links between our questions, experiment with As, While and Then. Leaving But out of your vocabulary will help to maintain rapport and keep minds open.

Avoid long and multiple questions

Most people find it difficult to follow a spoken question/ statement of more than about 20 words. Again, see many (client and agency) topic guides for a 'how not to . . .' illustration. Also, you could do worse than tune into many political or current affairs programmes on TV or radio, to hear how the question is often longer than the answer. This does nothing but annoy, confuse and baffle. Keep them simple, either specific or genuinely open. KISS formula rules here . . . Keep It Short and Simple.

ELICITING VALUES

NLP provides a good definition of what values are and how they operate in humans; they are the emotive reasons why people invest time and money into doing or not doing something. One thing is clear, if you want to motivate someone to do something, whether it is to buy something or to join you in exploring an idea, then an understanding of values and how they operate is vital. In business, being able to recognise and then work with a person's or organisation's values is critical to success. In research, it is at the core of many projects, and no less is it at the heart of a successful interface with a client's brief.

Values are our standards for evaluation. Feeling great, having fun or being reliable are all standards against which any possible choice or experience could be measured. Values are usually stated in abstract words, for example faithfulness, honesty, trust, caring, intimacy, affection, fun, acceptance. They apply just as much to corporations and to individuals.

Key points regarding values

Values:

- govern and provide up-front energy for our actions (motivation);
- are used for post-action evaluation of both self and others;
- are drivers of true purpose;
- provide the organising framework for our beliefs;
- provide the blueprints for our lives today;
- provide the terms of reference for:
  - taking action or not taking action
  - evaluating yourself and evaluating others;
- can change or be changed!

Values are those things that we move towards or away from. They either attract us or repel us. They are what we are willing to invest time, energy and resources in to achieve or avoid. All human decisions are based on values, which are usually outside of conscious awareness. Values are the basis of the criteria on which all decisions are made.

Values find conscious expression in our ideas of good–bad, right–wrong, beautiful–ugly, enhancing–diminishing and desirable–undesirable. In short, many brand values.

Three types of values which determine state, and so behaviour, are:

- *Power values* – what we want, such as: freedom, control and choice.
- *Operational values* – how we get there, such as: money, respect and achievement.

• *Determination values* – how we judge and evaluate, such as: truth, honesty and integrity.

Part of your approach when taking the brief should be gently to ascertain both the personal values of the client and the company values. There are two main methods for finding these values, first by asking questions such as:

'What is important to the company about this project?'
'What are the key needs that the project has to fulfil?'
'What is important to you about a successful project?'
'Is there anything else important that I should know to make this a success?'
'Are there any lessons that you learned from other projects that would be important for me to know about when completing this work for you?'

The second method can be more subtle and requires some observational skills on your part. Values are always displayed by our behaviours, so some people-watching with intent to notice values can be a great way to reveal them. This leads to you making assumptions, but you cannot just act on them, you will need to test the assumptions in order to verify you have gleaned a useful bit of information.

Exercise

Take a selection of current clients or people you know. Observe behaviours and ask questions that will reveal possible values. Create a profile and test your assumptions. One way of doing this is to offer the opposite of a value you think the person has and watch for the reaction. If the value is held strongly then you will get both a verbal response to verify the value and a physiological body language shift. This takes practice and experimentation in non critical environments in order to become adept. Be curious and stay in rapport.

Example Questions

'You seem to be the sort of person who . . . ?' (here you can give the opposite or play back the value you have assumed and notice the reaction)

'In this project is it important to . . . ?'

'Your company/department seems to believe . . . . Have I got that right?'

So, how could this work? Let's examine an example of the type of assumptions we could make and how to test them.

Take a client that you know something about. For example, this client likes to know that there is a procedure and that it is being followed. We may assume that there are high values placed on procedure, methods, rules, order, systems, policy and regulations. In terms of behaviour, we might observe the way meetings are run, how an office is arranged, whether the paperwork is neat and systematised. If this is your assumption, then some questions around the assumed values can reveal if you have made a correct best guess. These can then be used as a basis for constructing your action plans to reflect those assumptions.

Value matrices

We can think of values as a matrix, and as a first pass, we can make some assumptions about a person's value matrix by observing their key qualities, listening to the way they talk about their business and their job. Then we are able to focus questions so we can test our assumptions. Here are some examples.

If you know a client values efficiency, then you could assume that they also may value:

* precision
* order

Evaluation experiment

Think of a person that you deal with in a client organisation. Focus on the last time you communicated in person, especially where you had a personal as well as a business interchange.

* *What value(s) come across strongly?*
* *What assumptions might you make about their matrix?*
* *What would you expect to see as behavioural and material manifestations of these value matrices?*

Make your assumptions then check them by asking questions. This can be done in a casual conversational way and can yield much information.

- regulation
- reliability
- repeatability.

In NLP it is fine to make assumptions so long as you test them for accuracy.

If you know the client values winning and their talk indicated their competitive nature, you could assume that they may also value:

- game playing
- achievement
- examining competition
- innovation
- tenacity.

Finding out what is important to a client becomes an essential part of taking a good brief. We always want to fulfil the clients' values in a study, that way, even if the study does not show what the client hoped, our chances of retaining that client will be increased if we have been able to fulfil their values.

The key question is: What is important to the client? This may not just involve the parameters of the project or study, but also the way it is conducted and presented in alignment with the personal and corporate values of the person requesting the work and the business context.

It is also inevitable that both the individual client manager and the company have a complex set of interactive values (and beliefs) at work. It can be hard to pull them apart, but they will be there: it is impossible for them not to be. In the same way that people have their own specific *filtering system* (see later chapters), so, too, do they have their own *values system*, which dictates how they perceive stimuli around them. Remembering a foundation of NLP, communication is what is *received*. What you have said/asked/written is decoded by the recipient in *their* terms, not in yours. It makes sense to know as much as you can about their world.

Examples of research briefs and client values

The following is taken from an advertising research brief. What do you think you can tell about the research manager's values from this?

Objectives

The key objective of this research is to evaluate the advertising and to identify a direction for the follow-up campaign.

This research *is not* meant to measure the awareness, recall or launch impact, but it is supposed to be an in-depth exploration of the campaign.

Key areas of interest

- Gauge overall perceptions of the TV and print advertisements
- Test strengths/likes and weaknesses/dislikes of the concept and uncover reasons
- Explore appeal, relevance and understanding of the advertisements and get reactions to them across the (geographical) markets
- Understanding of the main and secondary messages
- How unique and innovative is this advertising?
- Is it memorable?
- What does the ad say about the brand?
- Is it relevant/credible for the brand?
- What kind of images does it give to it?
- How does it position it (i.e. is it unique, innovative, etc.)?
- Explore perceptions of who the target audience is

- Evaluate specific elements of the spot:
  - music, messages, mood/tone/style, claim
  - are there any missing elements?
- Determine impact of the advertisements on the brand
- What does it say about the brand? Does it fit with the brand or is it surprising? In what way does it change brand perceptions? Why might people be attracted to the brand from what the ad is telling them?
- Is the communication relevant/credible for the brand?

Methodology

- Qualitative research: two focus groups will be conducted in each of four markets: France, Spain, Belgium and Denmark.
- Each focus group will last two hours.
- Composition of the focus groups:
  - one group male, one female
  - age 25–35, singles and couples living in urban areas
  - modern mainstream:
    - progressive people with balanced and active lifestyles
    - individualistic, smart, multicultural and information seekers
    - key values: self-expression, enjoyment of life and wellbeing
  - current car ownership: small low and small high leading models (list to be provided), which are the main vehicles in the household
  - open to brands (i.e. would not reject a specific brand)
  - screened for sensitive occupations
  - only one respondent per household
  - open to advertising

Compare and contrast the above with the following brief, from an FMCG company. All examples are inevitably doctored to preserve anonymity and confidentiality.

Category understanding

Background

At present we lack understanding of how consumers and shoppers interact with the category. We can make assumptions as to why consumers choose certain products, but do not really know why the choices are made. Currently the market is segmented by retailers and suppliers in terms of the production process, but consumers do not fully understand these terms, let alone segment the category by them.

Aims and research objectives

There is the wider issue of why a consumer will choose one (product segment) over the other. We are looking at a full understanding of the take-home market, and not expecting a full understanding of the impulse market, but just some top-line views on purchase.

The first brief illustrates a client with a history of using market research, the second illustrates a less-experienced client and the briefs are, therefore, more or less specific and useable accordingly.

Values and their relationship to beliefs

Values and beliefs are closely related and often the difference is blurred. In general terms, we can think of values as the *principles* and beliefs as the *rules* which allow those principles to be followed or not; together, they form a matrix.

Take an example of a value, say honesty. We will see that in order for this value to be activated, there are beliefs or operating rules that must be in place.

In research, we are frequently asked to examine why people have reacted to, or will react to, a new product or a new concept in a specific way, or to review an existing product's performance in the market. Inherent in these projects is the concept of re-spondent/market values and beliefs.

Examples of these issues are to be found in the automotive industry (what about fuel consumption?), domestic issues (greenhouse gases, fossil fuels), FMCG (organic farming, packaging, recycling), B2B projects (corporate social responsibility, recycling), and so on.

These are examples of issues that are becoming important in marketing, and thus research. In any context, we need to understand what these values and beliefs are, in general, before we can make any real sense of how and why someone is responding in a particular way to our questioning. This wider contextualisation is significantly helped by the use of both NLP concepts (and indeed any wider values and beliefs theoretical model) and by the specifics of the questioning possibilities in order to obtain such an understanding.

Vitally, in order to obtain access to some intimate and personal issues, a greater rapport, and specific knowledge of how to achieve and maintain it, is also critically important.

See? It all fits together nicely!

SETTING THE SCENE – NLP FRAMES

NLP frames are enormously useful; they set the ground rules and allow you to control the direction of meetings. They set a context for a purpose, and we can put things into different contexts to give them different meanings. For example, a high wind at a beach picnic would be annoying, but the same high wind while sailing a boat would be exhilarating. Here are some useful ways of framing events.

Imagine sitting in a meeting with a prospective client. The meeting grinds on, and at the end, you are left not much clearer about what has been requested, decided or agreed. It appears that no-one has set the 'terms of reference' – the *frames* – especially the *outcome* frame or the *evidence* frame. What is the meeting intended to achieve? What are the time constraints? What are the end products?

Using the NLP concept of *framing* will ensure that you all agree why you are there, what is expected and how you will know that the goals have been achieved. Let's look in a little more detail at these requirements and frames.

Outcome frame

This involves evaluating situations in terms of outcomes. You want to leave the meeting clear as to what the client wants and able to get on with writing the proposal. The client wishes to know that you have understood the brief and that timescales are clear and met, both immediately – when the meeting should end – and longer-term – when the research/proposal is required.

First you need to understand your own required outcome. Is it well-formed? Is it positive and under your control? Second, you will need to understand the outcomes of any other people involved, and to help them clarify what they want. Third, integrate the outcomes. Once you have all the outcomes, you can see how they fit together; you may need to negotiate on any that are incompatible. Lastly, look at the integrated outcomes and see if you are moving towards them. If not, you clearly have to change direction.

The outcome frame is a very useful way to view your activities in a business. If a team (especially a management team) does not have a clear view of its outcomes, it has no firm basis for decisions and no way of telling whether a particular activity is useful or not.

Meeting going off track? Side arguments and discussions taking up space and time? Sound familiar? The question, 'How does (this) relate to the outcome agreed upon for this meeting?', is a challenge to use to any statement which, in the perception of the information processor, is not relevant to the outcome.

This procedure demands that the information source justify his statement relative to the context. It is impossible in the absence of an agreed outcomes frame. Thus, the latter is imperative for the smooth running of any meeting that is not to meander along until everyone is thoroughly confused.

Evidence frame

This frame is concerned with clear and specific details. How exactly will you know when you have achieved your outcome? What will you see, hear and feel? This is a useful frame to apply to the criteria within the outcome frame.

Ecology or consequences frame

How do my outcomes and actions affect the wider environment of family, friends, social and business interests? Do they support my overall integrity as a human being, and do they respect the integrity of any other people involved? One can sometimes find that opportunities which look very attractive when viewed in an outcome frame look very different through an ecology frame.

I was recently asked by a client to disclose the details of the respondents (name, address, etc.). This is an easy one to refuse, as it contravenes most of the Data Protection Act, ESOMAR and MRS Codes of Practice, but equally, it goes against the ecology frame. It would do the agency and the respondents great damage, and as such, does not match the conditions of the ecology (consequences) frame.

As if frame

Meeting stuck in discussion of a point (maybe of basic sample strategy) with no apparent solution? The as if frame can help.

This is a way of creative problem solving based on pretending that a different set of circumstances exist, in order to explore new possibilities. You can start by saying 'Let's suppose that . . .' or 'If that were the case, then . . .'. For example, 'How would we handle the sampling problems if we were based in Spain?' or 'Let's look a year into the future; how did we get here?' This frame can be a powerful way of generating ideas and of breaking deadlocks.

Backtrack frame

This is simply reiterating the information you have received so far, using the other person's key words, phrases and voice tones in the backtrack. This makes it very different from a summary, which often distorts the meaning of the other person's words. Backtrack is useful to open discussions, update newcomers and to check agreement and understanding. It helps build and maintain rapport, and clarifies the way forward should you get lost at any point.

Maybe use it at the wrap-up stage of the meeting, when you are near to finishing the brief-taking, to ensure that you have really understood, and have an agreed plan of action.

CHECKLIST FOR TAKING THE BRIEF

Timing

Take control of your time. Easy to say, but the reality is that time *is* under your control. Arrive on time/early, as there is nothing worse than being tense because the train was late. However, if the worst happens, you can control your response to the drama by using your anchor. I often travel (if not a local meeting) the night before, to make sure that lateness is not an option. Cutting it fine is not practical. It may seem macho ('I am so important, I have to attend all these meetings and have absolutely no time to spare'), but in reality it's just unsound.

Like the old safety campaign used to warn, 'Arrive alive'. Arrive in time and in control. The meeting will go better and the outcome will be better.

Preparation

Create a checklist of useful items so you can be certain that you will have everything you need. If you are unprepared, the tension this creates will hinder your performance, but all is not lost.

Dress/image code

The way you dress is an important part of creating rapport with the other parties in the meeting. What you are wearing may look great at the new music festival you went to at the weekend, or at your granny's 90th birthday party, but is it appropriate for a new client pitch? The way you dress gives a wide range of clues about the type of person you are, what your values are and how you feel about yourself, but equally, it gives a parallel set of clues to the observer, which may not translate the same as you intended, so it is important to understand how what you wear may appear to others.

CHAPTER 2

RESPONDING TO THE BRIEF

WHAT'S IN THIS CHAPTER?

- Proposal or action plan?
- The framework
- Creating positive mindsets
- Language
- Utilising values
- Setting outcomes and objectives

WHAT'S THE POINT OF WRITING A PROPOSAL?

The next step is writing the proposal. How often do we think about exactly what and how we are writing? What effect will the way we write, the words we use, have on the recipient? First thoughts: communication is what the other person has understood; communication is the response you get – not necessarily what you intended. Apply this thought to your communications to get the best impact.

PROPOSAL OR ACTION PLAN?

First we will deal with the construction to get the framework sorted, then we can use NLP language concepts to create a proposal with impact.

Let's start with the word 'proposal', what does that word presuppose? First, that the person is in mental consideration mode, therefore not in action mode; second, that this is not the final offering and so it opens the space for negotiation on project parameters and, more importantly, the price. So, you may have written the definitive plan, which you know will deliver, but because it is couched as a proposal, the client is at liberty to change and question the entirety or parts. Your stance is then defensive and this is a very undesirable place to negotiate from.

So what is the answer? How would it be if, instead of creating a proposal, you created an 'action plan' to deliver what the client needs? This removes the price negotiation implication in the

I (Roger) worked with a company that delivered research projects to medical companies, and the whole process had some interesting language wrapped around it. When we started to examine the assumptions contained in the language, it became clear that this was conditioning the approach the team had to presenting their proposals to clients.

The language of the brief was all about an 'invitation to bid', this implied that they did not go out looking for work but relied on their reputation in the field to bring them invitations. This was a very reactive stance and, in fact, this is exactly how they behaved. Once they had received an 'invitation' and written their 'proposal', they went to the next stage, which they called a 'proposal defence meeting'. Imagine their state of mind and attitude in front of the client in this defensive stance!

Action Plans

- *Determine the steps needed to reach an outcome*
- *Are achievement-orientated*
- *Recommend a course of action*
- *Are fact-based*

word 'proposal' and puts you in a position of adjusting a plan rather than rewriting the proposal. This is much easier to handle, with less room for misunderstandings.

What we want to develop is a structure that will lend impact and clarity to our action plans, so that when the client receives the action plan, it is very easy to say yes.

THE POWER OF WORDS

Every word we know is packed with specific meaning for us and will not be exactly the same for another person. So, it is a good idea to repeat back the client's words, as the specific meaning for them will be carried by those words. This approach will also help maintain rapport through the document. The principle, of course, works in person as well.

There are several ways to write an action plan, analyse/present findings or indeed to relate to your client or colleagues. Which do you think works best?

Proposals

* *Examine what might happen in the future*
* *Seek to persuade*
* *Recommend a certain decision*
* *Express opinions – supported by objective facts*

Experiment

Using the client's words exactly is also rapport building. We all code our words differently, so experiment with a few friends, six would be good, by choosing a word, say Love or Education, and asking them to write down five things that word means without the others seeing.

Find out how many have exactly the same five words.

Language use

Do we, or should we, use the first person personal pronoun, 'I' or 'we', in the writing of the action plan or not, and, if so, which one? NLP helps here, with the notions of *association/dissociation* and *perceptual positions*.

Association is the state of personal, direct involvement ('I or we think your problem is . . .'), while '*dissociation*' is one removed, acting as the objective outsider ('It appears as if the client's problem is . . .'). The former gives a much more involved feel and a personal, emotional relationship is implied, while the latter gives off signals of professional detachment. Which is best (which communicates more effectively) depends on the client's requirements and style, and is also likely to do with the nature and scope of the project. Advertising agencies are very keen to appear on the client's team/side, so typically use 'we', whereas researchers have often opted for a more distant, objective stance.

Creating positive mindsets

The objective is to create positive mindsets at the start of your action plan. In the brief introduction, you have an opportunity to begin to influence how your plan is received. There are some very simple language structures that will help you open the clients to your suggested solutions. There are also some simple words that, used unwisely, can undo many good ideas.

Creating rapport with language

Cover all bases

The first useful language pattern is called *cover all bases* and creates rapport by aiming to induce a feeling of inclusion. This is achieved by addressing *all* the possibilities that the reader might have in their mind about the project or about your company. Here is an example:

> PQR Agency has been asked to respond to the 'Widget Development' brief. The proposal must be available to the client by Friday this week. The decision to proceed with the research will be made on the following Wednesday. PQR Agency is delighted to have this opportunity of working on this project.
>
> 'We are delighted to respond to this brief, especially as we have conducted several projects for your company in the past. Some members of your project team have worked with us before and know our agency's value, others of you, we understand, have been given copies of our previous work and some of you will be working with us for the first time. In any event, we are confident that our experience will be extremely valuable and that this project will be a great success.'

Yes sets

Another pattern allows you to repeat back the facts that you gleaned at the briefing interview plus a brief idea of your solution. This is done in sets of three undeniable facts, then your solution or idea that you want to be accepted – i.e. fact 1, fact 2, fact 3 and then your solution. Here is an example:

> The XYZ company has been in existence for ten years. It is located in the south of England and its product to research is Wizzy Widgets. ABC research suggests they undertake a series of focus group interviews to establish the market for XYZ Wizzy Widgets in the north of England.
>
> Fact 1 = The XYZ company has been in existence for ten years.
> Fact 2 = Located in the south of England.
> Fact 3 = Product for research is Wizzy Widgets.
> Solution = Undertake a series of focus group interviews to establish the market for XYZ Wizzy Widgets in the north of England.

This construction is known as a *yes set*. The effect of three undeniable facts put before your plausible idea sets up in the mind of the reader three consecutive yeses. The mind then tends to say yes to the next thing that comes along.

Words to watch out for

Words contain presuppositions or assumptions that, when we hear or read them, are processed in a particular way by our brains and generate specific responses.

Presuppositions are the assumptions that lie behind the language we are using; not all are immediately apparent. They can have effects on the listener that the communicator never intended. The key words to watch out for are 'if', 'try' and 'but'. Although each has its own pitfalls, they can be used to create powerful messages to elicit a desired response. This is not about manipulation, but about putting your message across with the maximum chance of getting it heard.

There are two ways to go with this information, one is to use the words to obtain a conscious effect and the other is to replace them with more definite, and probably more empowering, words. The alternatives to these words are 'when', 'do' and 'and'. Look at the following examples.

If

The use of the word 'if' presupposes that you have a choice. You should only use it when you mean to be offering someone a choice.

'If you can arrange a meeting for 4 pm . . .'
Probable result: no meeting. 'I couldn't arrange it.'

Try

The use of the word 'try' presupposes failure. Only use it where you want to increase the chances of someone not being able to do something.

'Try and get it done by Friday . . .'
Probable result: 'Yes, I gave it a try, but I didn't finish it in time.'

But

The effect of 'but' is to negate the previous statement. Be careful to use it correctly, because when used incorrectly, the effect is to build resistance in the listener.

'Yes, we have considered your idea, but we are going to . . .'
Probable result: 'They ignored my idea.'

Consider what is presupposed in the following statements and the likely effectiveness of each of them:

'When you have arranged a meeting for 4 pm . . .'
'If you could try to hire me a car . . .'
'If you wish to retain your current hardware . . .'
'Please do it by Friday . . .'
'I'd like it delivered by Monday, but, if you can't, next Friday will
    do.'
'Try and find a better deal than we offer . . .'
'Try and deliver it by the end of the month.'
'Yes, we have considered your idea, and we are going to . . .'
'Ours is an excellent machine, but it's cheap too.'
'Yes, I know there are cheaper alternatives than ours, but have you
    considered the reliability?'
'When you need more information, do call me.'

It is far more effective when you start to use the language patterns that presuppose what you *do* want, rather than what you *don't* want.

A useful way of beginning to unravel the structure of the language we habitually use and to start using the language that will get our desired outcome is to listen to other people speaking. Take each of these patterns and notice when they are used. What was the effect? This then leads you to adjust how you personally communicate.

USING VALUES TO ENHANCE THE ACTION PLAN

As we learned in Chapter 1, being aware of, and using, a client's values forms one of the most important ways of connecting powerfully with a client's motivation to do a project. Satisfying the client's need to know that you are going to meet their value set, both personally and also the values of the business or department, may be more crucial to future business if things don't go according to plan than meeting their precise objectives.

Using the values elicited when taking the brief, we can replay these when writing the action plan in order to connect with and motivate the client towards your plan. These can be written as yes sets or cover all bases and here are a few suggestions:

1. Values of Speed, Accuracy, Price and Timing in a yes set format:
   'In order to reach your research objective, our plan has been designed to be delivered speedily with maximum research accuracy within your price constraints. It will require a go-ahead decision by (date) in order for this work to be carried out within the timing framework.'

2. Values of Creativity, New Ideas, Solutions and Innovation in a yes set format:
    'Our action plan will initiate the creativity needed to generate the new ideas that will lead to innovative solutions that you will be able to implement next season.'

3. Values of Cost Effectiveness, Thoroughness and Precision in a cover all bases format:
    'Our action plan covers thoroughly all the key areas that the briefing meeting with the accounts, sales and marketing departments highlighted. The action plan has been designed to deliver a cost-effective and precise review of customer satisfaction for your service.'

DOCUMENT STYLE AND CONSTRUCTION

Length/detail

Is your client a detail person or a big picture person? The NLP concept of *chunking up/down* gives a model for responding to clients in the most effective (compatible) manner, according to the way they handle information. Being aware of your own preference and how you like to handle information is also essential. If you like detail and your client wants the big picture, then by delivering too much detail you will either break rapport or fail to

I (Neil) recently lost a project because my proposal was too long, too detailed and too much for the internal client user. I had never met the internal team – only the research manager, who I know well, and who I know understands research well. I neglected to build in the required simplification for non-researchers: I thought I had this covered by walking them through the recommendation in detail, but clearly they were big picture people, at least as far as research went. My proposal was 40 pages, the winner was 8 pages.

generate rapport, and your action plan will have less chance of success.

Chunking

Sometimes people experience and talk about the world in general terms. We may set ourselves broad outcomes for what we want to achieve. On other occasions, we may be very specific, dealing in small items of information.

In NLP, we tend to talk about these as being big and little chunks of information. To move from the general to the specific and vice versa is known as *chunking* (see Figure 2.1).

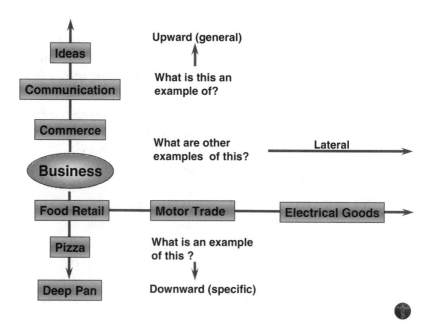

Figure 2.1   Chunking (The Hierarchy of Ideas).

Take the word 'business':

To chunk up, you would ask yourself *what is this an example of?*

To chunk down, you would ask yourself *what is an example of this?*

Moving from the general to the specific can be useful, for example in translating corporate goals into specific targets for individuals. It can be useful to move someone from the specific to the general to show how their particular behaviour fits into the larger picture.

Chunking can be especially effective when negotiations are stuck on a detail. Chunking up to a general area where both parties can be in agreement, then moving carefully down through the detail will often bring resolution.

This concept (The Hierarchy of Ideas) is about types and classes of information and was originally created by Bertrand Russell and Whitehead who began to use this notion to solve mathematical problems (Russell, 1902). The linguists got hold of the idea because it explained, in some way, how different people hold and disseminate information. Just think of the communication disparity if you have a detailed specific bias and the person you are dealing with is more comfortable in the more general 'big picture' area. You will be infuriated by their lack of information; they will be overwhelmed by too much.

Sensory preferences

Creating rapport is possible through the documentation using yes sets, cover all bases formats and enough sensory-based language to be sure that whoever reads the document will have their sensory preference met and matched.

When thinking of matching sensory systems, here are some useful hints on how to use a mixture of VAK approaches and to address your suggestions to all the three main senses (visual, auditory and kinaesthetic).

- Use diagrams and pictures to appeal to the visual sense.
- Use text and lists to appeal to the auditory sense.
- Use action-based metaphors and phrases to appeal to the kinaesthetic sense.

There is good reason, in the light of our knowledge about rapport, to pay attention to the client documentation style. Instead of producing your action plan in your own house style, experiment with using very similar fonts and layouts to your client's style. Your action plan will then have the feel of familiarity to your client. I (Roger) have used this approach often when bidding for work, with great success. Comments received from the clients have included 'Yours was the approach we were most comfortable with' and 'We felt your action plan was closer to our company's aims than the other bidders.'

I (Neil) used to work for a company where a formal template was the norm for all written communications – everything looked the same. Equally, I used to run my own research agency, where I used to encourage research staff to use whatever typeface and layout they felt best fitted what they were doing. It remains a fact that different typefaces engender different emotional context, and that the careful use of this fact allows the physical presentation to harmonise with the words. So, too, with choosing the format: which will be more rapportful, a 'word(y)' document or 'bullet-point' format?/an end-point-focus or linear and logical sequence?

Setting outcomes and objectives

Outcome statement

Start with an outcome statement, which states the outcome of your project, its impact on and benefits to a target population as

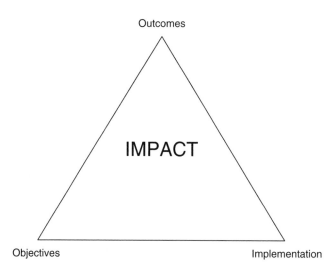

Figure 2.2 Impact!

a result of the achievement of your objectives. This should be stated in the positive.

Example words associated with 'outcomes' include:

Improved	Strengthened	Changed behaviour/ attitude
Standardised	Expansion of	Integration of
Advanced	Experience with Promotion of	Updated prediction of
Increased/decreased	Adoption of	
Innovative	Enhancement of	

For example, 'This research project is designed to deliver innovative enhancements of the product range and suggest ways to change and influence attitudes towards the products.'

Clear objectives

Once we have an outcome statement, development of clear objectives is the next step. An objective is a precise, measurable statement of what you, or your plan, intend(s) to achieve during a specified period toward a particular desired outcome. An objective is a statement that captures, in specific terms, the intended/anticipated results of your project.

Why are objectives important?

Objectives are important because they are the measurable factors by which the success or failure of one's efforts, a project or a programme is decided. Furthermore, strategies developed with specific roles and responsibilities are based on objectives.

Setting and stating clear objectives up front can outframe many misunderstandings or areas of confusion. It helps you pitch the action plan in the most suitable way for the reader and keep a clear focus. The action plan will have more clarity and will be easier to write and to read.

The basic elements of an objective are:

- a description of the activity or service to be provided (e.g. interviews);
- the expected result of the activity or service (e.g. increased understanding of the consumer);
- a tool to measure the impact of the provided service or the quality of the provided product and the standards of success the project hopes to meet.

When creating objectives, consider the following: who is the action plan for? What is their level of knowledge on the subject? What will they use the research for? What aspects do they particularly want covered? What does the proposal not need to cover?

Objectives should be SMART:
Specific: defined, relating directly to the issue being addressed.
Measurable/observable: the end result.

Attainable: within a scheduled time, budget and conditions.
Results-oriented: steps to achieve the end result.
Targeted: to the identified need and desired impact and benefit.

When creating SMART objectives in line with the parameters above, there are some words that it is useful to employ. Examples are given below so that you can design SMART objectives in a way that matches precisely the client's needs.

To create *specific, measurable and results-oriented* objectives, it is helpful to finish the sentence: 'Desired results of this project are . . .' Start with an observable action word that captures specifically what your desired result is.

Examples of words you can use within SMART objectives at various levels of thinking are below.

Specific

Avoid ill-defined terms that are open to variable interpretation (for example, understand, learn, grasp); use, instead, terms that

Table 2.1 Specific words for use in SMART objectives.

Knowledge	Application	Problem-solving
Define	Apply	Analyse
Disseminate	Calculate	Assess
Identify	Conduct	Construct
Present	Demonstrate	Create
Quantify	Introduce	Develop
Share	Measure	Establish
	Train	Evaluate
	Use	Implement
		Institute
		Redesign
		Refine
		Synthesise

describe directly observable results. When necessary, specify criteria concerning expected standards (for example, 'Identify and utilise an instrument with demonstrated validity and reliability').

Measurable

How can outcomes/success be measured? Table 2.2 shows some ideas for you to consider.

Attainable

To create *attainable* objectives, consideration should be given to the current level/status of the problem/area of identified need.

Table 2.2 Measurable words for use in SMART objectives.

Measure what?	Measure how?	Quantify how?
Achievement	Checklist	Categories
Attitudes	Clinical trial	Comparison to standard
Development	Content analysis	Difference
Effectiveness	Focus group	Frequency
Efficiency	Interview	Grade
Fit to purpose	Observation	Increase/decrease
Improvement	Questionnaire	Instances
Opinions	Self report	Percentage
Perceptions	Statistical analysis	Rating
Performance	Survey ratio	
Progress	Test score	
Quality		
Rate		
Satisfaction		
Timeliness		
Values		
Usefulness		

Also, consider the conditions under which work on the project will take place (for example, time, funding and other resources, support, facilities, staff, etc.).

Results-oriented

The first question is, 'What results are possible within the framework objective?' Then analyse the steps to be taken, how the results will be analysed and what method will ensure they are accurate.

Targeted

State the need and desired client impact required (use client values here) and give the benefits of your action plan.

To create objectives targeted to the identified need or desired impact, ask yourself whether the desired impact requires knowledge, application and/or problem-solving. Match your action verb to the desired level (see lists of words above) and match the objective with appropriate methodology.

A useful question to ask yourself is whether achieving the objectives can be expected to achieve the desired impact.

Outputs

The last element when writing objectives is to let the client know, or restate, the agreed output from your survey or research project, ensuring that what you present will be in alignment with expectations. Some clients will require a lengthy and detailed report with data, analysis and recommendations. Others may want you to present the outline of your findings at a meeting so they can have input before the final report. Yet others may require the results to form user guidelines. Below are some of the possible outputs from a project. Meet a client's expectations by discussing and agreeing the form of the output from your project.

- Curricula
- Minutes
- Protocols
- Documentation
- Papers
- Websites
- Instruments
- Presentations
- Tools
- Manuals
- Programmes
- Publications

Avoid confusing outputs (products) with outcomes (impact/ benefit) and objectives (action statements articulating desired results).

THINKING LIKE THE CLIENT

NLP provides a powerful tool for helping us think like the client. It can also assist in resolving communication difficulties that may develop between individuals, and can form the basis of a conflict resolution intervention. This is a useful practice to add to your repertoire. Once you have constructed your action plan, use the perceptual positions concept described below to apply a critical eye to your work and begin to get some notion of how the client will receive the action plan. This is a great way of playing 'devil's advocate' if you have no-one to take that role for you.

The three perceptual positions

There are (at least) three ways in which you can look at an experience or a communication. These are called the first, second and third perceptual positions, and using all three is a powerful way of increasing the flexibility of your thinking.

First position – me

In the first perceptual position you can look at the world exclusively from your own point of view, from your own reality and from what you think as an individual from your own personal experience. You think 'What do I want?' or 'Where am I going?' You are completely associated with the experience, and not taking into account anyone else. This position tends to reflect your own personal values and beliefs. First position is a good place to be if you want to focus on your outcomes and how to achieve them (Figure 2.3). You do not take anyone

Figure 2.3 Perceptual Position.

else's point of view into account, you simply think: how does this affect me?

Second position – the client

In the second position you can consider how it would look (or sound or feel) from the client's point of view. It is clear that the same situation or behaviour can mean different things to different people, and in communication (and especially in conflict) it is essential to ask, 'How does this appear to them?'. This does not imply that you have to *agree* with their viewpoint, only to *understand* it. This is sometimes called empathy, and the better rapport you have with a person, the easier it will be to attain the second position. This is a very useful route for both engaging a client's attention and support for your action plan, and debrief/recommendations.

Third position – an observer

The third perceptual position (sometimes known in NLP as the *meta-position*) is that of the entirely independent and uninvolved observer. This gives you an independent 'fly on the wall' viewpoint, which is on a different (but not superior) level to the other two positions. Third position is useful for taking an objective and resourceful view of your own behaviour, so that, in a difficult situation, you can create some useful alternatives. This is a useful skill that can help you avoid the stress that can be caused by hasty decisions.

Third position is remote, wholly objective and acts as a neutral observer. This is very much akin to the scientific detachment style of qualitative moderation, much advanced in the mid/late 1970s, and borrowed from Rationalist style. The picture is the eagle-eye view of the whole (assuming you are of a visual tendency). This never really made sense to me (Neil) as a moderator, though the instruction given in those days was often, 'Don't smile, don't get involved in the group, don't become one of them: the moderator is there as a neutral observer, so stay aloof'.

To be able to step into third position is an extremely useful skill. In situations of conflict, you will be able to see the interaction and understand how it could change. Whenever you step into third position, you are leaving your emotional attachments behind.

All three positions are equally important, and they are extremely useful when you develop the ability to move easily between them. A person stuck in first position will tend to be very egotistical and care little about others. A person stuck in second position will be strongly influenced by the ideas of others. In permanent third position, a person will be a detached and unmoved observer of life.

An example in a research context would be as follows: a client asks a question. From your viewpoint (first position), the answer is so obvious that you cannot understand why they have asked it. Taking a moment to imagine yourself in their shoes (second position), you realise that there must be a key point that they have missed. Now, looking at the situation as an observer (third position), you may notice just what is missing. By bringing the missed key point into your answer, you will enlighten and satisfy your client and enhance your relationship.

The three perceptual positions help us to understand situations or behaviours better, and to see the world in different ways, which leads to a greater range of choices in how we deal with it. Inventive solutions come from seeing things in different ways.

ACTION PLAN WRITING GUIDELINES

- Remember the power of words.
- Create positive mindsets.
- Use visual, auditory and kinaesthetic language.

- Attend to the client's values and play them back in your action plan.
- Understand the level of detail appropriate to the client.
- Assess your document style.
- Set out clear outcomes, objectives and implementation plans.
- Think like the client!

CHAPTER 3

THE SAMPLE

WHAT'S IN THIS CHAPTER?

- Characteristics
- VAK subquotas
- Recruitment approaches
- Rapport skills
- Briefing and training

RECRUITMENT

The typical recruitment processes for consumer research seldom include any reference to the respondents' own personal qualities, values or beliefs, save for the occasional 'creativity' criteria, often self-ascribed. Accordingly, they treat all respondents as essentially the same, just with different objective criteria, such as age, gender, occupation, consumption/usage/awareness, and so on.

NLP criteria or principles are not used in market research recruitment, but this issue has been examined by a friend in a conference paper in 2003 for the AQR/QRCA (Hoskin, 2003).

This work suggests that we may benefit from recruiting respondents according to their modality preferences, using their visual, auditory or kinaesthetic preferences as a screener question. This allows the moderator and respondents to be more closely aligned, and the topic guide, stimulus materials and phrasing of questions to be related to a specific respondent profile, i.e. V, A or K, or even O or G where the occasion is right. One of the most important findings from the paper was the less than satisfactory likely outcomes of using, for example, wordy A4 documents as stimulus pieces with people whose primary system is visual, not auditory. Why show words to someone who tends towards thinking in images? Why show pictures to someone who tends to think in sounds? The risk is that the concept/ad/communications piece will be more likely to be criticised or rejected because it has not been well 'filtered' by the respondent's own internal systems, and not because inherently the concept was flawed.

There are several other really interesting issues raised by the notion of segmenting respondents by their VAKOG preference, and the paper is well worth reading.

If we are serious about getting deeper into respondents' world perceptions, it surely makes as much sense to classify them by their communications preferences as by their product usage. Equally, it surely gives the recruiter more chance to obtain an appropriate sample for qualitative research if he/she is given some additional (NLP) skills to assist with recruitment.

Let's look at the recruiter's task in a little more detail.

CHARACTERISTICS

Recruiter

The recruiter has a central role in the qualitative process, but aside from a couple of days' training, is largely expected to possess

the appropriate characteristics for cold recruitment and interviewing. A number of recruiters I have met are indeed very skilled
in this interface, but some are not. In any event, the crux is that
it is largely a hit or miss affair, and the monthly supervisor check/
accompaniment does nothing to assist.

The key skills of a good recruiter are those of getting people's
trust and engaging at least their curiosity, if not their absolute
excitement, so that they turn up for the qualitative session. We
know from every field of human interface that we have a relatively
narrow window in which to make first impressions, and given the
hows and wheres of qualitative research, we really do give ourselves a difficult task. Some recruiters specialise in (i.e. prefer/feel
more comfortable with) on-street recruitment for mainstream
shoppers, others, for whatever personal reasons/qualities, feel more
at home recruiting business to business depths, maybe on the
phone, or recruiting medical depths, again on the phone. Why is
this? Sometimes it is simply because they have some personal
affinity with the subject (medical depth recruitment after having
been a nurse perhaps), but more often it is due to their own
preference and self-perception – of using a telephone, meeting
people face to face, and so on. This itself may give a clue as to
the VAKOG preferences of these people, though to the best of
our knowledge no work has been done on this yet in an NLP
context. Again, do they tend to recruit people like themselves?
What biases are we importing, unconsciously, into the interview
sessions?

In addition, relatively few research recruiters are given much,
if any, real training in the basic concepts of the qualitative research
rationale, or the role they play within it. The essence of the interface between the recruiter and the fieldwork department (and
indeed, too often, between the fieldwork department and the
researcher) is one of conflict. What the one wants, the other sees
as too complex, unrealistic or downright silly. In truth, often the
recruiter has a much more realistic perspective on the recruitment

than does the researcher, but that is somewhat outside the scope of this book. It is a structural problem, driven by seeking to reduce costs, maintain quality and satisfy clients: all at the same time.

However, a truism of most human interaction, and certainly no less so in market research, is the tendency we all have to 'like people like ourselves'. Indeed, NLP has much to say about this, and it is a norm for us to seek out those with similar views, orientation, experiences, etc. For a recruiter, this poses a very particular challenge: how do we engage with people who are very different from ourselves? NLP has many lessons here.

Respondent/sample

As with the recruiter, our qualitative sample usually is comprised of people who are prepared to participate, based on self-ascription or demographic/behavioural criteria, not beliefs, preferences or other characteristics. We might recruit people who are self-described as 'pro-advertising' and reject those who self-describe themselves as advertising-averse. But why are these criteria important? Is the population not made up of just such a wide cross-section? Do we only want to talk to people who are predisposed to our products and services? If so, all well and good, but by excluding people who we think won't respond well, we are unlikely to push many boundaries.

How much better would it be to recruit on the basis of critical outlooks and filtering mechanisms such as:

- *General–specific*: do respondents think BIG or small? Are they detail or overview people?
- *Sameness–difference*: do respondents respond to things/products/ads that are different or things that are the same?

- *Internal–external frame of reference*: does the respondent's response to, for example, advertising come from within ('it seems to make sense to me') or externally ('I think people would like this')?

These filtering mechanisms are basic NLP material, and we return to this area later in the book.

VAK SUBQUOTAS

Following on from the lessons in Frances Hoskin's paper, there would also seem to be the possibility, probably suitable only for specific project types, where a much more detailed knowledge of respondent communication references may be helpful (for example, new product development, communications evaluation, ad testing), where suitable, short version questions could be asked at a screener to elicit some measure of sensory style. This would enable us to utilise the VAKOG, or its short brother, VAK, as a basis for recruiting separate groups of probably visuals, auditories and kin-aesthetics, from which we would be able to achieve a much truer picture of how respondents were processing and responding to the ideas, questions, products, etc. to which we were exposing them.

This is a step on from seeking a 'creative' group, which is often done, and treats the respondent as a more important part of the mix than just simply a 'lab rat'. Implicitly, we also have to think differently for each group in terms of both stimulus materials and questioning techniques/phrasing/wording, but this section is concerned with how to recruit group members.

The second part of NLP's involvement with recruitment is concerned with the interface between the recruiter and the target respondent.

RECRUITMENT APPROACHES

Imagine the typical scenario. Does this strike a chord?

Recruiter: 'Would you mind answering a few questions?'
Respondent: 'Yes.'
Recruiter: 'Would you be free next Tuesday to attend a group discussion?'
Respondent: 'NO!'

The approach to a potential respondent is critical, and NLP has something to offer the recruiter as well as the executive. The above question is maybe apocryphal, but it is typical. The presupposition (another linguistic component of NLP) inherent in the wording is that the respondent may very well mind! It allows the respondent to mind. Like the well-used example, 'don't think of an elephant wearing pink socks', the human mind cannot NOT think of something, so instantly conjures a picture of what it has been told to ignore. Planting 'would you mind?' allows/creates a 'yes, I would mind' in the head.

Rapport skills and yes sets may allow these tasks to be accomplished more effectively.

Rapport skills

Rapport is probably the most significant skill here, and we speak at length about rapport throughout the book. The essence of this is that people like people like themselves: people recognise in others signs of sameness. They respond to these. So, why make life difficult for them? Why ask them to recruit people so patently different from themselves that they are at a disadvantage to start with? Recognising the nature of people's style, interests and affiliations is at the heart of this stage, and it rests on the fieldwork department, as well as the interviewer, to seek a better match between target and recruiter. Of course, this is sometimes difficult when a mixed sample, or a random sample, are involved, but that does not stop a common-sense approach being taken to matching the parties. It also requires some considerably greater thought on the part of whoever plans the allocation of researchers to the project, to ensure that the harmony between them and the respondent is greater than normal.

Why match a 20-something with a 50-year-old moderator? Seeking some form of rapport is not only common sense, but also good NLP practice. This extends into dress codes, and while there are no arbitrary rules here, it is clear that non-rapport clothing, dress codes and symbols will not enhance rapport. 'Hoodies' are a generational statement, thus, matching these will only be likely to happen within a specific social/generational/lifestyle group. Expecting it to work outside this is asking for problems. All it takes is a little advance planning and knowledge of whom/what particular project requirements are involved.

Rapport skills are never more to the fore than at the first meeting point. Within a matter of seconds, the initial rapport framework has been established, or not. Holding a clipboard to one's chest and uttering the magic words 'can you spare me a few minutes, I am doing market research?' creates so many barriers. So, arms down, pleasant smile, open body position (face to face, not angled) head/spine/body posture matching that of the target, now we are starting to match!

Recruitment on the phone? The same applies, but voice dynamics are to the forefront here. Listen for instant clues when the target responds with his/her name or number. Key 'measures' are:

- *Tone*: warmth, friendliness, positiveness, confidence (not arrogance) are all great starting points, and it's worth recalling some basic telesales training here. When you are on the phone, SMILE, as it will show through in your voice. This is basic

NLP, and shows the power of the state influencing the physiology, and vice versa.

- *Loudness*: think of your voice as your own personal instrument, and play it accordingly. Soft passages are usually interpreted as being gentle, intimate, respectful and ingratiating. Loud passages are usually interpreted differently, and can seem aggressive, overconfident, rude, abrasive, and so on, but a modicum can be confident, positive and outgoing. Use carefully.

- *Energy*: usually denotes enthusiasm, belief and commitment. Imagine yourself on the receiving end of a recruitment call where the voice is distant, low in energy/passion and belief. 'We're doing this survey,' the tired voice says, 'it's about pension planning in the year 2050. Would you like to come along for a couple of hours to discuss this?' Try saying 'yes' to this gem.

- *Speed*: often associated with energy (above), but has a few more risks, as too fast a delivery can lose energy and move swiftly into low/no comprehension, with associations of nervousness, embarrassment and pressure.

- *Timbre*: harsh, soft, melodic, uplifted or downbeat? The choice is yours, and the effect and effectiveness will be context-dependent. What impression do you seek to make? Practise the same introduction several times in different styles, and get someone to offer some reactions to each one. Or, over time, you'll find you get better and can gauge for yourself.

- *Phrasing/phrases*: one of the core components of NLP is creating rapport. You have read this so often now that you'll not need to think about what it means any more. But stop and reflect, now as you read this, on how the rapport you create physically will also be enhanced/created by the words and phrases you use. In a B2B interview I conducted a while ago, I was interviewing transport and distribution managers about the ways in which they moved large volumes of loose materials, such as sand, gravel, cement, etc., around. One of the ways involves very large bags, made of very strong, heavy duty polythene/nylon. Colloquially, they are known as 'big bags', and more correctly as flexible IBCs (flexible intermediate bulk containers). Very jargon-ish, but using a common (and accurate, contextually) language is essential for rapport and communication. So it is imperative, before the outset, for recruiters and research/interviewing personnel to get a good handle (very kinaesthetic language, please note!) on the terminology, to ensure the glue is available between them and the respondent target group.

- *Confidence*: 'I'm not sure about . . .' means they won't be either. 'I know it's hard . . .' means they'll find it (too) hard, too. Use confident language and a confident tone, but not arrogant, to create a 'will do . . .' response.
- *Use of names (forenames, etc.)*: this is really difficult sometimes. If in doubt, go slightly formal until you see the respondent's style. Use Mr, Mrs, Doctor, etc. to start with, and be ready to use forenames if the respondent does. This probably applies more to interviewing rather than to recruitment, but the lessons and process are just the same. Using matching addressing terminology helps to create rapport. If you use forenames and the respondent uses surnames, or vice versa, you are creating problems for yourself. The principle is matching language and harmony. Rapport means that you are, literally, speaking the same language, so be aware of what these language dimensions are.
- *Formality/informality*: this applies to language, as outlined above, and also to dress codes, referred to elsewhere. However, and much more subtly, it refers to a more general (and also particular) exchange style where some measure of old-fashioned respect and courtesies are either present or omitted. Again, this might be more often seen in face-to-face interviewing or recruitment, but it can also be present in telephone work. It reflects a sense of deference, of protocol and of hierarchy. I

(Neil) am not big on deference, but there is a time for a bit of forelock tugging if it improves the interview or recruitment process. Face to face, this will mean allowing the respondent to sit down first, standing up when they enter a room, asking permission to place a coat on a rack/chair, etc. Or not! Call me old fashioned, but I also think that the civilities which have gone out of fashion are extremely useful, such as holding a door open or allowing a female respondent to go first. Again, showing respect, creating rapport and some measure of recognition that they are the more important party in the equation, by a very long way. These clues are often subliminal, but go to make up a very important part of the interview.

All these things are contextual. Follow the lead of the respondent. When in a B2B interview, also remember to thank the receptionist and/or the secretary who led you through the maze of corridors to the respondent's office. Thanks are also due to whoever brings you the much-needed coffee. Personally, I hate coffee, but I always take it, as this improves the rapport and acknowledges the intent and gesture of welcome offered by the respondent, consumer or B2B.

The key here is to match and, where necessary, to pace the target respondent.

Using one's voice is a fundamental skill, and harmonising the exchange via voice is pretty much all you have on the phone, other than the content of the research itself, to encourage and incentivise respondents, before you even have a chance to mention the physical incentive (cash, charity, report, etc.). It's an essential element in the recruitment, but one which is largely left to the recruiter's own natural skills, or lack of skills.

Once we have some degree of harmony between the research side and respondent side, we must adopt the normal routines of rapport building. It cannot be emphasised too strongly, or often enough, that we have a very limited window in which to create rapport. If we miss this first chance, we get little opportunity to recapture the rapport that should underpin the whole interview framework.

Briefing and training

The adoption of these skills and approaches will take some time and training to achieve, and will possibly be seen as being for only a specific segment of the total interviewer force. While we might argue that full (basic) NLP training would be seriously good for the health of the entire interviewer force, we suspect that the time, costs and logistics of implementing it would be seen as prohibitive by many agency field directors trying to persuade the board. Indeed, it would be hard to justify.

So, practically, what can we do when there is no realistic opportunity of full interviewer training? Well, it is quite possible that the basics of rapport could be covered in the interviewers' initial briefing, and that the lessons could be backed up with maybe a short video/CD covering the principles of nonverbal communication, sent out to each one. The use of specific words and phrases ('Would you help me with this work I am doing on XXXXX? It's very important and I need to talk to people like you'), rather than presuppositional negative language will also be important.

Equally, yes sets can help here.

'Hello, it's Monday morning, you haven't met me before and will be wondering what I want! I need your help with something I am working on . . .'

At the same time, specific project briefing would allow details to be tailored to the task in hand, and functional practice could be given to the field team. This would go some way to alleviating the lack of formal training on rapport building, which is such an important part of the qualitative recruitment process.

Sample respondents

While fully acknowledging the increased time, cost and complexity of the above implications, it nonetheless remains true that matching people with others 'like themselves' can have serious benefits for an interview process. This is not only from the viewpoint of the researcher, but, given our tendency to prefer being with people like ourselves, imagine, if you can, now, the improved group discussion dynamic to be had were respondents all 'speaking the same language', with matching, or at the very least not un-matching, VAKOG tendencies.

Group dynamics is one of the big challenges to moderators, and while experience teaches a range of adaptive coping strategies for handling mismatches, matching would certainly produce better rapport, especially where less-experienced moderators are concerned.

While it is not a specific element within the NLP canon, the matching of moderator/interviewer gender to respondents can also have a specific role in rapport. This is in addition to the role and gender of the recruiter, and relates to the next stage 'down', where the sample respondents are assembled in some strange studio or hotel or house, ready (we hope) to play their part in the research.

The significance for research sample design lies in the nature of the task set for qualitative research in general and for any given qualitative research project in particular, and the needs of the respondent to be given a relaxing, comfortable and non-threatening environment in which to respond. In short, for them to be in the most appropriate state for the interview process, and indeed for the initial sample stage.

Typically, qualitative research is asked to discover, explain and explore things that are incompletely or not understood or known. To do this, the qualitative researcher needs to get more from the target respondents than simply rational, left-brain responses. That is the essence of what we do.

The extent to which we are able to 'get more from' respondents is determined by a range of factors, including the skills of the recruiter, the moderator, but, equally, the degree of gender-sensitivity inherent in the project scope. The hypothesis must be that there are certain situations where a mixed-gender group fails the acid test of enabling respondents to achieve communications freedom, either by creating inhibitions (by the presence of the opposite sex) or by failing to recognise the different communications traits of the sexes. This can have a similar effect to failing to take account of the different filter tendencies of respondents, recruiters and interviewers – reality is 'concealed' by failing to allow it to emerge in a recognisable and actionable way.

The evaluation and planning stage of any project includes a review of the structure of the groups, location of interviews and many other factors, and it is the authors' view that this review should include sole- or mixed-gender formats, not from the viewpoint of quota setting, but from the viewpoint of the criteria above.

Single-sex vs mixed-sex group format

As a very experienced and senior Head of a Qualitative Research unit (worldwide experience) once wrote:

'The main consideration is, will respondents be more open in a single-sex group or mixed, and also, is the subject one which is single-sex-specific or if the sexes might behave differently either when using the product (or whatever) or in discussion in the group. For example, I don't think it is appropriate (yet) for men and women to discuss doing the washing in mixed-sex groups, as the women might patronise. I think with technical subjects, men can pretend they know more and women less – e.g. in groups about engine oil. Though you have to consider each group separately. I have mixed enthusiastic SLR camera users because the interest in photography overrides anything else, and I would mix people who change their own oil in a car, but not when discussing the subject in general. With some subjects I like a mix of single- and mixed-sex groups if budget allows – e.g. alcohol – people go to pubs, etc. in different modes – boys' night out, with mixed groups, etc., or just with partners, and I like to replicate this in the sample. With financial subjects, I have conducted dyads with couples and then brought them into single-sex groups – you get quite different information. Wives sometimes pretend they are led by men, and husbands like to make out they are in control in the depths and then in the groups you get a different story and have to work your way round this to find the "truth" – so you need both. Same with decorating – although I have done mixed groups on DIY, but not with couples, having had my fingers burned – "I do it", "no I do it", etc.'

In debating the single- or mixed-gender format, it is also necessary to include other constituent elements of the potential mix, as there are a variety of influences at work in any group dynamic. These cover age, gender roles, the ease/rapport of the moderator and, of course, the subject matter itself, as the following extracts from conversations with a range of practitioners illustrate.

'Younger and older mix better – the middle are more of an issue. Life stage is more of a problem – women with kids have to take too much responsibility, whether they are working or not, and groups give them a forum to air this – they wouldn't if men were there.'

Neil says, 'Usually, women are easier to interview – especially older women. Having said that, this week I had a nightmare with this subgroup and a ball with mixed groups of under 22s. Single sex can be easier, because there is no posturing and the groups warm up faster. As an addendum, north of Watford[1] is easier, and you can't mix the genders in some markets – Far East, etc.'

'Some products/services can have an obvious gender bias, which would come out in groups and tend to dominate. Men tend to discuss more rationally than women, who are more emotion-driven.'

Little evidence is available to suggest that men's responses are changed by the presence of women in groups, though moderators often report an element of 'showing off' by males to females in the groups.

The only negative would be in the fact that some women have confided to recruiters in the UK that they would either be more likely or would think harder about accepting a group invitation where men were also present. This probably has as much to do with culture as with anything else, and experiences reported by moderators and clients *across countries* point to certain cultural differences that are gender related, but not on the basis of different response patterns, rather on the basis of cultural norms for gender mixing.

The following points are also worth bearing in mind:

- Don't let all the girls sit together in a mixed group.
- Younger groups are generally less concerned about giving gender-specific comments in a mixed environment.
- Cultural mores in some countries, for example China, may preclude mixed-sex groups as there could be too broad an age span.

---

[1] For non-UK readers, this refers to the popular notion that UK respondents get easier to interview, and are more 'open', the further north of London one travels.

Observation and viewing facilities

Though, strictly speaking, not a subject for a recruiter, interview location is an increasing issue in research, and, as such, it affects the 'selling-in' of the research by the recruiter to the respondent. Hence, observation is mentioned here.

The differences between male and female responses to being observed in viewing facilities are also important, and are a subject in themselves, but experience shows that women have a lower worry tendency here, perhaps due to the socialisation effect that encourages women to be more aware of themselves, how they look to others and more able to act 'naturally' in spite (or because) of this attention. It also probably has to do with the nature of male competitiveness and a search for acceptance for their views, or a basic 'show-off' tendency.

What is clear is that the role of the interviewer is crucial here, in creating appropriate rapport with the respondents. Equally, the role of the studio/venue personnel (homes, hotels, offices, etc.) is critical in ensuring that the rapport is maintained. All too often, hosts/hostesses at an interview location see themselves as purely administrative, and simply there to meet/greet/seat respondents until the researcher is ready. Not only is this poor rapport on their part, but it also gives the researcher, when the interview time comes, a more uphill struggle to create rapport than would otherwise be the case. Thus, a case is easily made for not only the recruiters, but the interview location personnel too, to be made aware of the importance of rapport.

It also remains for the reader, with experience, to decide about the role of cross-matching recruiter/respondent gender. This may be especially significant in more traditional B2B markets, where, in spite of increased female management incidence, there remains, often, a male-dominant culture. The extent to which a male–male or a male–female relation will achieve best results is unclear, but at the very least it should be taken into consideration.

Recruitment is frequently a female preserve, though there are many honourable exceptions. This does not obviate the need to be alert to the nature or the exchange between recruitment personnel and target respondents, and alert to the rapport and communication consequences and context of this exchange.

CHAPTER 4

RESEARCH INTERVIEWS

WHAT'S IN THIS CHAPTER?

- How we create our reality
- How does the process of filters and communication work?
- Reframing
- Envirometics
- Voice and energy
- The topic guide
- Groups vs depths
- Projective and enabling states

OVERVIEW

The main thrust of this book is 'the hidden art of interviewing', and this chapter deals with the core of this subject, but let's pause for a moment and review why it is even necessary to do this, let alone how to do it.

Perhaps it is because we, in the West, are still in the grip of the 'post-modern' tradition of thinking, still in thrall to the notion of Rationalism and cling to the concept that we are rational beings (for whatever psychological imperative), still adhere to the notion that marketing is a science, that market research is a science and that interviewing is simply getting on OK with people and asking them questions.

Perhaps it is also inherent in the increased structure and ownership of research agencies and client companies/organisations, that the belief in this conscious, rational target market still exists. After all, most companies are heavily oriented towards share price, balance sheets, accountancy/law, and agencies are following suit, with corporate bodies now acquiring agencies to add to a profit portfolio. Not much matters except pursuing the profit line, for both parties.

I have stood in front of many client audiences over the years and heard qualitative research criticised for being too 'woolly' and lacking in precision, and for not coming up with answers that can be acted upon. Whether this is a realistic goal or context for any qualitative research is hugely debatable (actually, it's wrong, misguided and plain daft) and is the subject of another book, though in reality it would be quite a short one!

It is especially sad, as during the early stages of the qualitative research tradition, in a commercial sense, we were fortunate in having critically clever, educated and skilled role models. The Fathers of Motivational Research, in the late 1950s, 1960s and into the 1970s, such as Dichter, Schlackman *et al.*, were able to use Freudian, neo-Freudian, Jungian and Rogerian concepts, with skill, in solving some consumer-related problems of the day, and persuading clients (or showing them) that such ideas had real commercial value and relevance. Maybe it's increasing age, but I do not recall those early days being overlain with cynicism, simplistic solutions or purchased by the metre by clients who had no real idea what was being bought and sold.

Old researcher's ramblings? No, I do not think so. What we have, far too often, now is something which *looks like* qualitative research, in the sense that a group of eight or so people meet in a room, where someone with a script (the moderator) reads out specific questions for them to answer (seldom discuss . . . just answer). This is compounded by the various codes of practice and quality standards, which seek to control the way in which qualitative research is done by suffocating procedure and logistics. The tapes must be labelled, the topic guide must be signed off by the client, and so on.

At no stage does this explain how really good, insightful qualitative research gets done.

So, too, with client buyers and users. I had a client who asked me to re-do a presentation, adding verbatim quotes to every 'Conclusions' and 'Recommendations' slide, justifying them by showing him that the respondents had indeed said the things I had concluded. Without these, he argued, how would he know that my conclusions were accurate? If the respondents had not said these things, how could he know they were true?

This is extreme, but not atypical. The linearity and assumption of conscious decision-making and communications is clearly a major part of today's corporate culture, and indeed of societies, in the West, and especially in the UK and the USA.

Across many sectors, especially Telecoms and Automotive, but, thankfully, decreasingly in Pharmaceutical research, there exists a direct questioning tradition which flies in the face of most of what we know about decision-making. Professor Zaltman at Harvard, Malcolm Gladwell with the Tipping Point and many others are beginning to offer hugely valuable insights into the reality of the way we work in our heads and with our emotions. Neuroscience is also beginning to offer concrete evidence that verbal responses may not match up to what is thought (in part of the brain).

So, where does this leave NLP and the hidden art of interviewing? The key issue here is that with the above as a context, we must look for ways to offer our clients better insight. We must seek new and more penetrating ways of discovering a respondent's own truth, their own perception of reality, their own way of decoding and filtering the world around them and the multitude of stimulus material thrown at them hourly by a sales-hungry marketing sector.

NLP shows us how to make the most of a respondent, by:

- improving rapport building ('getting on' with the respondent and putting them at their ease);
- using language that reflects the respondent's own, and explaining why this is important;
- providing a better understanding of how they relate to and decode the world (and communications) around them, using and developing specific projective and enabling techniques.

Your first project is about to go live, you have successfully navigated the brief-taking, writing an action plan that secured the work and you have selected your sample respondents. The next step, the research interview, is what forms the core of what we do, though some agencies and clients seem to feel that the key areas are at the front and back ends – the initial encounter and the final one (presentation), as long as these seem to go 'well', then the project is a success. We disagree.

The core of the research is undertaking an interview of such quality and insight that the answers to the research brief cannot help but be found. The interviewing skills of the qualitative researcher – the ability to put people at sufficient ease and to conduct the exchange with real ability – are what makes qualitative research what it truly is.

It is NOT a process: it can only seldom be prescribed as a formula, a route plan. It is a dynamic interchange between human beings, with all the complexity and subtleties that this entails. Done well, it is a real art form. This chapter deals with this most central aspect of qualitative research – the interview – and offers

NLP models and techniques to approaches to its successful conduct.

One of the key aims of most qualitative research is to seek to understand how an individual, or group of individuals, thinks/feels/behaves/perceives the subject area in which we are interested. This is inevitably going to involve the need to understand their own view of reality. There is seldom any single, objective truth in our target area. We do not see the world as it 'really' is, we see it through the prism of our own realities, our own experiences, our own sensory strengths and weaknesses, our own sensory filters.

If there is any basic disbelief regarding this, we need only take an 'objective' measure and look at the police force's experience in interviewing witnesses to any event. Each will have remembered it in a particular way, each will have a slightly/greatly differing recall of people, events, and so on. No truth there. Equally, imagine a favourite book, movie, painting or piece of music. Each individual will have their own specific set of perceptions and enjoyment (or lack of it), and these experiences are subjective.

The search, in qualitative research, for 'the consumer view' is doomed. All we can realistically achieve is an appreciation of the range of views present, and whatever degree of overlap, or differentiation, exists. To do that, we need to understand what filters, predispositions and past experiences, etc. the subject brings to the interview. NLP offers much here, and so, to start, let's examine how realities are created and used.

HOW WE CREATE OUR REALITY

We use our senses – sight, hearing, feeling, taste and smell – to explore the world. However, it would be impossible to take in everything presented to us, and therefore we all have our own perceptual filters that screen what we take in and what we leave behind. Neuroscientists suggest that we are processing over 2 000 000 bits of information per second. This includes all our external awareness of the world, such as light levels, noises and their location, distance and volume, the sensations of air movement, and so on. When you also add all the bodily signals and activities we are processing, from your breathing and heartbeat to signals from your proprioreceptors in your skin, you can begin to get a sense of how overwhelming this would be if we were to access it all in our consciousness. Miller (1956) suggests that our conscious mind can only handle 7 ± 2 bits of information, and, as a rule of thumb when working with people, it is best to assume that four is the maximum that you can input, as there will already be attention within the person taking up 2–3 bits.

This is a key notion when dealing with interviews and when asking questions – we can quickly be overloaded by too many instructions or too many questions. In this situation, our minds will simply filter out some information. Have you ever given a set of instructions to a group and then had some of them ask for clarification or to check their understanding of the instruction, and on doing so, found that some parts were just deleted? Thinking about how we deliver information is critical to successful interviewing. Understanding how an interviewee's map is constructed can make our job easier, more accurate and therefore successful in finding out just what people really think.

Our filters are individually based on our own unique experiences, culture, upbringing, beliefs, values and assumptions. As we explore reality, our perception comes from the inside. We may think that we perceive reality, but we are, in effect, creating our own personal reality, which may be very different from that of other people.

A useful way of thinking of this process is to compare it with map-making. There is a territory, and maps help us to make sense of it. However, maps are selective, and the type of information in them varies according to their purpose. For example, an AA road map may be very different from an Ordnance Survey map designed for walkers. It is important to remember that the map is not the territory that it describes.

We can have control over our personal map-making by changing our filters. Narrow, impoverished beliefs will lead to dull, limited maps. The very same world can become rich and exciting if we change the filters through which we perceive it.

It is important to remember that other people will have very different maps of the world. If you said the word 'beauty' to a group of people, one might see far-off mountains, one a sunny beach, one their lover's face, one may hear singing, another may experience an internal feeling.

We use our maps to describe our experiences to others and ourselves. To be able to communicate effectively, we need to understand and appreciate other people's maps of the world. When we are interviewing, in essence we are exploring the other person's map, either to gain information or to understand if our maps have enough common ground to form a relationship.

Figure 4.1 summarises some of the most important filters that affect our communication.

Thought experiment – Filters

This is a simple experiment that shows how our filters shift and, in consequence, how our perceptions are changed.

Spend a few moments visualising, thinking of a colour of your choice – see, feel and hear that colour. Next, put the book down and take a 5-minute walk around your environment and allow yourself just to notice what you see.

What did you notice? Did you see many examples of that colour, or perhaps you noticed that it was absent? Just by holding a particular thought, our minds are automatically programmed to notice it.

How could this affect your taking a brief and many other things?

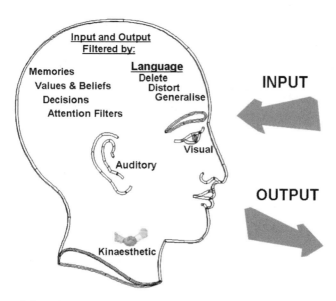

Figure 4.1   The most important filters affecting our communication.

HOW DOES THE PROCESS OF FILTERS AND COMMUNICATION WORK?

When something happens outside of us (stimulus), we take in information through our five senses (what we are seeing, hearing, feeling, smelling and tasting). Neuroscientists say we are processing some 2.5–3 million bits of information per second. Our filter system helps us pay attention to what we are interested in or what is important to us at that moment.

The Rule of Threes

A useful rule of thumb is the rule of threes. As some of our chunks of attention will be placed on the inside, we cannot tell how many chunks of attention are available. Breaking an instruction into threes prevents overloading of the consciousness.

Usually, this is restricted to between five and nine bits of information. Have you ever been so absorbed in the TV or a book that you have not heard your name being called? Your filter system helped you ignore that information so you could focus on what you were doing. The information thus filtered creates an internal representation (an NLP term meaning the pictures, sounds, feelings, smells and tastes in your mind). This internal representation affects your emotional state and your physiology, which then become the drivers of your behaviour.

Try this. Can you name more than seven products in a given category, say, breakfast cereals? Most people will be able to name two or three products in a category of low interest, and usually no more than nine in a category of high interest.

If we did not actively delete information all the time, we would end up swamped with incoming information. In fact, you may have heard psychologists say that if we were simultaneously aware of all the sensory information coming in, we would go crazy. That is why we filter the incoming information.

In NLP, there are three filters that operate to help us filter the massive amount of incoming information, these are: *deletion*, *distortion* and *generalisation*.

Deletion

Deletion occurs when we selectively pay attention to certain aspects of our experience, and consequently overlook and omit others. For the most part, this is an unconscious and automatic process – we don't think about what we say before we say it (at least not usually!). Think of your response when a colleague asks you how your weekend was on a Monday morning. Our responses are usually limited to a few sentences, or even just a word or two. We have not had to think about the level of response required; our filter system automatically knew, because

What do you see?
The snake in in the grass.
Paris in the the spring.

of the context, just what and how much information to delete from our internal map of the weekend. We also delete incoming data – how many times has someone told you something and you have no recollection of it at all? This is a universal human experience. Without deletion, we would have far too much information for our conscious minds to handle.

In an interview situation, noticing those times when information seems to be incomplete and exploring further with questions can reveal gaps and inconsistencies.

Distortion

Distortion occurs when we make shifts in our experience of sensory data by making misrepresentations of reality (Figure 4.2). There is a well-known story of distortion in Eastern philosophy, in the 'rope versus snake' analogy. A man walking along the road sees what he believes to be a snake, and yells 'SNAKE!'. A few passers by rush up and see the snake as well. Coming closer, however, they discover that it is really only a piece of rope. For a few moments, the passers-by shared the distortion of the man who yelled snake – they saw what they expected, or what their filters were set for by the language.

Distortion is the process of the mind continually trying to fit what it receives from the outside world into our belief systems and perceptual experiences. In an interview system, this effect can

Figure 4.2 Distortion.

cause people to align with the viewpoint of a strong individual – literally seeing the world from that perspective.

Generalisation

The third process is generalisation, where we draw global conclusions based on one or two experiences. Generalisation is one of the ways that we learn, by taking information that we have and drawing broad conclusions or rules about the meaning of the effect of the information.

This can be a rapid process. Imagine this scenario: you are driving cheerfully along the road and you are cut up by a white van. This causes minor annoyance, but then, a few miles later, another white van cuts you up. Your mind begins to form a generalisation about white van drivers and their skill level or attitude. Once this is done, your mind will sort for 'white van driver' and begin to assemble evidence to support your belief. Our filters are set and our map of reality changed, at least until we have enough contrary evidence to loosen the belief.

So, the question is, when two people have the same stimulus, why don't they have the same response? The answer is because we delete, distort and generalise the information that comes in through our senses, based on one of five filters. This is a fundamental part of the interview process, and of question and answer techniques.

Imagine the respondent who says, 'No, I never buy that type of product/watch that type of programme/watch TV ads/buy well-known brands/etc.' Do they really mean that they never, ever do so? Or do they simply (or actually, complexly) mean that they have a predisposition not to admit to doing so? Do they really never buy/watch?

When faced with this type of summarised and simplified presentation statement of behaviour, our first question must be,

'What, not ever? Not once in your life?' Almost invariably the answer will come back (with sufficient probing) 'Well, there was once, when I saw it by chance . . .'. So, we discover that the solution to this nature of generalisation filter is in asking a semi-challenging question.

Questions, questions, questions

The way in which we, as qualitative researchers, obtain more and more information is by asking questions and/or by observing behaviour, responses and actions. Whether in an interview, where words and a range of projective and enabling techniques are our main tools, or in ethnographic or observational situations, where watching, decoding, forming hypotheses and amplifying feedback are the main tools, it is the response we get from the respondent that is the informing element. The 'questions' are meaningless unless we obtain a response, verbally or otherwise, on which we base a further interrogative stage.

Simply asking questions and taking the first, 'at face value', response is just such a big waste of time. However, it seems to appeal to some researchers and clients, who delight in producing 10–15 page topic guides in the belief that simply asking these specific questions will get them to their information goal. Information jail, more like!

We need questions to add to and move along the interview from start point to understanding, and the questions themselves must be based on the responses to the preceding one(s).

One of my favourite questions/question styles, coming directly from what I learned during NLP training, is 'What is the best question I could ask you . . . ?'. I use this one a lot, and find that this very general, nondirective question is very useful, both at the outset (once rapport has been established) and also at the end of the interview (when the defences are well and truly down and we are entering the 'nearly finished' stage). The latter needs a slight change of wording (see below).

The real benefit is that this allows the respondent to use the intuitive part of their response mechanism to provide for the things they really wanted to talk about. Providing it is asked in a suitable way (i.e. not allowing too much time for manufacture), the answers are really useful for discovering important issues.

There is no limit to such questions, in wording terms, and certainly no absolute list. However, we have put our heads together, and offer the question examples below to give you further food for thought. Some simply offer variations on a main theme, using different wordings. The general principle here is that we offer more space for the respondent. Some questions are simply encouragements to answer again, in more detail/in a different way. Some are seeking clarification, using some form of feedback/clarification mechanism, by paraphrasing or rephrasing, or reframing, an answer previously given. Some are moving towards a projective or enabling format, to allow the respondent to answer in a different way. Try them out. It's only by use and experience that you will get to understand when to use which question.

Note, *these cannot be written into a topic guide*. The interview must be dynamic and interactive. It must not be a monologue with each party taking turns to have their one-way speech. Your question follows the response previously given. The next question is predicated on this last response.

- What question would you like to be asked?
- What is the most useful question I can ask right now?
- What is the best question I could have asked you at the beginning?
- What don't I know now that would make a difference if I did know it?
- What question would get me closest to where I need to be?

- What question should I have asked already?
- What question would you ask, if you were me?
- What exactly are you saying?
- What exactly does this mean?
- How does this relate to what we have been talking about?
- What is the real nature of . . . ?
- What do we already know about this?
- Can you give me an example?
- Are you saying . . . or . . . ?
- Can you rephrase that, please?
- What else could we assume?
- You seem to be saying . . .
- How did you choose those characteristics?
- Please explain why/how . . .
- How can you prove or disprove that?
- What would happen if . . . ?
- Do you agree or disagree with . . . ?
- Why is that happening?
- How do you know this?
- Show me . . .
- Can you give me an example of that?
- What do you think causes . . . ?
- Are these reasons good enough to . . . ?
- Would it stand up in court?
- How might it be refuted?
- How can I be sure of what you are saying?
- What is happening here?
- Why? (repeated, for laddering)
- What evidence is there to support what you are saying?
- On what authority are you basing your argument?
- Another way of looking at this is . . . , does this seem reasonable?
- What alternative ways of looking at this are there?

- Why is it necessary?
- Who benefits from this?
- What is the difference between . . . and . . . ?
- Why is it better than . . . ?
- What are the strengths and weaknesses of . . . ?
- How are . . . and . . . similar/different?
- What would (archetype) say about it?
- What if you compared . . . and . . . ?
- How could you look another way at this?
- . . . then what would happen?
- What are the consequences of that assumption?
- How could . . . be used to . . . ?
- What are the implications of . . . ?
- How does . . . affect . . . ?
- How does . . . fit with what we learned before?
- Why is . . . important?
- What is the best . . . ? Why?
- What was the point of asking that question?
- Why do you think I asked that question?
- What does that mean for you/others/the interview?

These are not rocket science questions, but allow the questions to do more than elicit a direct, specific and somewhat sterile response. They allow us to obtain further information, and from this, we move forward into another question, which moves us closer to our goal of understanding the viewpoint and filter process of another person.

Did we mention that these questions cannot be written into a topic guide? Well, to be clear, they cannot. You should be listening to the answer given and responding accordingly, not simply reading out the next question in the topic guide.

Questions seek to reveal more about the person's perceptions and filters, and the language used is a great starting point. What do they leave out? What do they alter (distort)? From what do they generalise?

These are not, however, the only filter systems at work! Oh, no!

Specific filtering processes

We are also in possession of a number of other filtering systems. These filters can be summarised as follows, and are dealt with in the following chapter in detail:

- attention filters (or meta-programs);
- belief systems;
- values;
- decisions;
- memories.

These are yet more ways of filtering the world around us, and the communication we give and receive in it, and are more really useful lessons from NLP for us Qualies!

REFRAMING

Imagine the respondent who says, 'I never get through to their help line. They obviously don't really care!'. This gives you the opportunity to ask about perceived motivations, perceived staffing levels or call levels, etc., and an opportunity, also, for the client to design communication better, 'Some of you have had problems with getting through. We have recruited more staff/put in an extra line . . .', responding directly to the notion of the initial complaint and reframing it in a different way.

All meaning is context dependent. One of the main charac-teristics of being a human being is to seek meaning in life. We do not just take in external events objectively, we also use our internal map of the world to give them our own personal meaning. Sometimes these interpretations are positive and useful; sometimes they can get in the way and be unhelpful.

In NLP, we use reframing to change and challenge the statements that people make about how they experience the world. Behaviour and events are problems only in the sense of the frame in which they are presented. When the frame is changed, they are experienced differently. There are two main ways of using reframing: *meaning reframing* and *context reframing*.

Meaning reframing

We use meaning reframing to enable a person to place a different meaning on an external event. In this type of reframing, the stimulus in the world does not actually change, but the meaning that is attached to it, the person's response, does. One meaning is being replaced by another. A negative feeling about an external event is changed into a positive one. For example:

Typical statements (often a complaint): 'This makes me feel . . .', 'It means that . . .', 'When this happens I . . .'
Analysis: What else could this mean? What positive aspects of this situation have not occurred to this person? How else might this situation be described?
Reframing responses: 'Have you considered that it could mean . . .?', 'What else might it mean?'

A typical meaning reframe might be:

Statement: 'When he buys me flowers it means he has been unfaithful.'
Reframe: 'Buying you flowers may mean that he finds it difficult to say the words "I love you"'.

Context reframing

We use context reframing to enable someone to see that the behaviour or event that they are complaining about can be useful in some contexts. It loosens up a person's model of the world by helping them to see that they have made a generalisation about a behaviour that occurs in a specific context.

Typical statements: 'That sort of behaviour always irritates me', 'It makes me mad', and 'I wish I could stop doing that, she's too . . .'
Analysis: In what other context might this behaviour be useful? Where else might it be appropriate?
Reframing responses: 'Is there somewhere in your life where that behaviour would be useful?' 'Where could it be useful to you and what for?'

A typical context reframe might be:

Statement: 'I can't stand people being bossy.'
Reframe: 'Sometimes you have to be bossy to get what you want.'

Imagine interviewing a difficult respondent, or any respondent about an especially sensitive subject. The respondent is unwilling to confront whatever the subject is and is being evasive. Try moving the 'perceptual position' from the first to the second or third position – you will find the respondent will ease up! This is because it allows them to take a step back, away from the 'immediacy' of the issues they have, and look more dispassionately at it.

ENVIROMETICS

Envirometics is the term we use to describe the physical environment we find ourselves in when we interview. Retailers, home builders and the police all acknowledge how important such ambience is, in the way it helps/hinders behaviour. In research, we seem to feel that this is either outside our control or simply to be accepted/tolerated.

Our view is that it is an equally important element, and that serious qualitative research can learn a lot from NLP, using what we term *interview feng shui* to describe all aspects of our working environment.

Interview feng shui

Feng shui is the art of creating a suitable, harmonic environment for the purpose, by use of space, colour, etc. This is particularly important for interviews on (so-called) neutral territory, i.e. anywhere that isn't the respondent's home territory, whether this is the office, home or whatever.

We invite the unsuspecting respondent to a cold, austere studio, a hotel with dodgy wallpaper or someone's front room, with the garden chairs brought in to make up the last three seats, and expect them to relax, just because we give them a few pounds and a cup of coffee. Over the past 30+ years, I have visited most studios and major hotels, and while great improvements have been made, I would not say that there are many, here or overseas, that I would consider comfortable and appropriate for a relaxed and comfortable interview.

Here are some dimensions that we believe to be important. The extent to which you can exert some measure of control over these may be limited, but at least if you know what to look out for, you will be in a better position to take ameliorative action.

Seating

Mostly, our respondents will be strangers to each other, or at best (we hope) will have only a passing acquaintanceship, if we are recruiting from a very small base. This being so, and given the norms of interpersonal/societal behaviour, seating seems to be an important aspect of how we run interviews. For example, certainly in the UK, and also elsewhere, shoulder-to-shoulder touching while seated makes many feel uncomfortable. Where we can, we should be allowing respondents their own space.

Studios, please let your old sofas go! Give us individual chairs. However, seldom do we benefit from upright chairs around a boardroom-style table. This creates an atmosphere of structure, of formality, and also prevents the moderator seeing half of the respondent's body. Low coffee tables and individual, comfy seating is to be encouraged.

Upright, formal and work-style is to be discouraged, even for a business-to-business session. If something is required for writing on, try clipboards or separate tables away from the main interview area.

Arrangements

The interview environment should be warm, dry, comfortable and safe. Obvious points, but from a respondent's viewpoint, they are being asked to enter new territory, with little or no knowledge of what is to come (if this is not true, check the recruiter for recycling respondents!). Give them as little to offend them as you can (have tea, coffee, soft drinks and alcohol, if allowed), make sure they know where the toilets are, etc. The hostess (studio, home or hotel) may be doing this, but check anyway. Make sure lighting is good, so they can see where they are going.

Meeting and greeting

Some years ago, I did a survey at a conference on viewing studios. I asked how many moderators went into the holding room to say hello to the group as it was signing in. I asked the same question in several different places, subsequently, and the answer was always around the 1 in 5 mark. So, that means that in 8 out of 10 moderators/groups, the first the moderator sees of the group – and vice versa – is when they enter the discussion room.

From either point of view, this a waste of rapport time, as it takes some time to build the group/interview dynamic, and changing the dynamics by altering location and personnel is just silly. Go and say hello, begin the forming process (see the group dynamics information later in this chapter) as soon as you can. Use rapport-building to relax the respondents and create the optimum atmosphere. I always use pretty much the same lines when I go into a holding room of consumers, though adjusted instantly, based on the response I get when I go in. 'Hello, I'm Neil,' I say, 'I'll be your pilot for tonight.' Almost without exception, someone says, 'Where are we going?'. To which I can easily reply, 'Where would you like to go?', and before you know it, we have a conversation going, and the beginnings not only of rapport, individually and as a group, but, on my part, the process of learning about the respondent/s, what they like and dislike, what their aspirations and concerns are, all of which form the basis of the actual interview.

Trite and unfunny some of you may say. Well, think up your own line! But mine works.

It does, though, raise two extremely important matters of moderator style and persona, as well as technique. They are linked, but I'll treat them separately.

Humour

I (Neil) once had a client with whom I did a tour of his company's five factory sites, presenting a series of workshops about the findings of an employee survey and the board's responses. I would do my bit, then he would do his, and towards the end of his presentation, he would tell a scripted joke. He was a really nice man and a caring manager/CEO, but he could not tell a joke to save his life. Each time he told it, it would fall flat on its face, and so would he. I told him this (nicely) and he agreed to omit the joke from the last presentation/site. Come the spot in the presentation where the joke had been, he announced that there had been a joke there but he had taken it out because he could not tell it properly. To his amazement, everyone laughed. It was the first, and probably only, time anyone laughed at him in this way, and he just did not get it. The moral is, if you can't tell a joke, DON'T. Think of another option for your introduction.

I also start the group session by saying something like, 'As you know, my name's Neil . . . I have a wife, twins and an old dog. If you had a wife, twins and an old dog, you'd go out every night doing this too!'. Not funny, eh? Maybe not, but the intention is to give them some insight into me and my family set-up, and to use a little humour to relax them and get them on board.

Seriousness

I was in a viewing studio the other evening, and had made some comment to the hostess which made her laugh. 'What a change,' she said, 'a moderator with a sense of humour. We don't get many of them.' This is true, I suspect. I have heard from many sources – recruiters in their homes, studio personnel, by observation and even as an instruction by so-called qualitative experts – that moderators should be/are often a serious, self-absorbed bunch, full of some sense of self-importance and liable to act as stars of the show.

Well, I am sort of humble enough to know that it's the respondents who are the stars. We are just facilitators of the evening. We are the conductors of the orchestra, not the soloists, even though many clients judge the success of an evening's groups by whether the moderator has asked all the questions on the topic guide and has stuck to the (absurd, precise, wholly meaningless and obstructive) timings on it. Frivolity is not what I am advocating, in any sense whatsoever, but a little humour never hurt anyone, not least of all a dull subject like pensions research.

In normal, everyday exchanges, we often use humour to express something, and to cover up a sensitive area. Using it in qualitative research is as much a part of creating rapport, and obtaining a valuable answer, as any other technique, and sitting at the head of a horseshoe group discussion staring seriously at a bunch of respondents is fruitless, discourteous and unproductive. Naturalness is the key here, and respondents will see through your falsehoods very quickly. Don't put on a Cockney accent if you're from the mid-West of America, and don't pretend to understand hip-hop if you were brought up on classical opera. Be natural, respect differences and seek rapport where it is available, using voice, posture, tone, etc. – they will respond accordingly.

My (Neil) wife used to have a dish-drying cloth with 'the shortest distance between two people is a smile' written on it. Fairly nauseating to have on a tea towel, but the sentiment is NLP speak for rapport-building and pacing. There is more on this later in this chapter.

Music

This is a really fascinating area. Seldom is music used in qualitative research interviewing, though there is everything to be gained from it. Welcoming music, playing as respondents arrive, creates a welcoming, safe environment. Trial research has shown this to work extremely well.

As a background, softly playing so that it is hardly heard, it acts (subject to the choice of music) as an excellent state generator. Trance-style tracks push respondents into an Alpha state, allowing more by way of intuition/unconscious responses to be obtained. The choice of tracks is important – no words, no drama (cut out the Gregorian Chants and Leonard Cohen) and no Led Zeppelin! I have used a lot of acoustic guitar instrumental tracks and some melodic jazz, again nothing heavy or discordant, and this has worked very well. It creates an ambience and a relaxed environment that seeks to mirror the feeling you would get at a cosy dinner party, at one level, and an introspective ambience at another.

As with all these things, some research topics do not require/lend themselves to this approach, so be choosy, but do be aware of the possibilities. Any subject that requires 'mood' and/or subjective exploration/responses is appropriate.

Introspection is vital for some types of research subject, and music is very helpful here.

Host(ess)ing

The host/ess can make or break the success of an interview. Make sure you have briefed him/her as to what you require. A good recruiter can match the style you want to set; a poor one can mismatch it and make it much harder.

I can take you to at least five main line studios where the respondents are placed in a holding room, with little if any instruction or context, and left alone to fend for themselves, except for a 'help yourself to coffee' instruction.

RAPPORT

This is the heart of this book. Good rapport with a respondent is a core skill, and a requirement for a qualitative interviewer. Without it, no interview can hope to be conducted to any level of satisfaction. Rapport is one of the key NLP learnings, and this section is therefore essential for the reader.

Rapport is far more than just getting on with someone. It is offering respect and recognition of the other person's world; it implies trust, an active relationship and an appreciation of their perspective. It comprises several dimensions, including words, body language, tone, breathing, dress/appearance, and so on.

As mentioned in the caution on dress codes earlier, turning up to an interview inappropriately dressed encourages mismatching and lack of rapport. Paralleling body language is crucial. Watch close friends or good acquaintances speaking, and one outstanding impression/clue is the harmony of their positions, voice tone, head angle, etc. It is particularly important to create this communications bridge with people right from the off in an interview. Matching this series of nonverbal and verbal clues is known as *pacing* in NLP. Subsequently, having established this bridge, we are able to lead the respondent into the areas we want, such as introspection, open disclosure, comfortable engagement with projective techniques, and so on.

Self-disclosure

We want our respondents to be open with us, to trust us and to open up. Why should they do this without some measure of reciprocity? The first stage is therefore to practise self-disclosure, within the construct of a research interview. So you had a bad night, so your partner is having an affair, so the trip up was terrible, this is probably not helpful to use as an ice-breaker!

Good rapport relies on understanding the way in which the respondent communicates and sees the world, and offering your respect and appreciation for this view by your own acceptance of their world. During the warm-up stage, when names and details are exchanged, I wonder how many of you include yourself in the process? I once heard a moderator introduce himself by saying 'I'm XXX. I interview people'. Hardly personal details.

Voice and energy

How would you like to be a respondent in a group/depth, in a strange place with a strange interviewer? Not much, I guess. Well, often, respondents, too, are somewhat anxious or just not especially looking forward to discussing orange juice packaging with you for two hours. So, let's start by trying to put them at their ease. Partly, we do this by meeting and greeting but we also use our voices to encourage rapport, and, throughout the session, we use our voice as an instrument to encourage/discourage, to probe/prompt and create openness. We speak louder and faster when we wish to inject energy (energy is good for creativity), or we quieten down when we want to discuss emotions, intimate details, etc. We use it like an instrument – louder and faster vs softer and quieter, to achieve different dynamics.

Tone and loudness

Also, we use our voice's tone to mean a question, a reflection, a statement, and so on. Softer and gentler for intimacy, harder and harsher for a different effect.

Moderator style is extremely important, not only at the selection stage of who should do the interviews, but also as a tool for use during them. What styles are there?

Dynamic is the overt, showman/woman style – lots of excitement – and may be used especially with a dull, energy-free group or interview, where we need to pace the respondents into a more urgent style of thinking or responding.

Classic/analytical/detached is, literally, the classic, 'scientific' style. It is often used by less-skilled moderators and by client-moderators, and often sounds like a marketing person asking a marketing question of a non-marketing respondent! There is no personality, no humour and little life here. It is also, often, a reflection of simply reading out a topic guide. This style (if it warrants the name) is unlikely to engage the hearts and minds of the targets, and will result in a purely factual and rational response level. It's almost impossible not to respond in this way to a flat and measured delivery. 'Just the facts ma'am,' as they used to say in TV cop shows. Well, that's all you get!

ROLE

Using all the above as variables, you must decide for yourselves what role you are being asked/want to play in the interview. I see it as a conductor of an orchestra, where the individual respondents are the different players, and where my voice, body language and tone are the instruments by which I make sounds from the orchestra's members/instruments. If they're playing out of key or at the wrong tempo, if I want to illicit a different feel, then I have to adapt my own style to do this. Knowing how this works is a fundamental NLP skill.

THE TOPIC GUIDE

One of the banes of the qualitative researcher is the topic guide. In its place, it is at best a way of signposting, to clients, the general direction an interview is anticipated to take, though the danger is that with a prescripted interview, all that will emerge is direct answers to those prescripted questions. At its worst, the interview becomes a matter of reading out the questions, in turn, producing a travesty of a real qualitative interview, and one which is capable of being performed by just about anyone, with no training. The topic guide also runs the great risk of determining the language used in any given subject area, taking no account of either the group/interview dynamics or of the preferred modality of an individual respondent. It is as bad as pre-scripting the questions/language/sequence used by a psychotherapist in a therapy session. It simply doesn't work this way.

Neither should a topic guide be 10–15 pages long. I have, in front of me, a topic guide left behind in a studio recently – not one of mine. (Additional tip: check before you leave the room, and leave nothing behind!) It is 17 pages long, though it has 1½ line spacing, so we can be generous and call it 12 pages. The subject is 'New Product Development in Computer Peripherals', and it starts like this . . . (honestly, it does say all this!)

Introduce self, interview process. Explain video recording, confidentiality (1 minute)

Interviewer reviews information from pre-interview questionnaire with respondents, including: (15 minutes)

What type of products or services do you use?

What type of multi-function devices do you use, personally, on a regular basis?

What type of printers do you use, personally, on a regular basis?

What type of copiers – black and white and colour – do you personally use on a regular basis?

What scanners do you personally use on a regular basis?

What percentage of your documents currently use any amount of colour?

It finishes with the glorious final question . . .

Person A: Now I have just one final question. What is the one most important thing that people responsible for the development of (this product), like the one you have just been looking at, need to know about designing or marketing their product to people like yourself?

Person B: Thank you all for coming. Before you go, I want to mention just a few things:

* importance of participation
* contribution
* confidentiality
* gift.

After participants have gone, insert all materials into packets.

Total time: 60 minutes

In between these two extremes, it goes on to give 16 pages of questions, with answer codes (or *probes*, as it describes them), including volume and cost questions, before finishing at minute 60. I'm unclear what happened if the moderator went beyond 60 minutes! It is split into several sections, but in total there are around 100 individual questions and probes.

I don't know about you, but this strikes me as the best example of how not to do qualitative research I have ever seen. Besides needing no skill whatsoever, it is impossible to do it in 60 minutes, and the close is longer than some sections, but is allocated 1 minute, in spite of containing THE most valuable question of all!

This is an extreme example, but illustrates the point. A topic guide should be short, as loose as possible and with as little pre-scription as is humanly possible. Don't put words into the mouths of the moderator or the respondents.

While on the subject of the topic guide, this can be reviewed not only in terms of structure and content, but also in terms of key questioning styles, tasks and general group dynamics.

You will all be familiar with the oft-quoted five stages of groups. I'll not repeat them in detail, but each stage has different characteristics, and, using this model, we can plot, using a range of NLP techniques, some critical dos and don'ts. This is shown in Figure 4.3. We call it the *Venturi principle for topic guides*, since

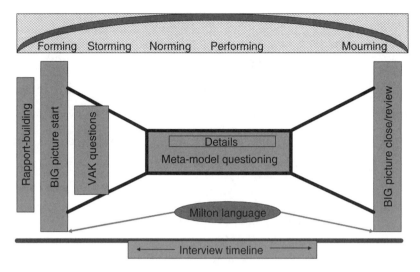

Figure 4.3   Topic guides: the Venturi principle.

the funnel shape resembles a Venturi. It shows the critical stage at the commencement of the group, when rapport must be established. This is why it is difficult to incorporate people into the group who arrive late. They are, effectively, one or more stages behind the rest of the group. In my own experience, all-female groups make up this gap much more quickly than all-male groups (and, in passing, also seem to create better rapport in the holding room than do male groups).

This is followed by the 'Forming' stage, at which time, in NLP terms, we are beginning the 'big picture' information-gaining process. Here, we ask open, unstructured questions using the Milton language approach (see below for an explanation of this).

We then follow on to the 'Storming' stage, when things are beginning to motor and it is right to seek information about the group's VAK (sensory filtering) preferences. This will help us to phrase our own questions to match their filter preferences, and help to explain their answers.

After this, during the 'Performing' stage, we encounter the meta-model specific question stage, when we are chunked down into detail, before emerging into the bright sunlight of the 'big picture' stage towards the end of the interview timing, announcing the imminent end ('Mourning' stage) and resorting to Milton-style questions again to wrap up.

Milton language: general language

This is the notion of using 'artfully vague' language patterns to pace another person's experience and access unconscious resources. Based on the language used by Milton H. Erickson MD, the 'father' of modern hypnotherapy, it seeks to allow the respondent to define and create as much of their own reality in the answer to a question area as possible.

You may be interviewing doctors about some class of drug therapy, and your key objective is to establish brand imagery/identity. Rather (at this early stage) than asking a direct and contextualising question about specific drugs/brands, we might just ask . . . 'Antihistamines, what about them?' and wait for the respondent to construct an answer context all by themselves. They might choose to talk about effectiveness, efficacy, drug reps, drug companies, social medicine, patient types, etc. What we might ask later on (see Meta-model below) will be different.

Meta-model: specific language

This is a model developed by John Grinder and Richard Bandler. It identifies categories of language patterns that can be problematic or ambiguous, and allows us to use the concept of chunking down to achieve a much more specific response framework than would be the case above.

Here, we would ask for specifics such as, 'What antihistamine drugs do you prescribe?', 'What do you think when I mention XXX brand to you?', and so on.

We have chunked down into detail, as opposed to chunking up into very general and nonspecific terms of questioning, and we would also maybe look for the respondent's use of sensory-clue language, such that we could enhance language rapport with them by accessing and reflecting their own preferences.

HANDLING INDIVIDUALS

Anchoring

You can use the NLP concept of *anchoring* to link a respondent/group to a particular state. Imagine that you have asked for new product solution ideas, and they come up with a few, fairly quickly. Anchor this 'productivity' and engagement by a simple anchor – clapping your hands a couple of times and telling them how helpful they are being. Try tapping your paper pad on the table a couple of times for the same effect. The next time you want that level of energy, try tapping the pad again, or clapping, it should bring them back to the productive state.

Anti-rapport

Sometimes, we don't actually want rapport. For the handling of difficult people, or when it is time to move away from one topic onto another, the use of anti-rapport techniques is important to master.

Difficult people

All group/depth moderators will, at one time or another, encounter difficult respondents. These can range from the silent
ones, for whom giving their name in a group is hard, to the
loudmouth who dominates the group and has an expert opinion
on anything and everything, through to the respondent who
arrives or gets drunk in a group. Being able to handle these
people without undue disruption to the rest of the interviewing
is a critical task, and NLP has a number of strategies to assist.

The Mouse: won't say a word until asked directly, speaks very
softly, does not elaborate on a single comment.

Response: use matching tone, level of voice and body posture. Lean in
towards the respondent (do not crowd or ape them), use positive eye
contact and shut out the other group members. Softly encourage them
with phrases like 'That's great, that's right, that's just what I need . . .'.
This uses NLP techniques for getting in rapport, emphasising the close-
ness of tonal and postural communicating.

The Hog: won't stop talking. At each new area, he/she has
THE definitive view, dominates the group and frightens/bores everyone else to silence.

Response: use mismatching body posture and negative eye contact.
Lean back/away, turn away, obviously towards someone else and direct
a specific question to another respondent, shutting the problem out.
Break synchronicity and use contrasting language patterns and tone. If
all else fails, ask him some 'difficult questions' – 'How can you be so
sure you are right? What evidence do you have? Have you really driven
every car on the market?' until he gets the message. This uses

anti-rapport techniques, communicating clearly that a given behaviour is not working/acceptable.

The Sheep: this individual/group take(s) their lead from a Hog, or someone else with a strong view: either they do not care much or are being subdued by the Alpha respondent/s. They are really not helping the information elicitation required in the group.

Response: encourage differentiated views being expressed by challenging the consensus, using the rules for deletion, distortion and generalisation. 'What, no-one has ever had a problem with that make of car? Not one of you?' 'Are you all saying that TV ads never have had any effect, at all?' 'Are credit card companies really just out to put people into debt? Is that really what you all think they are planning to do?'

The Goat: this respondent (usually male in my experience and more common in the UK) is a show-off, and either makes fun of or makes jokes about the subject throughout the session. He is a disruptive influence, and is usually not appreciated by the others. Occasionally, when recruitment has been poor, or when, for other reasons, some of the subjects know each other, two respondents may have some joke dynamic going on between them. This is far worse.

Response: as with all 'difficult' people, withdrawing your rapport, and/or turning the power of the group against them, is the best form of defence. If all else fails, say to the group, 'Sometimes in these groups, we select one person at a time to sit out part of the group, and we draw a number between 1 and 8 from a list and that person sits out the next section. This time, that person is YOU.' Take the person outside and get the recruiter to pay them off and ask them to leave.

ANIMATING THE GROUP

In France, a moderator is sometimes called an animateur, one who animates the group. Whatever the name, the responsibility is to ensure that the brief has been met, that all respondents have been allowed to participate and contribute all that they have to give, and that all the information needed to do the job has been elicited. This latter part probably goes further than simply asking all the questions on the topic guide.

As this book shows, people are able to give us many clues as to their real selves, and this information, on their communications preferences, values and general approach, is vital for a real qualitative research approach to be adopted. I once worked with someone who complained to the fieldwork department about a group, which 'just would not talk'. Well, the fault is the moderator's, not the recruiter's. In NLP, we refer to this phenomenon as 'There is no resistant person, only a lack of rapport'.

A competent moderator should be able to animate most mainstream groups; a really good moderator should seldom be confronted by an impossible group. This book, and experience, should enable you to tackle most, if not all, subjects and groups.

Creating rapport and body language

Watching people will lead you to an appreciation of the myriad of clues offered by the human body in any exchange, from eye movements to skin tones, from body posture to voice tone. It is a fundamental aspect of human communication that we neglect at our peril. Indeed, the irony is that so many of our everyday communication skills are dependent on this, but once at work, we seldom seem to pay much attention to it. This is especially significant, as, often, respondents will be unable or unwilling to offer a straightforward, direct and unambiguous response in qualitative research (or indeed, in any form of research interview). It has been said that over 90% of communication in a situation where the meaning is ambiguous comes from nonverbal sources, thus, awareness and sensitivity towards these clues is an essential part of the research exchange.

NLP training offers sensitisation to the range of sensory changes. This is especially useful in the context of depth interviews, as it is easier to concentrate on a single respondent rather than many, and also, typically, the interviewer/respondent are in closer physical proximity in depth interviews.

So, learn to 'calibrate' the normal skin tones, expressions and behaviour in the respondent at the outset, and then learn (by watching and being observant . . . there is no mystery to this) the ways in which skin tones change, especially around the throat and neck, around the eyes and cheeks and also the lips. See how eye muscles contract (crease up skin), how shoulder muscles also make shoulder levels rise or fall (tension or relaxation), how breathing changes according to the experienced state (relaxation, tension, excitement, anger, etc.) – this is best observed by watching the shoulders themselves and the upper chest, though be a little careful when watching this area in a female respondent, lest your motives be misunderstood!

These are key clues to watch out for, especially when much of the value in the interview itself comes from nonverbal expressions of response. But these skills need practice. It requires a conscious attempt to decode exhibited behaviour, and needs to be done systematically, working through:

- Calibration (what does the respondent 'look like' normally?)
- Monitoring (how is the respondent's appearance changing?)
- Context (what/why has a change occurred?)

Context is critical here, and sometimes the obvious explanation is the correct one (she is crossing her arms because she is cold!). It is the responsibility of the interviewer to get the context and diagnosis right, and to query a feeling with the respondent if it is unclear what is happening. This takes the use of nonverbal analysis to a far deeper level than is conventionally quoted against simplistic examples. It is noticing small changes that are really important, especially where they concern those behaviours that involve unconscious changes, such as skin tone, eye movements, breathing level/speed/depth, etc. These take practice even to notice, let alone decode.

Peripheral vision

Within a group, or indeed any interview situation, there is much to be gained by continual observation/awareness of respondents' actions outside the main, direct line of vision, using our peripheral vision. This is a common part of any group interview, where, typically, the interview is in the shape of a horseshoe or rectangle. Implicitly, when focusing on one or two respondents talking, the remaining respondents are 'free' to have side conversations, make faces, or whatever, largely out of the direct line of sight of the moderator. Here is much important information contributing to the continuing interpretation/exchange of the interview process.

NLP training assists here by enhancing our ability to refocus on a broader perspective, literally allowing us to 'watch' all of a group discussion while still giving attention to a single group respondent. This involves all our five senses, and should be as much a part of the group discussion analysis as text analysis or word analysis.

The reactions and behaviour of the non-speaking members of a group discussion are vital clues for the moderator to pick up, but the peripheral vision skill is one which few people in general, and even fewer men, find intuitive or easy. NLP teaches us how to defocus vision and how to allow a wider circle of vision to be absorbed – with specific points taken up thereafter.

Peripheral audio

Similarly, with hearing, it is beneficial to train the ears to hear more than one conversation at a time, at least to the extent that you can pick up key discords, or agreements, from other respondents in a group.

Practise this in a meeting, in a restaurant or bar, or at home (assuming you do not live on your own!). Begin by listening in to one voice/conversation, then just let other voices be heard, while not losing touch with the original one/s. It will be hard at first for many of you, but the trick is not to try too hard. By concentrating too hard, you simply block other sounds out. Allow them to enter your consciousness.

You can try it now. Listen to the sounds around you. When you begin, you may hear road noise outside or the hum of a computer or the sounds of someone in another room. As you listen, you will also hear some music or a conversation somewhere else (remember not to lose the original sounds).

This is what it is like in a group. You are happily exchanging detail with a particular respondent, but you become aware of two others having a side conversation. Some moderators/clients will ask them to hold the conversation until 'we can all join in' or 'so that the people in the other room can hear'. I think these are lame. You should be able to pick these situations up and turn to them, saying, 'That's important also . . . I don't know if you all heard that, but Jim over here was saying to Fred that he never saw the point of having four wheels on a car that only does 70 miles an hour'.

This ability has several benefits. First, it gives you the sense of what more people are saying – even if you don't hear all the details, at least you can follow something up afterwards. Also, it shows you are truly listening to the group. In addition, it tends to exert some gentle control over the group, much like the see-all teacher at school, who had eyes in the back of his head and saw you as you misbehaved!

Practise, practise and practise!

Language

One of the most useful tips from NLP is the use of particular types of question. One that I use a lot, often at the beginning of the interview, is 'What is the most useful question I could ask you now, about . . .?'. When asked/responded to without thought, what frequently transpires is indeed a really useful, deeply felt issue, from the respondent's viewpoint. It gives numerous clues as to deep emotional worries, concerns, etc., and the way it is phrased gives language and modality clues. It is truly an open question.

There are variants on this question, and there is no definitive version. A fuller list is given elsewhere in the book, but here are some examples of how this works.

What don't I know that would really help me understand?
What question would get me closest to understanding?
What question should I have asked you before now?
What question would you ask, if you were me?
What question would you like to be asked?
What question would you not like to be asked?

Also, we can valuably adopt some questioning from the chunking up/down framework and from the structure of deletion, distortion and generalisation (see page 101).

GROUPS vs DEPTHS

In qualitative research and interviewing, we are faced with the basic choice of group discussions or in-depth interviews. Are there differences or similarities in the way in which NLP can assist or be used here? Let's look and see, and while we're about it, what about Ethnography and Observation more generally?

Movement

After sitting in a meeting or an interview for a while, the brain seems to associate the location in which you are sitting with a mental position or role. It helps a lot to find some reason for the respondent/s to move around. If there is no obvious reason, invent one, by saying something like, 'I'd like you to come over here and look at this material more closely'. Or, you can explain the problem in a different way, such as, 'I know you've all been sitting here for a while now, how about a comfort break, so we can all stretch our legs and maybe get something to drink?'. Even if only a few actually move, physically, it may well be enough to kick-start the brain. There is some evidence that the brain works in 90-minute rhythms called *Ultradian rhythms*, 90-minute cycles of psychophysiological processes (Rossi, 1986). The effect is to require re-energising around the 90-minute mark, and, at the least, to start us on a diminishing attention curve towards the end of that spell. Funny how it coincides with the fatigue point in standard 1½-hour length groups, eh?

OK, so maybe around the 45–60 minute mark (irrespective of whether it is a 90- or 120-minute session), get them to take a break at a suitable point in the conversation. Get them to walk around, and ideally to change seats when they come back. Folk are quite territorial about changing seats, so you may need to explain it by saying that you want to divide the respondents into two teams of people who have not yet sat beside each other, and get them to do a simple exercise, such as one group 'for' debating against the other 'anti' group. The content is slightly academic, but the effects after they have resettled can be very productive.

It is a little harder for depth interviews, but I usually use the same 'take a break' moment and subtly shift seating around, so at least the facing positions are altered. While on this subject, take a moment to look at Figure 4.4 and see what you think is wrong with it. It was the arrangement set up by a major studio for some one-on-one interviews I conducted recently with consultants in major teaching hospitals.

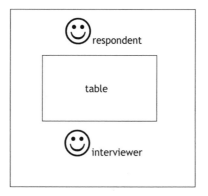

Figure 4.4   Initial one-on-one interview set-up.

No big prizes here. The table, set directly between us, acted as more than a psychological barrier, and an 'us and them' (or more accurately a 'me and him') barrier, it acted as a block to half of all respondents' bodies. So, how did I change the room? Take a look at Figure 4.5. A much happier time was had by all concerned!

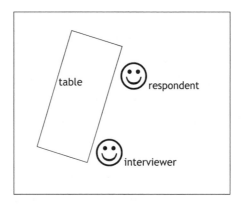

Figure 4.5   Amended interview set-up.

PROJECTIVE AND ENABLING TECHNIQUES

The Disney strategy

The Disney strategy is named after the famous studio boss and cartoonist Walt Disney, and has a lot in common with the spatial anchoring/archetype model referred to below. One of the major elements of Disney's unique genius was his ability to explore something from a number of different perceptual positions, a key NLP skill and concept. An important insight into this key part of Disney's strategy comes from the comment made by one of his animators that:

> '. . . there were actually three different Walts: the dreamer, the realist and the spoiler. You never knew which one was coming into your meeting . . .'

This was not only an insight into Disney but also into the process of creativity itself, and refers back to the notion, described above, of getting folk in interviews to change their positions, physically, in order to free up their brains as well.

Creativity as a total process involves the coordination of these three subprocesses: ideas, practical review and objective appraisal, called the *dreamer*, the *realist* and the *critic*.

A dreamer without a realist cannot turn ideas into practice. A critic and a dreamer without a realist just become stuck in endless debate and discussions, while a dreamer and a realist might create things, but they might not be very sound ideas without a critic to keep their feet on the ground. The critic helps to evaluate and refine the results of creativity.

Unfortunately, what usually happens is that the dreamer and the critic get into a fight . . . The dreamer and the critic go in conflicting directions until, finally, the realist says, '*** this, I'm off!'. At least, mentally.

Everybody already has the dreamer, realist and critic inside him or her. Equally, in group discussions, we often find that the same roles or people are also present, so we find that this ongoing perceptual battle continues, and unless these roles are recognised and channelled, the group will end in stalemate.

One of the tenets of NLP thinking is that 'the map is not the territory'; in other words, the idea is not the person. By commenting on or criticising the idea, we need to be clear and separate the person from the idea.

Part of why Disney could function so effectively was that he did not criticise his team or himself; he criticised the plan to accomplish the dream. What keeps the critic and the dreamer from being stuck in a polarity response is the realist.

Below is a simplified form of a strategy that you can use, which involves the three different points of view – dreamer, realist and critic. In research, individual respondents can take different or rotating positions, and the technique is also great for use in in-company brainstorming sessions, or even for your own problem solving!

1. Select the problem you are going to deal with. Choose three places in front of you that you can physically step into, just

as for the perceptual position technique described earlier, one for your Dreamer, one for your Critic and one for your Realist. (I use flip chart pages, maybe inscribed as a text/visual reminder, placed on the floor, though it can take up quite a lot of floor space.)

2. Take the problem or idea you want to work with. Step into the Dreamer location and let your mind be loose. The Dreamer does not have to be realistic. . . . Do not let reality dampen your thoughts. Brainstorm. What would you do if you could not fail? The Dreamer can be summed up in the phrase 'I wonder if. . .' When you have finished, step back to the uninvolved position.

3. Step into the Realist position and think about the plan you have dreamed about. Organise your ideas. How could it be put into practice? What would have to change to make it realistic? When you are satisfied, step back to the uninvolved position again. The phrase for the Realist is 'How can I do this?'

4. Step into the Critic position and check and evaluate the plan. The Critic asks, 'Is there anything missing?' If the plan needs other people's cooperation, what is in it for them? What do you get out of it? Is it interesting? Where is the payoff? What is in it for me? At the end of this, return to the uninvolved position.

5. Step back into the Dreamer position and change the plan creatively to take in what you have learned from the Realist and the Critic. Continue to go through the three positions until the plan fits each one.

NOTE: it is essential actually to move your body into a different physical location for each of these roles. You will have a different physiology and neurology in each of the positions, and they need to be kept separate. Move from one to the other via the uninvolved position.

Spatial anchoring/archetypes/perceptual positions

One of the key aspects of NLP is the multisensory nature of our experience. Many 'techniques' in NLP involve recreation of positive states, using a range of sensory recreations to counter negative programming, and frequently using a spatial differentiation to accentuate these effects. Archetypes in Jungian psychology, and in NLP, allow us to permit the respondent(s) to inhabit temporarily a different personality, and by using this in combination with spatial anchoring, we can achieve some really useful insights. In the qualitative research process, the adoption of a different 'persona', with different characteristics (skills, outlooks, etc.), can be very helpful in unblocking thought processes.

In practice, this means encouraging respondents to identify a number of different characters, to identify their characteristics/ strengths, etc. and to identify a space on the ground into which they can step. This is probably easier in reality than it is to describe, but the sequence can be summarised as follows.

1. The respondent identifies key characters from reality, media and literature, or by way of archetypes, as appropriate. For example:
   Businessperson/architect/explorer/scientist/poet/sportsperson
   Richard Branson/Tony Blair/Michael Schumacher/Eric Clapton
   Superman/King Kong/Batman/Lassie
   Managing director/marketing director/salesman/production manager/shop-floor worker/customer
2. Each character is identified by a sheet of paper on the floor.
3. The respondent is asked to stand on each in turn and describe the special characteristics, using full NLP sensory state descriptions.
4. The 'problem' (or question) is then addressed using each spatial anchor in turn.

The result is the ability to step out from the respondent's own self-perceived limitations or 'programming' in NLP terms, and use the vision or outlook of their inhabited character to seek a fresh perspective on the issue.

This can produce some very powerful results, and in at least one case has resulted in the respondent jumping immediately away from a particular sheet of paper intuitively, as the 'vibrations' were so strong as to invoke a physical reaction.

Inherent in this approach is the notion of a *perceptual position*, and this is a wonderful skill taught in NLP. Perceptual positions enable us to adopt more points of view than just our own. They allow us to think outside our own box, and can work very well in groups (I find less well in depths).

The origin of perceptual positions is a very simple idea: 'Before you criticise someone, walk a mile in his shoes.' In other words, you cannot really understand someone until you have experienced what it is like to be in his situation. This contextualisation is at the heart of much NLP – understanding and being in rapport with someone else's view of the world, and using their filter system, not yours, to understand their perspective. I wonder how often this is a problem for some researchers, agencies and clients, who assume everyone has the same frame of reference as they do? I very well recall debriefing a TV commercial project, on beer, to an agency in fashionable London, near the really trendy wine bars. The fieldwork was conducted (since the TV commercial was to be launched) in South Wales, with a target of working-class, 18– 24-year-old males. When faced with feedback from the ad, and the description of buying behaviour, the ad agency planner asked what 'the brand specification language was'. He had some trouble with the answer, as it reflected life in a working man's club en- vironment in the Rhondda Valley, whereas he was used to seeking sophistication in the wine bars of Kensington. Worlds apart, and he did not see the other life at all.

The ability to see things from the point of view of another is a key skill in understanding people, and is important to communication processes in relationships, negotiation and interviewing, as well as to healthy boundaries and self-concept. However, NLP is not only concerned with *seeing* things from other points of view – i.e. visual representation – but also kinaesthetic, auditory and, to a lesser extent, olfactory and gustatory sensory systems.

NLP pays careful attention to linguistic and semantic representations inherent in beliefs, interpreted feelings, values, thinking patterns and identity – equally important components of how we experience ourselves, the world and the people around us. Further still, somatic aspects, such as physical responses, gestures, eye movements, voice tonality, posture, movement and other behaviours, all play important roles in mind–body states and the quality of experience for ourselves and for others. A perceptual position might contain as many of these components as the perceiver is aware of, or can imagine.

Consider walking a mile in another man's shoes. That is fundamentally a kinaesthetic and behavioural representation. If you were actually to do it, you would have many other perceptions as well. What you could and could not see, as you walked along in those shoes, would be important. What you heard in the environment around you, in your own head, perhaps words or a song, what people said to you . . . these would also be important to your experience. The state of your body while walking, your posture and internal physical sensations might be a big part of your experience. Add to all this what you believe about what you are perceiving. If you believe certain things, will that affect what you perceive? What other perceptual filters might you have working? How do you interpret what you do perceive? Are you cautious in interpretations or do you produce conclusions rapidly?

Now, imagining doing this as you read these words might be worthwhile, but if you were actually to walk that mile while imagining each of these perceptual distinctions, that would give you a much fuller sense of what the world was like if you walked in that other person's shoes. However, not many people are really going to walk a mile, and we need not be too literal here. Using NLP perceptual positions, you could create a very rich sense of another person's experience using only your own memory, imagination, physiology and very slight shifts in your spatial location.

Part of NLP Practitioner training can involve, literally, walking behind the 'subject', matching his/her way of walking, speed, arm swings, shoulder positioning, etc., with a view to enhancing an understanding of how it feels to be that person. Similarly, in qualitative interviewing, it is most helpful to get a sense of what it is like to be the other person, and thereby to understand better why and how they reach the beliefs/attitudes/behaviour that we are investigating: to understand from their viewpoint, not from ours.

Ethanography/Observation

This is where 'immersion' techniques are so valuable – in seeing, expriencing and becoming immersed in the subject's world/life. Spending many hours in the respondents context and company places particular demands on the researcher, and rapport and observation (of the respondents behaviour, language etc) are even more important.

CHAPTER 5

UNDERSTANDING WHY PEOPLE BEHAVE THE WAY THEY DO

WHAT'S IN THIS CHAPTER?

- Understanding people
- The five sensory filters
- Eye-accessing cues
- Primary interest filters
- Chunk size preferences
- Sameness or difference?
- Motivating attention filters
- Options or procedures?
- Past, present or future?
- Decision-making

UNDERSTANDING PEOPLE

This chapter is all about how to understand people, or as one of my (Roger) NLP trainers, Wyatt Woodsmall, calls it 'The Science of Idiots'. How is it that people react and behave in the way they do? What can we do about this and how does it help or hinder us in all areas of human interaction?

We each have ways of taking information in, manipulating it inside (thinking and feeling) and then generously offering it back to the outside world. These patterns in NLP, known as *attention filters*, *meta-programs* or *sorting principles*, are the models that people use to filter, sort and organise the sensory inputs they receive. Since the huge majority of these inputs (2–3 million, less 7 ± 2) are processed unconsciously, it is clear that most meta-programs must work at an unconscious level.

In order for the brain to deal with this amount of information, it must organise it into categories, and attention filters are the keys that help it to decide which categories the data are associated with. This provides the structure that governs what we pay attention to, how our internal representations are formed and how we interpret our sensory experiences. Thus, attention filters have a significant influence on what we do and what we do not do. These sorting principles are often context-dependent and, as such, it is unwise to use them merely as a typological tool. Attention filters will be operating on received data from outside, and also with our internal map, influencing thought patterns, states and behaviours.

During the processes of deletion, distortion and generalisation, which we employ to reduce our sensory input to a consciously manageable level, our individual attention filters tell us what to pay attention to and what to delete.

Attention filters produce patterns of behaviour based on the reference categories into which we organise our experience. Individuals tend to generate a typical configuration or cluster of attention filters, by which they organise their thinking and understand their experiences. By understanding their internal configuration, it is possible to construct a communication that will naturally and automatically get selected as 'of interest' by the recipient's meta-programs.

In order to obtain an understanding of a person's attention filters, it is necessary to study the language and the metaphors they use habitually. Information about our internal attention filters' configuration is constantly supplied in our day-to-day language, and there is a range of questions that can be asked to clarify which attention filters are operating.

To communicate effectively, you must match the recipient's attention filters, rather than your own perceptions of how the world works and what people are like. You must also develop a high level of sensory acuity in order to follow the route through the other person's attention filter configuration, noticing when one attention filter takes over from a previous one. Attention filters provide the key to understanding a person's motivation, and allow you to decide how you will communicate with them successfully.

It is vital to remember, however, that, as with eye movements, there are no concrete rules for attention filters. It is essential to calibrate individuals, and even when they demonstrate a dominant tendency to use a particular attention filter, understand that they may modify their strategy under stress or in other situations.

There follows a selection of meta-programs with some examples of characteristics, linguistic indicators and tips to help you. It is possible to group attention filters in many ways, but we will use a simple structure, grouping the programs into key areas that will help us utilise them for interviewing.

Let's examine some of these filters in more detail. We should note that although we are describing these activities in a linear and sequential form, we should remember that all of this happens in a millisecond − everything is parallel or even matrix-processed by our mind/body/brain system.

THE FIVE SENSORY FILTERS

In Chapter 1 we discussed how to use these filters to gain rapport, and in this chapter we take another look to find out how these filters affect the research interview.

The five sensory filters are visual, auditory, kinaesthetic, olfactory and gustatory. The last two, in the context of communication, are less important, so we will focus our attention on the first three.

With most things human, we have preferences. This is true for our sensory filters, too. Take a moment to think about how you best access information – do you like it to come in pictures so you can see it, do you prefer to read, talk or be told about something or do you rely on your 'gut feelings' to take in the information?

Thought Experiment

Imagine if I were to drop you into a totally dark room. Your job is to find the door. How would you do it? Perhaps you would find the walls with your hands and feel (kinaesthetic) your way to the door. Can you imagine how you could find the door using just your auditory system?

You may find that you have a bias. We often find that we use one preference for everything as this is easiest for our brain, unless we are forced by a situation to shift our preference, in which case we will use another sensory input channel.

We can tell which one of these filters is operating by listening to the language people use. This is known as our *primary system.* With practice, you will begin to hear just how people take in information. We tell each other in our language, but unless we have our communication filters set to receive this useful information, we ignore it.

Hearing, then matching a person's language is an excellent way of increasing your understanding of how a client thinks and gaining deeper rapport (more about rapport skills later). To be able to listen for these linguistic indicators of our representational systems enriches our own language and our ability to be understood by people with other preferences. In NLP, these words are called *sensory predicates.*

See Chapter 1 for a larger list of sensory-based language, but, for ease, here are a few examples.

- *Visual*: I get the picture, I see what you mean, let's get this in perspective, it appears that, show me, the focus of attention, looking closely, a blind spot, it's clear to me, a different angle, he's a dark one, there's a cloud on the horizon, this is the outlook, with hindsight, she's short-sighted, you'll look back on this.
- *Auditory*: that rings a bell, we're on the same wavelength, let's talk about it, who calls the tune, within earshot, let's discuss things, I'm speechless, shout from the hilltops, people will hear you, this silence is deafening, it's music to my ears, word for word, in a manner of speaking, turn a deaf ear.
- *Kinaesthetic*: he's thick-skinned, a cool customer, I grasp the meaning, a heated argument, I will be in touch, I can't put my finger on it, she's a cold fish, a warm-hearted person, we are scratching the surface, let's dig deeper, hit the nail on the head, you'll get shot, a lukewarm attitude, I feel it in my bones.
- *Olfactory and Gustatory*: it's a matter of taste, let's chew it over, I smell a rat, it's a bitter pill, that's an acid comment, it's a bit fishy, it leaves a bad taste.

How to find the sensory system

In addition to the language indicators of representational systems, we can also examine how each system handles the incoming data and how that can influence communication.

Different modes of processing produce observable behaviours. These are generalizations, but nonetheless useful, and provide us with clues as to how the person is processing information from the world outside in relation to how they create their own reality (see also Eye-accessing cues later in this chapter).

The visual system

The visual system, as the saying 'a picture is worth ten thousand words' suggests, deals with holding and processing simultaneous information. Our pictures may be stills or movies, they may be colour or black and white, we may even have a split screen and be able to see two movies simultaneously. The key feature is that our representation is all there at the same time. So when we communicate in this mode, we tend to exhibit certain general behaviours.

Watch for the following signs of visual processors: the eyes or head will move up; even when sitting or standing, the body is held erect and they breathe from the top of the lungs; they will often sit forward or lean forward when seated; they are generally good spellers and give fast responses to questions; however, they often have trouble remembering verbal instructions, as they get bored by long explanations and their minds tend to wander; they memorise by seeing pictures; they like how things appear visually and are often organised, neat and well groomed; they are more interested in how a person looks at them rather than what is said.

The auditory system

The auditory system is sequential – we can only utter one sound at a time. There are two parts – *digital* (words) and *tonal* (the variation in sound).

When the auditory system is being used, you may see the eyes or head moving from side to side or down and right; the breathing comes from the middle of the chest, and they typically talk to themselves and are able to repeat back conversations accurately; learning is by listening and they can be distracted easily by noise; they are often responsive to a particular tone of voice or certain words, and find spoken language easier; these people are logical and good at remembering steps, sequences and procedures.

The kinaesthetic system

The kinaesthetic system is responsible for our intuitive processing. It is the system that gives us that gut feeling, 'I just knew it was right/wrong', with no apparent logic present.

In kinaesthetic processors, the eyes or head will move down and left and the breathing comes from the bottom of the lungs, with the abdomen moving in and out; posture is often more slumped and they may talk slowly, the response to questions is also often slower; they will often stand close to people and touch them; they can be physically oriented – many athletes are strongly kinaesthetic; they need to move and memorise by doing or walking through an activity.

Communication across different sensory types

When we begin to consider the differences that each system brings in behaviour, we can see how mismatches in communication occur. To a kinaesthetic processor, the visual processor will seem too fast. To the visual processor, the sequential nature of the auditory creates impatience, as this style of processing may require the person, in effect, to go back to the beginning if stopped in mid-flow. Think about your work colleagues and family, can you understand how communication difficulties arise?

EYE ACCESSING CUES

Another method used to identify a person's thinking process is their eye movements. We tend to move our eyes according to which representation system and part of the brain we are accessing. In most cases, this is a reliable indicator of how a person is thinking, especially in relation to retrieval of information.

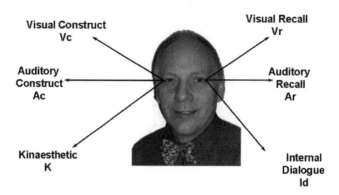

Figure 5.1   Typical eye accessing cues for a right-handed person.

It is important to remember that people can have different eye accessing systems. However, for a right-handed person, a typical pattern is given in Figure 5.1. The important thing to remember is to calibrate a client's eye movements before making judgements based on them. Think up a few simple conversational questions, which will indicate the processing patterns present for an individual.

When interviewing using a question and answer process, this system becomes very useful. By crafting questions, it is possible to calibrate a person's *lead* – this is the way they go inside and find an answer to a question or work through a problem. You will see sequences of movements as the person retrieves data from various parts of the brain or talks to him/herself about the question.

The basic pattern, which is true for a large proportion of the population, is shown in Figure 5.1. There are variations for left-handed people, although there is no rule, except that we must calibrate each person.

Rule of thumb

(as you look at the other person) *We generally tend to look upwards when we are using visual thought processes, to look side-to-side or down-right for auditory, and to look down-left for kinaesthetic.*

PRIMARY INTEREST OR FOCUS OF ATTENTION

This group of filters guides what we pay attention to, and is particularly useful when we know that we want to gain data in a particular area – for example, holiday destinations or a new shape of mobile phone. The primary interest will definitely influence the interest level and value of the data gained.

When we engage in a significant activity, we have preferences about what focuses our attention – some areas will have a high signal, some a low one. These particular sorting principles give you clues as to which contextual markers people use to access experiences. In other words, the markers that people use to retrieve memories. This becomes important in focus groups.

People

When describing something, this type of person will primarily focus on the people – for example, who was at a party. They like people, interact well socially, have developed good social skills, love to chat and help people.

Activity

When describing something, this type of person will primarily focus on what happened – what's going on, what activities occurred in some situation.

Place

This type of person will primarily focus on where they are, location – near or far. 'Where I am coming from is . . .'

Things

This type of person is interested in physical objects. They have a tendency to look for the 'right' car, the 'right' house, etc. They notice the tools, objects and products involved in a situation. They are task-oriented, get the job done and focus on the end result.

Information

This type of person wants to know what information, what data, is/are available. They like to know about ideas and you might hear them say things like, 'I just thought you should (or might like to) know this.'

Time

This type of person is interested, for example, in dates.

'Was it Tuesday or Wednesday when that happened?'
'Ten years ago, in 1986, I started to change. . . .'

The timescale for projects is an important factor, too. For example, imagine you are conducting a focus group around the topic of Holidays and you want to find out how the client can best market its new range of activity holidays. You go out and find a general sample group. Imagine how each attention filter will affect the respondents' view of the material. Only some will be interested in the activities, the others will initially want to access the material through their own primary interest. Moreover, the sort of questions you may hear are:

People: Who goes on this sort of holiday?
　　　　　How many people are involved?
　　　　　Who can do which activity?
　　　　　Do the reps help with the activities?

Activity: What type of activities are available?
　　　　　Are they dangerous?

Place: Where are they taking place?
　　　　　What sort of accommodation is available?
　　　　　Which country?

Things: What do we need to take with us?
　　　　　What equipment is provided?
　　　　　Who makes the equipment?
　　　　　What safety equipment is provided?

Information: What are the safety procedures?
　　　　　How do I book?

Time: How long do the activities take?
　　　　　Do I have time to do all the activities during the holiday?

GLOBAL–SPECIFIC: CHUNK SIZE

This deals with the chunk size of information people prefer. There are two basic styles: global and specific, with a lesser third style: lateral.

Within this meta-program there is also a natural preference for a direction – which comes first, the global or the specific, or do we just stay at one place on the continuum? Learning to move up and down this scale has an enormous effect on taking our communication skills towards excellence.

Global

The first style is what is often referred to as *global* or *big picture*, and the preference is for large chunks of data with little detail. This leads to deductive thinking, where the big picture leads down towards the details.

Global processors are often convinced by ideas and concepts, and will talk and consider projects in general terms, having difficulty in appreciating step-by-step processes. They will want to see the big picture first and then think about smaller details, usually concentrating on the overall direction of the task and wanting to delegate the details. They want to be shown the global scheme of things so that they can see how their activities fit in to the whole.

When speaking, some of the linguistic indicators to be aware of are: giving an overview of a situation with little or no detail; talking in concepts and abstracts; becoming impatient, or losing interest, if provided with too much detail; they may suggest you 'cut to the chase', or ask where this is leading; events may be described in a nonsequential way. Watch for large head gestures and/or the upper body moving back for the big picture.

Some key words you can use are: generally, basically, typically, overall, overview, perspective, framework, idea, concept, flexible, open-ended and spontaneous.

Useful tips are to present the big picture, or overall concept idea, first and refrain from using too many details, which the person will find boring. Concentrate on generalities and also be aware that they may 'read between the lines' and fill in details in a way that is different from your way.

Global to specific

Some people do like to have both sides of the coin. Global to specific requires the big picture first and then, when they are comfortable with that, they want the detail. 'Let's look at the overall picture before we get into the mechanics of things.'

Specific

Specific processors tend to perceive a task in terms of its constituent parts; they break down tasks into smaller, more specific and definite steps. These people concentrate on the details first, and need to have them before they make any decisions based on those specific facts. Often, they will miss the overall goal of a task because they get caught in the details. Watch for small head gestures and/or the upper body moving in for detail.

They will need to have details on the sequence of what to do and when, where and how to begin, what to do next and how each step contributes to achieving the whole task. Once they know the parts work, and only if they will work, they will consider the bigger picture.

Specific processors also have a need for concrete examples and often can be thought of as using a 'microscope lens'. When speaking, some of the linguistic indicators to be aware of are: giving you all the details and often going down several levels in describing and explaining something to you; talking about steps and sequences using lots of adverbs and adjectives; if distracted or interrupted, they will often need to go back to the beginning.

Some key words you can use are: exactly, precisely, specifically, first, second, third, next, then, before, after, plan, schedule, order, organised, structure, definite.

Useful tips are to break things down into specifics, emphasise the details and present them in a sequential fashion. Vagueness, too many generalities and a lack of sequence will tend to confuse them. Do not expect them to see and understand the bigger picture automatically.

Specific to global

This preference of the global–specific meta-program leads to inductive thinking. This is typical of Sherlock Holmes's style, where all the details are collected meticulously until they complete the big picture. 'Let's look at the details and then you'll see how the whole portfolio is made up.'

Lateral

The last style can be considered poetic, where a sideways move is habitual and one thing may be seen in terms of another. This is common in artists, poets and some scientists, particularly those who have made breakthroughs. We may think of Einstein in this category; the thought experiments he invented, where he imagined he was riding a beam of light, led to the famous $e = mc^2$ equation for relativity.

RELATIONAL SORT FOR DECISION: SAMENESS–DIFFERENCE (MATCHING–MISMATCHING)

There are two basic ways of operating mentally when we work with data. We can look for what matches what we already know (the same) or for what differs or mismatches. This meta-program plays an important role in our overall thinking patterns.

Hand gestures are useful to notice for these patterns. Gestures where hands are coming together and close indicate sameness, whereas hands moving apart and moving at odd angles indicate difference.

Sameness

This pattern is exhibited by a tendency to respond to the world of experience by looking for sameness, or, at least, similarity. For example, how what is happening now is like something that happened in the past. It is useful for people who organise by similarity to notice differences, because they have a tendency to generalise based on a few examples, especially when they discover what something is like.

Characteristics you might spot are: a tendency to look for 'what is there' as opposed to 'what is missing'; a perception of things in terms of what they have in common and how things fit together; a tendency to match what you are saying with something that they already know.

When speaking, some of the linguistic indicators to be aware of are: the use of words like same, just like, similar to, in common, maintain, keep the same, stay the same.

Useful accessing strategies are: emphasise sameness, maintenance, what there is in common and how things have not changed.

Sameness with exception

This is where the primary attention is directed towards things that are the same or similar, but with secondary emphasis on the differences. These people prefer change slowly over time and will resist major changes, except when seen as progressive and gradual. The category makes up the largest group in the population.

When speaking, some of the linguistic indicators to be aware of are: people who will tell you first how sets of objects or situations are similar, then what is different about them; the use of comparatives – more, better, less, or, the same except, but, evolved, gradual, although; a tendency to tell you how things have gradually changed through time.

'It is almost the same . . .'
'It is basically the same . . .'
'It is the same except . . .'
'My life is basically the same; however, I am having more fun.'
'My job is more or less the same, although I have more duties now.'

Difference

This pattern is exhibited by a tendency to respond to the world of experience by first looking for how things are different. People with this tendency may not understand the word relationship. It is useful for a person who mismatches information to also notice similarities, because they have a tendency to chunk down and may have some difficulty with patterning and generalising.

Characteristics you might spot are: the incongruities – how things don't fit together, how things don't match; an emphasis on how things are totally different; a tendency to sort for 'what is missing'; a strategy of mismatching data in order to understand them.

When speaking, some of the linguistic indicators to be aware of are: phrases like 'night and day', 'there is no relationship'; words like new, changed, different, revolutionary, unique, radical. 'My life has really changed in the past five years. I feel like a different person.' 'My job is totally different than when I started. I'm doing a whole new job.'

Useful accessing strategies are: emphasise how things are totally different; frame things as totally new and revolutionary; focus on creative, new solutions and change.

Difference with exceptions

This is when the primary attention is directed towards how things are different, with secondary emphasis on the similarities.

Characteristics you might spot are: first, somebody will tell how some set of objects or situations are different, then point out similarities or what they have in common. 'My life has basically changed; however, I'm still living in the same house.' 'My job is totally different, although I'm still working for the same boss.'

When speaking, some of the linguistic indicators to be aware of are: talking about rearranging things – it helps to point out the variety that comes from change.

Useful accessing strategies are: first emphasise how things are different, then note commonalities and continuities in passing.

MOTIVATING ATTENTION FILTERS

Motivating attention filters are those filters that handle data in ways that move us to some sort of action or judgement in the outside world.

Motivation direction: towards and away from

This filter directs the way we move in relation to our values. *Towards* pulls us to the positive benefits of our values. *Away from* pushes us from our undesired values, creating a sense of aversion. Since everybody moves towards some things and away from others, we have a natural propulsion system – away from pain and towards pleasure.

Towards

Characteristics you might spot are: having clear goals; the motivation to get or to have things, to achieve, to attain; a tendency to move towards what they like/want; a strong ability to prioritise things.

This type of person has trouble recognising what should be avoided. They often ignore negative consequences and fail to notice details going wrong. They are motivated by incentives or 'carrots'.

Watch for pointing, head-nodding and gestures of inclusion.

They talk about gain, achievement, accomplishment, obtaining, having and getting what they want. They will also consider things, people or situations they want to include.

Useful tips are: stress that you (or your product or service) can help them get what they want; restate their goals and what they want to achieve; use words like attain, obtain, have, get, include, achieve; recognise that they may not appreciate potential problems.

There is actually a range of gradations of the 'towards' attention filter, often characterised as follows:

- *Towards*: 'These are the objectives.'
- *Towards with some Away from*: 'These are the objectives . . . and that will avoid . . . xyz.'
- *Towards and Away from*: 'Well, here are the goals . . . which means we will not be able to . . .'

Away from

Characteristics you might spot are: an ability to recognise easily what should be avoided; a tendency to move away from, avoid or get rid of things they don't like or want; a tendency to focus on problems and what can, has or might go wrong.

This type of person has trouble working with priorities and formulating objectives. They are motivated by threats or 'sticks'.

Watch for gestures of exclusion, expressions of something to be avoided or removed, head shaking, the body moving back and expressions of facial tension.

When speaking, some of the linguistic indicators to be aware of are: talking about what they don't want and what they don't want to happen; telling you about situations to be avoided, people and things to be excluded; telling you what they will stay away from, get rid of, avoid.

Useful tips are: find out what they don't want, or want to avoid; stress that you can help them avoid what they don't want; explore potential problems and show how they can be overcome; recognise that it is difficult for them to define what they want; emphasise how easy your plan will make their life.

Here is the range of gradations of this attention filter:

- *Away from*: now we know what you want to avoid, we will be able to exclude what is necessary to get the best solution for you.
- *Away from with some Towards*: so, we know what to avoid . . . and these goals will give us . . .
- *Away from and Towards*: by avoiding this problem, we will achieve the objectives.

Frame of reference: self–others

In terms of 'self' and 'others', which option is a person compelled to attend to? Which one has the greatest signal value (commands their attention and focuses their behaviour)? We often find those in the caring professions have a very strong *others* focus.

This focus tends to shift as we mature, so, when interviewing, it is useful to consider the age of the interviewee. This can give a broad idea as to where their focus may be. Clearly, this is not an iron-clad rule, and a few questions can easily show just how a person is filtering the incoming information. As a general rule of thumb, the following is a guide to the main focus of different age groups:

Teenagers – self
Young, single adults – self
Young parents – others
Couples with grown up children – self (often, the self is the relationship they share)
Older people – self

Focus on self

These people attend to their own thoughts, feelings and/or behaviour, almost to the exclusion of others'. They are compelled to respond to the needs of their inner world. There is a tendency for someone who sorts primarily by self to be 'inside' a lot of the time, and they often seem to be oblivious to other people and to the outside world in general.

They evaluate the quality of communication with others primarily on their feeling about what is going on, rather than the responses they get.

Watch for an absence of head-nodding, saying 'uh-huh', little or no facial expression and a tendency to respond to content, not to nonverbal signals.

When speaking, some of the linguistic indicators to be aware of are: me, myself and I!

Also watch their behaviours, only nonverbal observation will reveal this pattern. If you drop a pencil, they will not pick it up, they will look at you then look at the pencil. There is no spontaneous reflex action, although they may eventually decide to pick it up.

Useful tips are: hinting does not work, nor does sarcasm. BE DIRECT!

Focus on others

These people perceive interactions primarily in terms of what they can do for others, who are the focus of their attention. Other people have primacy and the highest signal value.

People with this focus seem to be 'outside' and paying attention to people and the world around them. They attend primarily to other people's thoughts, feelings and/or behaviour. They evaluate the quality of communication with others primarily on the responses of the people around them. They attempt to facilitate the other person's understanding of a discussion. Because other people's responses are important to them, they often feel the need to try and anticipate other people's responses. They organise a situation to please the other person.

Such people may find it difficult or uncomfortable to be the focus of attention and may not be able to answer personal questions. Watch for head-nodding, saying 'uh-huh' and facial expressions that respond to nonverbal signals.

When speaking, one of the linguistic indicators to be aware of is: letting you lead the conversation, ensuring that all your needs are met. In terms of behaviour, they will pick up dropped pencils by reflex as an unconscious response.

Useful tips are: these people are responsive to verbal and non-verbal cues; they appreciate a depth of rapport.

Motivation source: internal–external

This is the primary focus for judging, evaluating, deciding responses and behaviour. It refers to where the source of authority and responsibility resides; where a person places the responsibility for their actions. It also refers to the source of motivation and validation for the self.

Internal

These people provide their own motivation from within, and they decide on the quality of their work. They often have difficulty in accepting negative feedback and will often question the opinion or judge the person giving the feedback.

They tend to rely on their own criteria, evaluations and judgements. Validation and the source of authority and evidence come from the inside. Things will be evaluated on the basis of what they think is appropriate, using their own feelings.

Their own feelings are also used to know that they have done a good job. Evidence comes from the inside for verification and validation of how they have done, how they are doing. They will decide that they have done a good job based on their own subjunctive criteria.

These people provide their own motivation and are convinced when you appeal to things they already know through their own experience.

When speaking, some of the linguistic indicators to be aware of are: telling you what they decide; they will say that they just know it, 'It feels right', 'I feel it inside', 'I decide', 'I feel satisfied about it.'

They resist when someone tries to tell them what is right for them or when someone tries to decide for them.

Useful tips are: don't tell them what other people think and decide; emphasise what they think and that they have to decide for themselves; help them clarify their own thinking, 'Only you will know if this is right for you', 'It is up to you.'

If you combine internal reference with moving away from, you get the following: 'You are the only one who knows what you would lose if you don't come to the meeting.'

External

When people are using external reference, they rely on other people's evaluations and judgements; they conform to other people's beliefs. The source of authority and evidence comes from external sources. They use external standards and feedback to develop their own opinions. Validation is sought from the outside; they need external approval.

They require direction from other people, using them to find out what they should be doing and how. They also tend to draw conclusions based primarily on the other person's reactions.

They have to ask other people what they think of their work; they rely on others to tell them when they've done a good job (using the other person's criteria).

When speaking, some of the linguistic indicators to be aware of are: telling you that they know something because other people or outside information and/or external sources tell them, e.g. 'Someone has to tell me', 'My friends tell me', 'I get a reward', 'The facts speak for themselves', 'This is the way it is.'

They may describe incoming information or respond to a suggestion, query or an idea as though it were an imperative, an order or a decision.

Useful tips are: when the frame of reference is external, you will want to know who they use for the reference; who is the authority that they are using? This can be elicited by the questions 'According to whom?' and 'Who says?' If the authority is not a person, you may want to find out what the information source is, for example, research. Emphasise what other people think and decide, especially significant others and authority figures, 'Other people think . . .'. Give them data such as statistics, percentages: 'The facts show that . . .'. Reassure them with a lot of positive feedback as to how they are doing.

If you wanted to convince this person to agree to something, you could have them talk to other people who have already done it, so they could tell them all the benefits. This is an external reference combined with moving towards.

External with internal check

Depending on the content, these people rely primarily on the criteria, evaluations and judgements of others. However, they also consider their own criteria, opinions and beliefs.

OPTIONS–PROCEDURES

We have two broad responses to getting things done or dealing with instructions – an options style or a procedures style.

Options

'Options people' can *develop* new procedures or strategies; however, they do not work very well when having to *use* procedures. They value alternatives, so search for innovative and different approaches and are good at starting projects rather than maintenance.

Commitment may be difficult because it reduces available options. However, they may be totally committed until the next thing comes along.

When speaking, some of the linguistic indicators to be aware of are: talking of the possibilities, of other ways, more choices, being stimulated, challenged with new things.

Useful tips are: 'Let's find a better way', 'I can break/bend the rules for you on this', 'This option will give you unlimited possibilities.'

Procedures

'Procedures people' like to *follow* specific and definite procedures; however, they may not know how to *generate* those procedures. There is a compulsive need to complete the procedure, and closure will be an important value.

When speaking, some of the linguistic indicators to be aware of are: they know 'the right way' and how to do things; they will tell you how they came to be in a particular situation and will use ordinal language.

Useful tips are: use numerical overviews, 'There are five steps to making this sale'; provide ways of dealing with procedural breakdowns, 'First you should do . . ., second, this . . .'.

TIME SORT: PAST, PRESENT, FUTURE

The English language allows for time distinctions to be made between past, present and future. This is made possible through the use of verb tenses. For example, 'I was curious' presupposes that curiosity was part of some past experience and is no longer necessarily part of the speaker's ongoing experience. 'I am curious' presupposes that curiosity is part of the speaker's ongoing experience. 'I will be curious' states that the speaker is anticipating being curious at some future time and is not necessarily curious now.

Through the linguistic distinctions of verb tenses, we objectify and externalise our imagery of the passage of time. There is a tendency to perceive time as linear, which is expressed in the verb tenses we use. Because of how we externalise the passage of time, this makes it possible for us to think we can organise, structure, manage and control time. Consider a few linguistic examples of how we quantify time: we lose and find time, spend and save time, waste time, are late/early.

We sort time into three zones – the past, the present and the future.

Past

Here, people think about what they have experienced and what that means to them. History is important to them and can provide a basis on which to infer or make predictions. They spend much of their time thinking about the past.

When speaking, some of the linguistic indicators to be aware of are: telling you about past events and using past tenses in language; referring to a past occurrence to understand situations.

Useful tips are: refer new tasks to past jobs; give examples of past successes and use case studies.

Present

Here, people think and talk about what is happening at the moment, using their senses in the present moment. They may fail to think of future results or consequences.

When speaking, some of the linguistic indicators to be aware of are: use of present language; telling you how they are now.

Useful tips are: refer to what is happening now and how things will change immediately once they take action in the moment.

Future

These people think and talk about the future, projecting their senses out into the future. They may fail to make plans or take action now to create their desired future.

When speaking, some of the linguistic indicators to be aware of are: use of future tense language; referring to what they wish to happen in the future.

Useful tips are: refer to what will happen in the future and how things will change in due course; demonstrate how open-ended the future is and how many options are available.

DECISION-MAKING

Our last category of filters contains those that help us come to decisions.

Decision-making using the NLP model is simple and has two phases: the *channel* and the *clincher*.

Decision channel

When we make a decision, it has to fulfil one or more of the following criteria. It must either:

- look right;
- sound right;
- feel right;
- smell right;
- taste right or
- make sense.

Thought Experiment

Think of two or three purchases in different categories and work out which channel, or combination of channels, you used to come to a decision.

We may vary our channel or combination of channels within contexts, or may stick to the same channel, which can have interesting consequences. Let's take an example – shoes. We all know someone, even ourselves, who has bought a pair of shoes just because of the way they look. The fact that they will hurt and cause blisters after a few hours does not play a part in the process. On the other hand, maybe you do not care what the shoes look like, as long as they fit and feel comfortable to wear. Some of us may have even tried on a pair of shoes that both looked right and felt good, only to find that when we walked across a floor, they squeaked or tapped unacceptably. Occasionally, even when we get most of our other channels aligned, the purchase does not make sense logically – it is too expensive or fragile perhaps. This may stop us, but the other senses may be strong enough for us not to make the sensible choice.

Decision clincher (convincer)

Now we have the channel, the final piece is the *clincher* or *convincer*, which completes the decision strategy. There are three possible ways that we may complete the decision process. First, how many times do we need to have seen the object? Let's go back to shoes. Frequently, we may see a pair of shoes that fits all the channel criteria, yet we don't take the action to buy until we have walked around the town to a number of other shoe shops – then we end up back at the first pair! Alternatively, we may have tried on several pairs before we are convinced that we have the right ones. Typically, and as a rule of thumb, three times is average for most people. Experienced car sales people will always show you more cars than the one you had selected, in order to fill this convincer. In car sales there are no be-backs (be back tomorrow!)

For some decisions, notably ones where we may be expending a large amount of money, we may need time to pass before the convincer kicks in. How many people do you know who find the house they want, yet take weeks, if not months, to start the purchase process? Sometimes they even wait too long and lose their favourite property.

The third type of convincer involves the quantity of information needed to convince us that we can complete. This was a tactic used in the past in insurance sales, by presenting to the customer in their own home. There is no chance of the customer going to other companies in the time you are with them, so providing more information about the product and working through personal details can lead to the buyer feeling that there is no more to be understood, and so their convincer is filled and the deal clinched.

USAGE

So, armed with the knowledge, how do you use this in research? Why should you use this in research?

The simple answer is to better understand people. The more detailed answer is to better understand how people make decisions (with which sensory filter, using what basic filter programme). If we understand how our respondents are going about their response to our client's services, products and communications, then we are better able to ensure that rejection of our stimuli is genuine, and that it is not simply a mismatch or omission.

CHAPTER 6

THE ANALYSIS

WHAT'S IN THIS CHAPTER?

- Recording the interview
- Analysis
- Eliciting this information
- Summary

TO ANALYSE OR NOT TO ANALYSE?

There is every indication in today's speed- and cost-dominated qualitative environment that the output of any depth or group project relies very heavily on simple reportage of 'what was said' by respondents. Indeed, one American client stated that almost all their qualitative reporting was in the form of transcript plus overview and summary of findings reporting, usually on a day-after-fieldwork basis, and it was on the basis of what was said/sought in answer to specific, direct questions, that the marketing and product development were set in motion. He went on to ask for verbatim quotations to support each and every conclusion and recommendation, and was unconvinced by the argument that analysis is just that – an analytical process which goes beyond what was said, into the areas of what the moderator thinks it means in the context of the client brief and objectives, and the respondents' context.

It is likely that this trend will continue to grow, whether by virtue of the corporate culture and the nature of short-term decision-making or whether simply because it is increasingly possible to ask for this. Technology, digital recording media and, before long, the use of auto-transcribing software will make this even more prevalent.

However, it won't improve the research reporting process one jot unless someone takes the time to read and analyse the content, and there will still be some clients for whom this will render a report largely meaningless. In fairness, it does give the moderator/analyst the chance for a systematic evaluation of NLP language used, and clues as to the nature of the respondents' make-up for more detailed review.

The issue here is that the words we use, and their context, give not only the mainstream content, but also the chance to learn a lot about the respondents' deeper structures and meanings. This is hardly a revelation, as psychology and literature have this as a major foundation of their existence. Discourse Analysis, Content Analysis and other techniques allow us to study form, structure and meaning, and so, too, do the language aspects to NLP.

Part of the technique here involves the usage of words, phrases and associative/metaphoric structure during the actual interview (or interpersonal exchange), but in this chapter we are concerned with the notion of post-interview analytics: what it means *after* it has been said. Before we focus on this, it is worth mentioning, briefly, the tools of the trade, i.e. the means of recording and analysing.

ONE WAY OF WORKING

Imagine you have been on the road all week, interviewing respondents, maybe undertaking some observational work as well, and you are now back to get your head round what material you have got and what it all means.

Your client, and maybe your accounts department, is screaming for the project to be completed, and your first temptation is to use memory, plus a few scribbled notes taken during the interviews, to create a nice-looking PowerPoint presentation, with some hastily assembled video clips. Maybe you also follow the topic guide structure and sequence, starting, of course, with an Objectives page, followed by a Methodology page, a sequential description of the (recalled) findings, and completed by a Summary page. Standard stuff. The client understands this. It is not too challenging, and, provided you deliver it fairly confidently (and don't shake too many client expectations as to findings), you'll be all right.

Job done, invoice in, on to the next project. However, maybe late at night you'll begin to wonder about *that* respondent, and whether she really meant what she said. You took it at face value, but did she really mean what she said? Because you care and you are professional, you want to go back and check out the raw materials again, watch the studio DVD, read the transcript. What do you do?

We'll come back to what you do, but, briefly, a word on the format of these raw records. You will have a range of formats with which to contend – video, audio tape, digital, transcripts, etc. – and each one has its own particular requirements, characteristics and offerings.

RECORDING THE INTERVIEW

Video

With the advent of portable digital video recorders, there is little reason not to video record all interview sessions, subject, of course, to relevant industry codes of practice, respondent permissions, and so on. The audio quality is acceptable, but can be enhanced easily by a rifle microphone attached to the camera's hot shoe, or equally, by the parallel usage of a good quality digital recorder, the sound from which can subsequently be married up to video images, if higher quality is required for presentations, ethnographic clippings, etc.

The use of video offers so much extra by way of contextual, nonverbal opportunities for analysis that it seems short-sighted not to use it! Many of the more modern/better refurbished studios now offer digital recording of interview sessions to 'take away DVDs or CDs' on the day/night, so there is little excuse for not having a high quality record of it, except that the camera lens/detail is severely compromised by the angle of view in many locations. Personally, when I use a digital camera, I set it up behind my shoulder, such that respondents are recorded at eye level, not from ceiling view, as the downward angle makes reading most facial expressions a waste of time, and little can be read into the proceedings. Subject to the room size and set-up, this produces perfectly acceptable results. Ideally, the moderator has someone helping to operate the camera, reframe/focus/change the tape, etc., though this is an extra cost. In a perfect scenario, we would have at least two cameras, set at 45° and allowing both 'sides' of a group to be recorded simultaneously (Figure 6.1).

Audio

Still, though, the standard fare is for audio recording, and though digital (and mini disk, for a while) is becoming standard, many interviews are still recorded on C90 cassettes, not least of all in many older studio facilities. I use a Sony digital recorder on HQ (high quality) and download to my laptop in between sessions, as the recording duration will not allow a full evening's session of 3–4 hours to fit on a single HQ recording, but this is a quirk

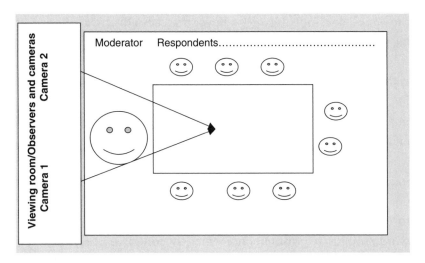

Figure 6.1   Two cameras recording both sides of the group.

of the machine itself, and there are longer recording length machines available.

Again, during the interview, notes (written by the moderator) will be made, and should be referred back to when replaying the recording. Why did you ask that particular respondent that particular question at that specific spot in the interview? Your notes should help here.

Transcripts

This is what it is about: to use them or not, and, if so, how? They represent the textual evidence for analysis, but should not be taken at face value in many circumstances, where there may be a sub-agenda. By all means accept that the respondent's name is Jane (factual, likely to be true, etc.), but do not accept that her view of advertising, as stated, is all there is to obtain, 'I never watch adverts: they are patronising, and, anyway, I am out all the time', does not mean she never watches adverts as she is out all the time!

Similarly, 'That's good' is open to a range of interpretations, and should be checked against context, tone, etc. (see below). Does it mean 'That is really great and I like it a lot'? Or does it imply sarcasm, 'That is meant to be good, is it?' or is it modest endorsement, 'That's OK'?

Transcripts are good for textual analysis in NLP terms, and indeed for any other form of text analysis. Personally, I have not got into using a computer analysis tool for text, but that may be to do with my own personal filtering systems, and I prefer spoken words/sounds to written ones when it comes to analysis. I also prefer to use DVD/video to enhance understanding by watching people and their reactions, but, again, this is just my own style. Others are quite comfortable with computerised analysis tools, and I really believe this is an important area for the future, especially when linked to the future of automated transcriptions.

So, I know I prefer to watch a moving record of the interview. What then? Well, analyse this!

ANALYSIS

Analysis of what? Well, content is the obvious answer, but within this there are several key areas which typically reveal some valuable findings, over and above the simple business of what was said, by whom, and in response to what. This is done with a view to relating it to an understanding of what the client needs to know, and what the context of the response by the respondent was. This usually means large sheets of paper, with lots of notes, verbatims, arrows and theme blocks. It also, increasingly, means using some visual tool for me, at least, such as a mind-map program, especially for top-of-mind association materials (with which I often start my interviews). Mind maps are great for setting out raw materials and for re-ordering sequences/layouts/ associations/groupings, etc., when using one of the modern pieces of mind-map software.

I have used several, but have now settled on Mindjet Mind-Manager, which I think is really useful. It exports to many formats, and drops nicely into a PowerPoint presentation. It is not especially expensive, even for the Pro version, and is a really worthwhile addition to your analysis toolkit. You can highlight sections to create colour-coded themes, move any element around, drop in floating notes and use a variety of formats to accentuate key findings. It is really helpful in an NLP sense, as responses/ideas can be grouped (and, of course, moved around) to reflect respondent profiles. It should even be possible (though I have not yet had reason to use this) to use it to highlight different responses from respondents with identifiably different filter preferences – see below (and note the use of the mind-map format).

Meta-programs

Meta-programs are the basic filter systems that we use in our day-to-day lives. In fact, there are some 50+ such mini-programs that we use to move us along the road every day, but the ones most often found useful in everyday research analytics are shown in Figure 6.2.

It should also be noted that these are capable of further development, additions and refinement by the reader/researcher, in the light of experience.

Motivational preferences

Some people are motivated by power, authority and influence over others, while others want to be liked. This is fairly obvious

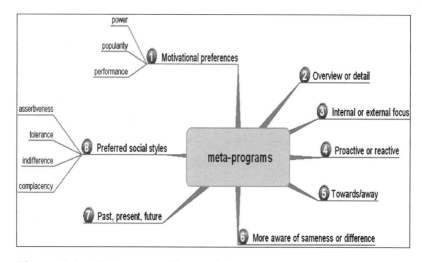

Figure 6.2 The most useful everyday meta-programs.

in itself, but appears to be seldom used in analysing the responses we obtain from respondents. Others are maybe driven by performance, achievement or functionality. How important is this when we are reviewing responses to, for example, a new car/phone/laptop computer? Does it not surely allow us much greater insight into why a respondent gives positive or negative answers? Using the concepts offered by the NLP notion of advanced filtering and decision-making motivational preferences, we are able to do much more.

Chunked up/down

As we have seen earlier in this book, the concept of chunking (big picture vs specificity/detail) allows our interviewing to be directed at particular levels, and shows us where our respondents are in their response structures. Here, the concept of chunking is valuable as an indicator of the individual's own natural chunk style. Imagine the (frequently) observed combination in partnerships (business, personal, etc.) where one has the ideas and the other has the executional skills.

This is the value and role of chunking in filtering preferences, and we can observe how (and why) respondents process and receive information. Are they responding/rejecting/filtering because of a chunked up or chunked down processing? How are we able to revise our (or our client's) communications to permit greater harmony between message and filtering preference?

Focus

Internal or external filtering refers to the direction of the individual's vision. Are the filters concerned with their external or internal structure? Do they evaluate stimuli in terms of their internal satisfactions/motivations, etc. or by reference to external points? Do we buy the new digital camera to 'show' other people that we have it, or because it has 4 million more pixels and we think it will produce sharper pictures?

Activity

There are some we interview who are, by nature, proactive people. They move forwards in search of their goals and preferences, seek out information and take action, on their own, to further them. Equally, there are those who tend to respond to stimuli from outside and need this 'push', and tend towards reaction/reactivity.

Direction

Why did the respondent buy the new Volvo car, in place of the old Citroën, previously owned? Was it because the respondent

AWAY   TOWARDS

Figure 6.3   Towards and away from.

actively wanted the Volvo, or was it that the respondent did not want another Citroën? Was it a definite move towards or a definite move away (Figure 6.3)? This is often critically important, and has very significant implications for our clients and our analysis structures.

If the motivation is towards, the selection/choice pattern is essentially directed at one option, though there will, of course, be contenders. If away is the motivation, the selection is much more complex, with multiple options.

Sameness

When we are faced with a choice of products, brands or options, what do we notice? Is it brands that are essentially the same as each other, or do we notice the brands that stand out as different? When comparing options, are we struck most by sameness or difference? What communicates most effectively for our clients?

Time

Past, present or future? Do we look back, ahead or in the now? Do we hark back to something, treat all as in the 'now' or seek to live in the future? Regret, acceptance or ambition?

Social standing

How do we interact with others? Do we tolerate, seek to dominate, are we indifferent? All these social styles are important in
the decoding of our respondents' responses.

Values and beliefs

Values are the essential beliefs that govern our responses to the
world around us. We should be listening for words and phrases,
as well as more direct statements of what makes people tick. What
aspects of their lives are important? What do they hold most
important? What really drives the central part of their lives, what
are the generalisations they make about themselves, others and
the world and their operating principles in it?

Values are the things that are important to the respondents/
people – not objects or people, but experiences/feelings such as
learning, health, wisdom, respect. They are nonphysical qualities
that we seek to have more of in our lives. We need to understand
what these are, in many projects, in order to come to an understanding of the respondents' responses to products, services, social
policy, etc.

Beliefs act as self-fulfilling prophecies that influence all our
behaviours. There is a full description of values and beliefs back
in Chapter 1, so have a refresher look there.

Body language

Over 90% of our effective communication can come via nonverbal communication; that is, voice tone, physical gestures, facial
expression, and so on. In fact, we unconsciously use this language
every day of our lives in the same way that animals do.

Why should we believe we stop using/needing this vast amount of additional information when we are involved in a market research interview setting? We process this information unconsciously, most of the time, but NLP allows for increased sensitivity to this source of feedback from others, allowing us to monitor what is going on in the background, as well as paying attention to the words themselves.

You will hear some people say that body language is easy to misread, and that simply because someone has their arms crossed, they are not necessarily being defensive, just comfortable or maybe even cold. This is true, and points to the real issue: that of observation of how people are, under normal conditions – no stress, etc. – and how they are when put under some kind of stimulus. This is critical, and one of the first lessons in NLP training is in sensory acuity – simplistically, watching how people are behaving/ looking, etc., checking for skin tone changes, checking for eye/ pupil dilation changes, watching (especially facial) changes. Even then, these observed changes may have a range of causes, and thus, researchers need to be especially vigilant and contextualise these observations. Not easy, but that does not alter the value and role of being able to compare and contrast between normal and unusual, contrasting words to other information, and so on.

The main areas for observed changeability, under normal interview conditions, are to be found in the face/chest area. Here, skin tone, eye movements and dilation, colouring, breathing changes, etc. are more observable. But be aware of all gestures, expressions and other clues. Try to match them to the obvious responses (words) that you have been given. Let the internal voice speak to you 'This does not add up,' it will say, 'what she is saying doesn't match what I am seeing'. This gives you ammunition to challenge or respond to what is being said. This is a difficult area for NLP practitioners, since the context of NLP tells us that interpretation is not what NLP is about. It seeks to observe such gestures/changes/states so that our rapport with another can be better matched, and so that we will be more able to create harmony by so doing.

In qualitative research, we must seek to involve, I believe, some measure of interpretation, or else we fail to do our job fully. The practical midpoint is, of course, to use the observed changes for both goals, but to be wary of making assumptions about someone's apparent changed state or appearance, and not to make the interpretative leap without checking with the respondent as to possible reasons for the changes. 'Something tells me you are not keen . . .,' you might say, when her breathing rate increases in response to a question. 'You don't look like you are enjoying the ad . . .,' you may say when his eyes take on that glazed look while watching. 'Does answering that question bother you?' you might ask, when probing for a more personal response. 'Why is that, do you think?'

Blink rate

Rapid, or increased, blinking is often associated with unpleasant feelings, and decreased blinking is associated with pleasant ones. Watch what they are doing, and, even better, use close-up video to record a respondent while performing a task. Follow this up with a question/s, during the interview, and with contextual analysis afterwards. Beware though, it might have been the studio air-conditioning! Context and clarification is key.

Body posture

We use this in two ways. During interviews, we can use body posture (leaning forwards, backwards, sideways) to enhance or break rapport. The closer the similarities in body posture, the more we are likely to be in rapport, and the more we communicate

Figure 6.4   The facial area gives us many clues.

effectively. During meetings, or in interviews, if we want the other person to respond better to us, we adopt a closer match to their posture. In interviews, we note that they are leaning back and may not be participating fully, or are not responding as fully as we would like, so we match their posture and then lead them into a leaning inwards and forward posture, which encourages closer communication. If you doubt this, go to a restaurant/pub/club or street and watch people. Watch those involved in more intimate communications and watch the closeness/forward postures. Remember this when interviewing. Use it to assist, too, in helping to decode, post interview, aspects of response, and maybe things that you missed during the interview. Maybe in a group, you just missed what one of the respondents was doing, and analysis is now possible to spot at what point they became more/less involved or disengaged in the discussion or ad.

In analysis, watch for this in the respondents and relate it to the questions/answers/materials, etc.

Breathing rate

As with blinking, above, breathing changes in response to stress, excitement, enthusiasm, discomfort, and so on. Watch what your respondent is doing. If they are breathing more rapidly, you might need to know why, so seek some self-analysis from them, 'Are you enjoying the new product's taste? You look like you are!'

In interviewing, you can lead a respondent into new territory by using your breathing rate, obviously presented, to quieten down or speed up an interview dynamic. My experience is that we have three basic gears for the interview: fast, medium and slow. A slow pace encourages introspection, reflection and intimacy, while a fast pace tends to create more by way of creativity and spontaneity. Dull, unproductive group? Speed things up, ask rapid questions, use faster breathing rates and move around. It is the emotional equivalent of running downhill: after a short way, you lose some control of your speed and end up running just to stay upright. So, too, with the brain (remember the NLP linkage between physiology and state) – at speed, our brains run into unconscious response mode (the conscious can't keep up, so the unconscious takes over) and we tend to get more unscripted or uncensored responses from the respondent. If we want the reverse, slow the pace down, get people to reflect, engage the conscious side more.

How do we notice changes? Well, they are easier to spot in women, who tend, in the West, to wear lighter fabrics and expose more of their necks. Being able to see the shoulder area and its movements – rising and falling – is a real clue to breathing rate and depth. Rapid, shallow breathing may well signify tension: but beware of snap judgements and check before diagnosis!

Again, in analysis, watch for this in the respondents and relate it to the questions/answers/materials, etc.

Energy level

Energy is something of a combination of symptoms and clues, but is easier to spot than to describe. It is a combination of speed/pacing, of breathing, of loudness of voice and of 'passion'.

I use this technique a lot in group discussions, and usually stand up and move around when I wish to use this approach to encourage respondents to perform certain tasks, such as top-of-mind word association. I often use this at the start of a group to get the group going and to create some dynamic and rapport. This last point is a generalised rapport, and seeks to create a sense of togetherness and unity in a group of strangers.

It also helps to jump-start a dead group! So, if it's all going horribly wrong and the group is just sitting there waiting for someone else to speak, try this approach. Get up. Move around. Use your physiology to change theirs, knowing that a change in physiology will help change their state. If it needs to go the other way (an unruly group), get down on the floor with some collage materials (or similar) and get respondents to join you on the floor. It quietens them down wonderfully! Again, in analysis, watch for this in the respondents and relate it to the questions/answers/materials, etc.

Facial expression/head tilt

This is one of the easiest areas to spot, as we are assumed to be interested (an essential part of interviewing) when we look at the other person. Link this to the eye-accessing cues referred to earlier in the book, and also to the way we respond to questions more generally. To things we don't enjoy, or untruths, we tend not to hold eye contact, we tend to offer uncertain gazes, we tend to narrow our pupils. Watch for this, along with tightening of skin around the eyes or mouth. Also, look for skin colour

Figure 6.5   Head tilt.

changes to clue us into what may be a change in their mental state or engagement. Always check this out with some more/less oblique validation question, but do watch for the clues: they are there to help us communicate with each other. If in doubt, check out the behaviour and communication of small children, babies or animals. Nature has efficiently developed this tool for us over millions of years, and it is insane to ignore it.

In analysis, watch for this in the respondents and relate it to the questions/answers/materials, etc.

Vocal qualities (pace, rhythm, tonality)

Much of the detail has already been covered in the sections above, but the key point is that the voice is both your instrument and theirs. Use it to encourage, probe, create or break rapport (the latter for use with difficult people), to start or end a topic section, to sympathise or challenge during an interview. Use it to give you clues, during the analysis stage, of what respondents were really saying when they originally spoke.

HOW DO WE ELICIT THIS INFORMATION?

Language and observation

This is the first port of call. We are, after all, in the business of words, and words represent the basic building blocks of qualitative research – our briefings come in word form and our interview guides are in word form. It is the basic structure of how we communicate with our respondents but it is far from the only way, and it is this that represents perhaps the biggest challenge in qualitative research: to stop taking respondents' (and indeed, clients') words at face value and to learn the next level/s of possibility. It should already have been understood that during the actual interview itself, the use of words will inevitably have had a significant effect on the responses we achieve, and question structure and words chosen are part of the equation over which we, as researchers, have control. This is a core skill, and must be learned and practised before the researcher can go on to the analysis stage, without which, the rest is largely meaningless.

The next step is evaluation of the actual words used, the construction of phrases and sentences and the selection of metaphors. All tell us something about the way our respondents think, behave and act. The more we understand, the closer our rapport will be, and the closer our rapport, the closer we get to being in their shoes and seeing their world construction, not ours.

Once, during a 'values and beliefs' type interview, a respondent described her husband and herself in terms of having a working partnership (nothing to do with any business enterprise, just on a personal basis), more than a relationship. This seemed to me (and still does) a very significant use of language and choice of words, with a significant meaning inherent in them, and equally for her motivations, values and aspirations for her choice of car (it was an automotive study). I said this to the video cameraman afterwards, and expressed the hope that he had captured this moment on tape for later review. He said that he had, but he didn't think it was very important, as relationship and partnership meant pretty much the same. He and I disagreed, and I hope he is a better cameraman than he would have been an interviewer!

Eye accessing cues

Like most nonverbal signals, eye accessing cues are not absolute. They require observation to plot what is normal, and they represent a tendency for the eyes to follow a particular direction when the brain is engaged in specific tasks or operations. If it were a simple matter of a 100% rule, it would be easy. It is not, and it's not easy. To utilise this skill automatically takes long practice. But this does not make it any less valuable.

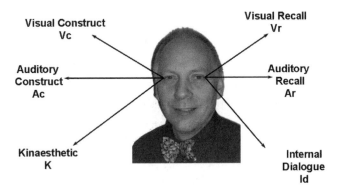

Figure 6.6   Eye accessing cues.

Remember that these are all techniques that allow you to compare what is being said/done at a conscious level with what is happening under the surface. Just as with a strange dog that you might encounter in a respondent's home, you will need to exchange some nonverbal information. It will have to learn that when you extend your hand, it is not an invitation to lunch, and vice versa. I used to have a Labrador bitch. It took most people about 30 seconds to learn that she did not have a harmful gene in her body, but did have an insatiable friendliness to humans, and indeed for food (it is part of their in-built breeding/genes: they all do it!). Thus, when she made a move forward, it was for pure and straightforward motives, and the expression of anticipation on her face was not about having your arm for a snack. Equally, I have met other dogs, cats, etc. in the course of 35 years of research to whom the same motives could not be ascribed, especially one pub dog, who took a deep dislike to me from the outset of the interview and did seem very interested in lunch, with me on the menu! You think this is a joke?

Just so with people. Each must learn the others tendencies and normalities. Why should the same exchanges not take place within the research interview context? They do, and they are normal between people.

SUMMARY

OK, so you have your tapes or transcript and you have your visual review of what they said/what they might really have meant. Now you have to do something with it all. But *what*?

This is not the vehicle to offer words about the broader context of qualitative analysis, as it is intended to focus on the active contribution mainly of NLP, but it should be apparent that the use of language is clearly an important aspect of NLP. Frequency of use of phrases, which may give clues as to the priorities, sensory filtering systems and beliefs of the respondent, is extremely important in the decoding of what was said and interpretation of what was behind the words.

Similarly, the words you select to phrase your questions and describe your findings will also be heard by the recipients (respondents and clients), and filtered by their own filtering systems and beliefs. Just because you said something, in a question or in a debrief, in a certain way, do not assume that your meaning will be that message taken by the recipient. It is such clues that we seek in the analysis process.

- What did they hear?
- To what were they responding?
- How were they processing the information?
- What did their responses actually signify?

I firmly believe your analysis is entitled (obliged) to point out your own interpretation of what was meant, not just what was said.

CHAPTER 7

PRESENTING YOUR FINDINGS

WHAT'S IN THIS CHAPTER?

- The presentation process
- Dealing with fear
- How to connect with your audience
- Feng shui for presenters
- Delivery
- Virginia Satir's five postural archetypes
- Dealing with difficult people
- Videoconferencing

PUTTING IT ALL TOGETHER

> 'The human brain starts the moment you are born and doesn't stop until the moment you stand up to speak in public.'
>
> George Jessell

You have done a great project, have some really great findings and have all the charts and materials sorted, but you have discovered that the brand team is bringing along the CEO to the debrief, and he is noted for a short temper and a worse attention span. You are getting nervous! Some of the approaches below are standard (know your material), but nonetheless vital. However, we have some additional routes into a secure and effective presentation for you that will give you the tools to make a really effective end to the job, enhancing your reputation and that of your agency, or indeed your (client) department.

The debrief is the end, possibly, of the project, and it is a great opportunity for you to get noticed by clients and colleagues alike, furthering your career and giving you that warm feeling of a job well done. Equally, it could be a chance to feel fear and make a total idiot of yourself, unless you decide to prepare yourself. More importantly, it is the chance to win or lose future business.

The truth is that few people are really good at presentations, and even fewer know why they are, even if it's true. A brilliant presentation does not just happen. It is always planned, rehearsed then delivered with flair and charisma. An excellent presenter is one who takes the time and learns the skills of presentation – not one who hopes for their natural talent to carry them through. Presenting is a set of skills rather than a talent. You can be a good presenter when you learn these skills. You will be a greater speaker if you find a way to learn from every presentation you deliver.

Imagine that you have an appointment to present to a group. An important question for you to review is 'Why am I delivering this presentation?' The answer, 'Because I was asked' will not serve you. Instead, ask why does this group need to hear from you? What do you have to tell or share with them, what is so important that you are taking up their time to talk to them? Be clear on the purpose of your presentation before you design it. Have something worthwhile to say. Start by knowing what you want to happen, then you will begin to create an effective presentation.

Telling stories and painting word pictures that create images in the listeners' minds and connect to the way they feel, means that they are more likely to understand and remember your message. The best presenters are storytellers. Use stories, metaphors and anecdotes to illustrate and reinforce the main points of your presentation. Learn to master the skill of storytelling. Listen to newscasters, comedians, entertainers and other presenters. Our most impactful stories are personal to us. This will make them easier to remember for you, and they will make your presentation unique. We will listen to stories. We hate lectures.

This is easier in qualitative research than in quantitative research, as we are essentially dealing in just this: stories. We are reporting the results of our exploration of people's attitudes, beliefs, behaviour and perceptions. If we can't make these into a good story . . . well!

That said, there are critical areas where the inherent interest in the raw material needs some help for it to be a really effective presentation, and you are a major component of that.

THE PRESENTATION PROCESS

To deliver successful presentations, they need to be structured. We will take you through a simple process using NLP techniques and concepts that will help you deliver presentations with poise and impact. Moving from how you appear at your best, through handling the information and connecting with your audience.

Let's look at the overview of what is needed to deliver an excellent presentation. The most important factor is you being in the best state to deliver – this is crucial to your success. Other factors are:

- setting your aims and objectives;
- knowing the audience;
- structuring the presentation;

- use of visual aids;
- delivery;
- rehearsal;
- handling questions and difficult people.

These techniques draw deeply on NLP understanding of how people make judgements and react in such circumstances. So, let's look at how NLP can help you not only get through this stage, but use it positively and to your advantage.

Being in the best state

'There are two types of speakers. Those who get nervous and those who are liars.'

Mark Twain

It has been often quoted that public speaking is one of the most stressful experiences we undergo, unless you are a natural performer. Assuming you are not one of those people, a critical first place to be is in a suitable state.

As we explained earlier, your own state is largely responsible for others' reactions and responses to you. Act like a rabbit in the headlights and that is how you will be perceived and consequently treated. All successful public speakers have tricks they use. Getting in the right state before the event is maybe the most important. But what constitutes the best state? It is possible that there is no 'best state' for all presentations: it may very well be that each demands some variation, or at least that there is a basic repertoire from which to select.

Let's dwell on that for a moment. For a very senior client who you do not know well/have never met, and who has had little to do with qualitative research, you may feel that a fairly 'serious', measured and authoritative style is most appropriate in order to connect, create rapport and get your message across. For a less-daunting audience, who you know well, a more relaxed style, almost informal, will be the most resourceful state.

Remember that the objective is to impart, convince and create belief in your findings. It may be that you will not know the best state until you arrive, but we can still equip you for all these eventualities – by controlling your physiology.

Physiology

We know that our minds affect our bodies, and the reverse is also true – surprisingly, our bodies affect our minds. The fastest and most direct way to change your emotional state is to change your physiology. Posture, breathing, facial expression and voice tone and tempo will all contribute to this effect. During a presentation, then, using your body is important to maintain a resourceful state as you progress through the presentation.

We all know that when we are happy, we smile. In fact, when we smile, we become happy, due to the body/mind effect. Actors are experienced in the amazing power of physiology. They pretend to sob and, very quickly, they find they are feeling the emotions that go with sobbing.

When we smile, more than 80 muscles in the face move blood to the brain, increasing blood supply. This increased blood supply alters oxygen levels in the blood and stimulates the production of particular neurotransmitters that make us feel better.

In passing, this also applies to phone conversations, so remember to smile when you are on the phone, especially with a difficult client/colleague. This in itself will improve your state!

One of the consequences of being in an unresourceful state during, or just before, your presentation (or before you go into an interview) is that this feeling will constrict your chest, affect your breathing (making you breathe more rapidly and shallowly), and make you sound nervous or stressed. If you find yourself in such an unresourceful mental and emotional state while you are presenting, change your physiology. Lift up your rib cage, smile, put your shoulders back, breathe deeply and shift your voice tone to confident and calm. This will help change the way you come across, just by altering your physiology.

We all have a physiology of excellence associated with resourcefulness and flexibility. That physiology can change with contexts, and it can be mapped across and used in different contexts. Here's how.

1. Think of something you do easily and confidently.
2. Imagine yourself in that situation. Get yourself into the physiology of that situation.
3. Pay attention to your posture, expression, breathing and your inner voice tone and tempo.
4. Now imagine yourself presenting with that same physiology.

OK, we do have to be sensible here and pick physiologies that will work in the context of presenting – you may have a great physiology when making love that might not transfer too well! On the other hand, if you shoot, or play a sport that requires body control to get results, using some of that physiology may work extremely well.

Fear

Addressing an audience is one of the big fears people have, and, although it is hard to believe, it is more common than the fear of death. If you have a fear of presenting or feel some anxiety, you are not alone. Even great speakers like Churchill and Kennedy experienced this fear. They worked on their delivery skills so they could deliver even when nervous.

Here are some of the ways fear manifests itself:

- *Skill level*: unsure of your skills or no practice.
- *Content*: being unsure you have sufficient knowledge.
- *Unforeseen situations*: will you know what to do?
- *Fear of being judged*: by self or others.
- *Fear of being vulnerable*: usually to verbal criticism, attacks or abuse.
- *Previous experiences*: memories of unhappy or unsatisfactory experiences.
- *Comparison with others*: believing you don't measure up.

Fear is a signal to you from inside yourself, what is important is how you interpret that signal. Do you run away and hide, keeping your head down and hoping you will not be the one who has to stand up and present the results? Well, most of the time, we know we will have to present . . . that is why we are in the meeting! On the other hand, are you going to receive the signal and take some steps to ensure that when you do stand up in front of your audience, you can present from a place of skills rather than fear?

Dealing with fear

When you recognise this fear signal, how can you deal with it? Here are some ways with which you can experiment to reduce your fear or even remove it.

Method 1: 'edit your movie'

This method is particularly useful for dealing with memories of unhappy or unsatisfactory experiences, even if they are manufactured by you imagining what might happen.

1. Find a quiet place where you will be undisturbed and recall the memory of a time when you had that unsatisfactory experience. Maybe you can do this in the car (if someone else is driving!), on the train or in the cab on the way to the venue.

2. Notice whether you are aware of that memory as if seeing it through your own eyes (associated). If so, then change your viewing position to that of seeing yourself and notice how your feelings change. You should be aware right away of a reduction in anxiety. Now we can begin to edit the qualities of your movie to reduce the fear even more.

3. If your memory is in colour, change it to black and white. Put a frame around it and reduce its size gradually to that of a postage stamp. Now allow it to become unfocused and blurry. Send the memory away into the distance until it becomes a mere dot on the horizon. Notice how you are feeling.

4. Evaluate the effect. A good way to judge the effect is to rate the experience on a scale of 1 to 10 – 1 being insignificant and 10 being uncomfortable with the fear. After editing your movie, has the rating reduced? Even a movement from 9 to 4 is a significant improvement.

5. Repeat the process with other unpleasant memories until you become more comfortable with the thought of presenting. Imagine yourself in the future and notice the differences.

We have been working with what, in NLP, are called *submodalities*. The modalities are our sensory apparatus, visual, auditory and kinaesthetic systems. The submodalities are the way we code our experiences, and there are submodalities for each system. Changing these can put us in control of how our memories affect us on a day-to-day basis. Any changes we make can, of course, be reversed, but who wants to feel worse? In fact, you can have a lot of fun enhancing your positive memories. Below are just a few of the important submodalities for each system, phrased as questions that you might ask. Experiment with changing the submodalities. What happens if you take a pleasant memory and enhance the qualities, say by making the movie bigger, closer, brighter, adding more sound, turning up the volume? Notice where the feeling is in your body and make it bigger and bigger.

VISUAL

- Is it a movie or still frame?
- Is it colour or black and white?
- Is the image bright, dim or dark?
- Is the image life size, bigger or smaller?
- How close is the image to you?
- Are you in the picture or watching from a distance?
- Does the image have a frame or is it a panorama?
- Is it three-dimensional or two-dimensional?

AUDITORY

- Are you saying something to yourself or hearing it from others?
- What specifically do you hear or say?
- How loud is it?
- What is the tonality?
- How fast is it?
- Where is the sound coming from?
- Is there an inflection in the voice?
- How long did the sound last?
- What is unique about the sound?

KINAESTHETIC

- Is there a temperature change? Hot or cold?
- Is there a texture change? Rough or smooth?

- Is there a vibration?
- Is there an increase or decrease in pressure?
- Where is the pressure located?
- Is there an increase in tension or relaxation?
- If there is movement, what is the direction and speed?
- What is the quality of your breathing? Where did it start/end? Is it heavy or light?
- Are the feelings steady or intermittent?
- Did it change size or shape?
- Were feelings coming into your body and/or going out?

Method 2: using anchors

Once you have had practice creating anchors, it is possible to use strong positive state anchors to remove negative states of anxiety. Here's how.

1. Create a very strong positive anchor. The best type of state for this is an energetic state, such as excitement, high motivation or enthusiasm. Test the anchor and make sure that you are able to initiate a good strong state.

2. Recall the memory of a time when you had that unsatisfactory experience, and as the memory comes back to you, fire your strong positive anchor. The effect will be to neutralise the feeling of the negative memory or even replace the feeling with positive feelings from the anchor. You have successfully recoded your memory.

3. Test by thinking about a situation in the future where you may be presenting, and notice the differences.

So, let's get your own state right. Think back to a time when you made a really great presentation. How did you feel? How do you think you looked? Imagine the 'stage' and recapture the feeling, the sound, the look, the taste. Anchor this feeling with a special touch point. Create a spotlight state (NLP anchor) that you can take with you to your presentation meeting, so you can be at your best.

Dress

We also are influenced by our dress code, as indeed are those we meet and those to whom we present. Getting the dress code right is sometimes tricky, balancing your own preferences with those of several clients. However, there are several basic themes, and, as for the advice on meetings, dress accordingly. Make it something in which you feel good and in control of your own state, be natural and be appropriate.

Your attire offers a series of communications clues to the audience, and their effect will either enhance or hinder your own presentation. I once employed an attractive young woman who returned from a debrief complaining that the, mainly male, audience seemed more interested in looking at her appearance than the charts. She insisted that wearing a short skirt and V-neck sweater did not give them the right to ogle her. Fair comment, but market research is unlikely to be able to change human nature. She was clever, she was correct, but seemingly not very wise. Be warned.

Equally, lest the reader feels this is overly sexist, a similar comment about a male colleague. He seemed, to a client, 'like a clothes horse – more interested in how he looked than in what he was saying'. Be doubly warned.

Aims and objectives

In Chapter 2 we covered the use of SMART outcomes, and here is another place to develop a SMART outcome for your presentation. In addition to this, NLP provides us with a tool called the *well-formed outcome*, which is designed to be brain-friendly and helps set your filter system in the most resourceful way, which will help you to be at your best.

A well-formed outcome

Use these questions to ensure that you have covered all the bases for yourself and have marshalled all the resources to achieve what you want. The more precisely and positively you can define what you want, the more likely you are to achieve it. We do this by ensuring that our outcomes, or desired goals, are well-thought-out and clearly-defined. You can have a colleague ask you these questions and allow your mind to come up with all the answers.

1. What do you want? Stated in positive terms. Your SMART outcome/objective is . . .
2. How will you know when you've got it? Stated in sensory-specific terms. Create a strong internal representation. What will it be like when you achieve your outcome? Create a detailed sensory internal representation, what will you see, hear and feel? Ensure that this is juicy, is it appealing? Does it draw you towards it? Describe it to a friend or colleague.
3. What resources do you need to get it? Identify all the resources you will need, from equipment and materials to help from colleagues.
4. How will doing an excellent presentation benefit you? State at least three benefits.
5. Do you want this outcome in any other situations? If so, where, when and with whom do you want it? Where, when and with whom do you NOT want it?

6. How will making an excellent presentation affect other aspects of your work life?

7. (a) What would happen if you did make an excellent presentation?

   (b) What would happen if you didn't make an excellent presentation?

   (c) What wouldn't happen if you did make an excellent presentation?

   (d) What wouldn't happen if you didn't make an excellent presentation?

Once you have created a well-formed outcome, then it is time to integrate this outcome with an NLP process called *stepping up and stepping down*.

Begin by stepping down, asking yourself the questions in Figure 7.1(a) or having a colleague ask you them. If you find a place where there is a loop, find a way out. If you do find a loop, this may be causing inertia, so ask questions that start 'what/how will you . . . ?'

Looping

Q. *What stops me?*
A. *Not enough time*
Q. *What do you want instead?*
A. *More time*
Q. *What stops me?*
A. *Not enough time*
   Ditto

Getting out of a Loop

Q. *What stops me?*
A. *Not enough time*
Q. *What do you want instead?*
A. *More time*
Q. *What can you change to free the time? How can you reschedule your work to create the time?*
   Time to get creative!

How to connect with your audience

As always, it is important to know the numbers and composition of the audience to establish the nature of the audience's expectations and preferences when you start. Ask them, seek information from

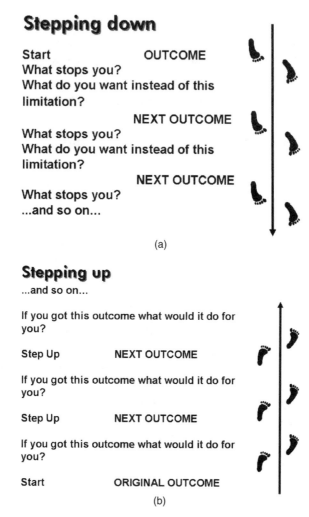

Stepping down

Start   OUTCOME
What stops you?
What do you want instead of this
limitation?
                         NEXT OUTCOME
What stops you?
What do you want instead of this
limitation?
                         NEXT OUTCOME
What stops you?
...and so on...

(a)

Stepping up
...and so on...

If you got this outcome what would it do for
you?

Step Up   NEXT OUTCOME

If you got this outcome what would it do for
you?

Step Up   NEXT OUTCOME

If you got this outcome what would it do for
you?

Start   ORIGINAL OUTCOME

(b)

Figure 7.1   (a) Stepping down; (b) stepping up.

your colleagues, pay attention or listen to their conversations and questions before the presentation. Know your stuff. Enough said . . . if you are not in control, reading this book cannot solve your problem!

Aside from the gathering of specific data about your audience, there are also some useful ideas centred around how people take in information that will advance your ability to deliver your results congruently and confidently.

What types of people are in your audience? There are many ways of describing an audience's response/requirement typology, including some less-charitable and polite ones, but in the context of this book, there are a number of points that we can usefully make about how to understand an audience better, and thus present in a more powerful way.

Based on the work of David A. Kolb, Professor of Organizational Behavior at the Weatheread School of Management, we have a useful way of thinking about presentations, which derives from the ways in which students learn and the ways of processing information. It is, thus, applicable to presenting ideas.

We can be aware of four ways of handling information. You will have each of these types in your audience, so knowing how to cover the needs of the types during your presentation can be a powerful way of formatting your information. I (Roger) use this method to plan all my presentations. The four ways are the following.

Why?

Those who are focused on the question Why? (Divergers) represent around 35% of the population. This question occurs in many forms for presentations. Members of the audience may be asking themselves questions like: Why am I here? Why do we need this? Why will this solve our problem? Why did we pay so much for the research? Why didn't we engage someone else? They may even ask you these questions before you get started, which, if you are not prepared, will impinge on your credibility.

The key drive here is a need to be motivated and to have a reason to engage. They are seeking meaning and involvement, and this means that you will need to think of, and have a way of handling, objections even before you get to present your findings.

Some of the questions it is useful to ask yourself are as follows:

- Why should anyone listen to what I have to say?
- What are the benefits to the participants?
- How does it connect to their needs?
- Why has this research methodology been used?
- What are the outcomes?

This is the largest group, so unless you engage them, they will have a tendency to drag the presentation off course until you have provided sufficient motivation.

What?

Those who are focused on the question What? (Assimilators) represent around 22% of the population. They are the seekers of information and will often want to ask questions that take you into detail. Members of the audience may be asking themselves, or you, questions like: What methodology have you used? What sample criteria did you use? What are your qualifications?

They like to think through and reflect on ideas. They will want to know what the experts think and have facts qualified and evidence available. They may also want to establish your credentials before taking you seriously. Assimilators are prone to standing back and examining in order to comprehend, and you should focus on the key features of your results, making them clear and with reference to evidence to back up your conclusions.

Some of the questions it is useful to ask yourself are as follows:

- Do I have all the facts?
- Are my facts logical and ordered?

- Do I have clear evidence for my conclusions?
- How do I establish my credibility?

Failure to engage this group can take you into defending your conclusions and being forced into greater and greater detail if you cannot satisfy the What question.

How?

Those who are focused on the question How? (Convergers) represent around 18% of the population. These are the doers and practical people interested in how they can utilise what you are presenting – how the results will be used. Members of the audience may be asking themselves, or you, questions like: How has this been done? How can I use this information? How will it work?

This group seeks usability of what is being presented and will be interested in the practicality of the results and taking action. They may want to experiment with what you present.

Some of the questions it is useful to ask yourself are as follows:

- How can my results be used?
- What will the results allow the client to do?
- What are the actions that the clients can take as a result of my presentation?

Failure to engage this group may mean that no action will be taken. Focus on usability for this group.

What (if) else?

Those who are focused on the question What (if) else? (Accommodators) representing around 25% of the population, are the possibility seekers. Members of the audience may be asking themselves, or you, questions like: What are the possibilities? Where will this take us? What else can we do with this conclusion/research?

Accommodators like trial and error and have a way of refocusing activities when new information is presented to them.

Some of the questions it is useful to ask yourself are as follows:

- What new options does my research open up?
- What are the new possibilities that are available through my research, and as a result of my presentation?

Focus on the benefits that will arise in the light of your research.

Structure – what makes for a great presentation?

A great presentation is one that:

- conveys knowledge;
- has order and clarity;
- makes sense;
- is fun;
- is inclusive.

Remember, this is all about effective communications: the meaning is the communication that is received, not sent. So, did you get your message across the last time you presented, or did you come away with a feeling (or knowledge) that you did not manage to persuade them or that they didn't really understand/ listen? If so, you failed in the communications stakes. NLP offers a number of lessons (see above) but also tells us a number of things about the way in which an audience needs to be spoken to, in order to be fully engaged:

- What is your outcome?
- Get their attention.
- Get them focused.
- Get them nodding their heads!
- Get them ready for the information.
- Pay attention to the group.

Format the receiver's mind for the information, like creating folders and files on a computer. If we know what is coming, then our brain can be ready with the spaces to collect the information.

How many boxes or files will you need for this information? e.g. three principles, five keys, six main points.

Keys to success

- Who are the target group?
- Know their jargon.
- Know their problems/stresses.
- Build an expectation.
- What do they already know?
- What are the major issues/challenges?

In-framing and out-framing

The concept of framing was covered earlier, in Chapter 1, but equally has relevance here. Besides being a great way to ensure that they are aware of what the presentation will/won't cover, it allows us to cover certain basics as well, such as timings ('This presentation will last an hour, as I know some of you have another meeting to go to'), logistics ('There will be an electronic copy available tomorrow on the company intranet') and protocol

('If you have questions, please save them until the end, so that we can make sure we cover the basics in the time. Then I'll be happy to stay on and answer any questions that you have').

The in-frame covers what is included, what they can expect and what will happen. The out-frame covers what is not included, what the presentation isn't about, what will not happen.

Using the why, what, how, what else grid

When preparing your presentation, working with the Why, What, How and What Else concepts can create a powerful way not only to organise your information, but also to structure your delivery.

We will take each quadrant and examine what needs to be covered and how you might think of doing it, in order to make sure that you connect to each group.

An easy way of collecting and sorting your information is to first brainstorm all the things that need to be in your presentation. Put them on Post-its, then sort the items into relevant quadrants on a large sheet of flipchart paper (as shown in Figure 7.2). This

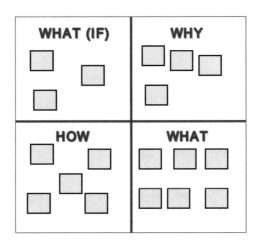

Figure 7.2 Finding out where your gaps are.

will give you a rough idea of where your gaps are, as we all present information closest to our personal style.

Creating a powerful **why** using NLP

Your brief introduction should include the following:

- an introduction to yourself that is short, to the point and establishes your credentials;
- a *mind-opener* or *hook* that will grab their attention and pull them away from thoughts of the next things they must do, or the pile of work sitting on their desk, or the argument they just had with . . . ;
- your intended outcome and how long you will take to present;
- an outline of what you're going to tell them and why they will be interested.

For the latter, put the main points up on a slide/flipchart to format the receivers' minds for the information, like creating folders and files on a computer. If we know what is coming, our brains can be ready with the spaces to collect the information.

Briefly say what they will be able to do with the information. Create meaning by connecting what you say to their experience of the industry or research area.

Next define the context – where you use the information. Engage the attention using story, metaphor and witness (point, incident, benefit).

Adults are knowledgeable and have many pre-stored experiences. Unlike children, who come to us with clean slates, adults have vast reservoirs of knowledge and experience. Great presenters can use this to their advantage. The fastest way to engage people is to link the unknown with the known. Since adults know so many things, opportunity for linking abounds. Simile and metaphor are useful tools. A simile uses the words 'like' or 'as' to connect the unknown with the known, for example, it tastes like chicken. I don't care what food I'm discussing, you now know how it tastes. Metaphors link without using the words 'like' or 'as'.

A facilitator in a training organisation used a wonderful bridge to set off a creative session on marketing ideas. He asked, 'Suppose we were in the business of attracting squirrels. How would we attract them? Maybe we could climb up a tree and act like a nut. Now, what kind of nuts do our squirrels like?' Employees laughed and joined in enthusiastically to offer new ideas for 'nuts' that would attract customers.

Begin to motivate the audience by giving a global why. Give reasons, and link these to potential personal values and to the company values. Use meta-programs to help with this.

Remember, in general, people are motivated emotionally by 'moving towards' happiness or 'moving away' from pain. When your alarm clock sounds in the morning, why do you get out of bed? If you answer, 'Because I love life and I can't wait to start another spectacular day', you are motivated by 'moving towards'. If you answer, 'Because if I don't get up now, I'll be late for work and get fired', you are motivated by 'moving away'.

Add an emotional element to your presentations by explaining to listeners the rewards of action (moving towards) and the consequences of inaction (moving away). Be sure to address both ends of the spectrum. If you only dangle rewards, the 'moving away' listeners tune out; if you only threaten doom, the 'moving towards' listeners sour.

Use the other meta-programs (mentioned earlier in the book) in a similar way.

Creating a powerful **w**hat using NLP

- Go through your points logically and in sequence.
- Summarise as you go along.

- Outline concepts.
- Define words and jargon.
- Explain the principles.
- Say why it works in a sentence or two.
- Set out the process:
  - use a flow diagram of the stages
  - what is the order?

Creating a powerful **how** using NLP

Show:

- how you did the project (summary);
- how the results were collected;
- how the results were analysed.

Creating a powerful **what** (if) **else** using NLP

- Summarise the key points.
- Contextualise/generalize your research conclusions. Give examples of applications in the client's business.
- Deal with questions.
- Plan for questions – don't be taken by surprise.
- Ask for them if none are forthcoming.
- If you don't understand a question, ask for clarification.
- Don't be afraid to admit you don't know. Tell them you'll find out and get back to them. Do get back to them!

Visual aids

Whatever you use, whether it's an OHP, flipchart or computer presentation, keep it simple and clear. Visual aids should add to the impact of your presentation. Learn to use software packages that are specifically designed to produce presentation material.

Keys to good slides

- Bullet points are most effective!
- Keep the point size large on slides – use 18–24 point text, with up to 32 point for titles.
- Use a sans serif font for clarity.
- Keep graphs large and simple, labelling graphics, graphs and maps clearly.
- Use colour to differentiate elements avoid yellow and orange text unless on a contrasting background.

Using colour

One of the most useful items you can get is a colour wheel, which will help you create combinations of colour that work together. Also get a book on colour theory so that you understand the way colour affects our mood and how we access information. In general terms, the box (right) gives a few tips to get you thinking.

Bold colours are light-hearted and cartoon-like, and if you use big chunks of black, you can create a window through which information can be displayed in an eye-catching way, and which will also compensate for pale colours.

Meanings of Colours

Don't use red and green together
Purple = royal.
Red has cultural differences –
China = good luck.
Red = passion, horror, danger, active, aggressive, impulsive.
Green = restful, calm, prosperous, youthful.
Blue = serene, loyal, peaceful, conservative, trustworthy.
Brown = mature, obstinate, reliable, relaxing, calming.
White = cool, pure, innocent, honest.
Black = authoritative, respectful, powerful, practical.

Colours have meanings in our culture. Purple and grey indicate a sedate and sophisticated atmosphere; strong primary colours will appeal to a younger audience. Try using colours that suggest innovation, such as lime green, bright purple and bright blue.

Layout

Our eyes trace a Z path (Figure 7.3) when we read slides and other visual material, and there are two key areas in which it is best to put your most important information – the *primary optic impact area*, which is top left as you look at the slide and the *secondary optic impact area*, which is at the bottom right.

Using uppercase text will slow the reading of your slides down by 17–20%, so unless this is an intentional strategy, using mixed case will create less fatigue, especially over a longer presentation.

When using different fonts, use a maximum of three, using families of fonts and styles in order to increase the variety. Only use a maximum of three styles within a family or you will create readability problems, leading to confusion.

When using graphics, they should have a reason to be there that is clear to the reader. They also need to add to the

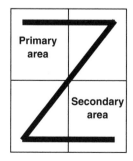

Figure 7.3 The Z path.

Figure 7.4   Make figures bigger and use mixed case lettering.

Figure 7.5   Think about the alignment of text.

presentation as a visual metaphor, rather than just being there for effect or to make the slide look pretty. If you decide to use graphics, do the unusual with them, make them big (Figure 7.4) and do not confine them to a border.

The rules of proximity and alignment

Our brains are designed to search for patterns. Text and images that are close together are interpreted as groups by the reader, and unconsciously we presuppose that there is a link. A helpful strategy is to ask the question 'What information does a reader expect to find together?'

Thinking about alignment of text and the messages it conveys is important when designing slides (Figure 7.5). Some simple rules can be helpful when working with alignments:

- total centring looks amateurish;
- centring conveys a formal, sedate and rigid impression;
- create white space.

Delivery

Feng shui for presenters

The chances are that you will have little real control over room arrangements in general terms, unless you are presenting on 'home territory', but that does not mean that you are totally at the mercy of events and arrangements.

Get into the room before your audience arrives, to check the set-up and get the feel of the room. This helps to make it your room. Walk around the room and sit in a few different chairs to take in the feel of your room and how your audience will see you. Check your equipment and put on your busiest slide to check for readability.

Key issues are: which side of a screen to stand (see below); when you give out any handouts (if you give them out at the start, be aware that your audience will then have two points of focus – you and the handout); whether you black out/darken the room (making the screen of greater/lesser visibility); and the extent and frequency of any questions (set the rules at the beginning using the framing technique from Chapter 1).

Where do you stand? This is not strictly NLP in any formal sense, but linguistics and stagecraft in the Western world tell us that an audience is predisposed to scanning (reading) from left to right. So, if you stand in front of a screen/audience, expect them to focus from left to right, meaning that if you want them to focus on you (not the screen), stand to the right as they look at it, and, conversely, if you want their attention more on the screen, stand to the left of the screen.

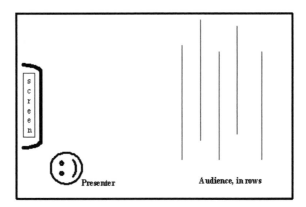

Figure 7.6 Where to stand 1.

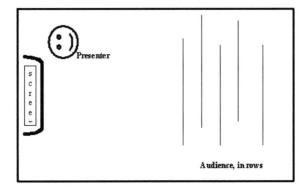

Figure 7.7 Where to stand 2.

Sounding your best

Drinking one or two glasses of warm water before you speak will lubricate your vocal chords. Breathing deeply and slowly will allow you to project your voice and pause when you want to – not when you need to. Speak slower than you normally speak. The audience needs to hear you, think about what you're saying and internalise it. Avoid the intake of coffee and other stimulants

– they have the effect of enhancing any nerves and speeding you up. This may get you through the presentation quickly, but not at your most effective.

A simple rule

Get attention. When I (Neil) do a presentation, I always stand up. The only situation for doing it differently, I believe, is when the presentation is more of a workshop or a round-table discussion rather than a direct results presentation. Standing up gives you authority, presence and allows you to command some degree of stage attention.

CAB (cover all bases)

This pattern, as we have already mentioned, is useful when building rapport with groups at the start of a meeting or at the beginning of a presentation. The pattern is tailored to the particular circumstance and can be used to initiate rapport and break down resistance. For example, 'I know many of you have been waiting for this presentation for some time and others of you found out about it a few days ago, whilst some of you have been sent along by your managers and others may have had to rush around to make arrangements so that you could be here at short notice.'

When you stand up, announce your presence by saying who you are and how pleased (if you are not pleased, fake it, or leave the industry) you are to be there. Clap your hands once, not too loud, starting with your arms wide, and welcome everyone, saying something like, 'Some of you will have met me before at the briefing session, some of you will have attended some of the research and some will come to this meeting without any previous contact . . .'

Later, when introducing the research techniques, use the same technique, 'Some of you will have been involved with qualitative research before, frequently, some will have had a limited experience of it and some none at all . . .'. This way, you have covered all bases and made everyone feel a part of the proceedings.

Yes sets

Public speakers, such as politicians, commonly use this pattern. By receiving three undeniable facts in a row, the unconscious mind is likely to consider the next statement true as well. For example, 'As you sit in this meeting room, just after lunch, you will quickly learn all about the market's perception of your company.'

Equally, when you begin, say something like, 'It's Tuesday morning, we all have lots to do later today and it's really important that we get through all the material by 12.30' (audience mentally says 'yes, yes, yes'), 'and I know you will find this information really helpful' (audience then mentally also says 'yes'), getting you off to a good and attentive start.

I (Neil) also recommend starting off the presentation, after the yes sets, by something auditorily and visually strong, like a clap of the hands, as if to say 'Right, we're off!'. This has the effect of immediately establishing your presence and authority, plus it will strike at most of the VAK chords in the audience. It also anchors the audience in the positive (hopefully) state you created by the yes sets, and can be activated again when required throughout (perhaps when you are trying to get a controversial point across). It is also useful to raise your arms (this follows neatly on from the hand clap), perhaps outwards to shoulder level, as this will engage their eyes, their brains and move them upwards (and outwards) to a state of readiness and openness, as opposed to looking down and inwards and not concentrating on you, the presenter, and the material.

Tone of voice

This is essential to a good presentation. A hesitant, uncertain voice will occasion an uncertain and hesitant response. A quiet voice will tend to draw the audience in, but it works badly when you are trying to generate response and excitement. An audience is entitled to expect your enthusiasm to show in the presentation. It is not simply a factual imparting exercise: it is as much of a show as any actor or musician will give. You have a short time to engage them and you need all the help you can get in order to cut through their concentration threshold and get them to listen.

Eye contact

Look at people in the audience, at everyone, repeatedly through the presentation. It makes them feel they are there and you are paying attention to them! Don't stare, though – anything more than 2–3 seconds per person is too aggressive unless you are answering a specific point they have raised. This is often called the *lighthouse technique*, and if you find looking directly into people's eyes difficult, look between their eyes as you scan the room.

Virginia Satir's five postural archetypes

When presenting, there are some archetypical gestures that are useful to know about. These gestures are very influential, and knowing how to use them in just the right way can create presence and initiate the sort of reactions you may want in your audience. Conversely, when we use these gestures inadvertently, they may have unintended consequences for the receipt of our information.

Virginia Satir was a leading psychotherapist and people watcher, especially in the area of family therapy, and her work was one of the models on which Bandler and Grinder based their original development of NLP. In addition to her other major contributions, she observed five archetypal gestures that people make that create mindsets and feelings in the observer – the blamer, placater, distracter, computer and leveller. These gestures are very useful to understand and can be effective when used in the right way.

The blamer

Uses words like *all, every, any, each time, you always*. Universal quantifiers abound and they use lots of negative questions – Why don't you . . . ? Why can't you . . . ? You don't have to . . . , etc. Points finger a lot. Has a loud, booming voice tone.

If you want to make a strong point, this is a useful gesture. It works best if you avoid pointing at people, as doing this you can elicit a negative or aggressive attitude. Pointing at the flipchart or furniture is much safer.

Figure 7.8 The blamer.

Figure 7.9 The placater.

The placater

Uses words like *if, only, just, even, could, would*. Prone to mind-reading. Adopts a 'cringing' posture. Has a whining tone.

Adopting this posture will invite those who want to attack or challenge to go right ahead. Use this gesture only if you want to elicit a sympathetic response, and do it for only a short time.

The distracter

Also known as the alternator, because they can switch from one type to another instantaneously. This could be called flexible, but it isn't! It is distracting to the listener, because you never know where the distracter is going to end up, and so they appear to be very unpredictable. Posture tends to be asymmetric – one hand up, the other down; one foot forward, the other back, standing 'lop-sided'. You will see this in many comedians – Norman Wisdom and Lee Evans being great exponents of the distracter style.

Pacing back and forth is a distracter activity. This will cause you to lose presence and charisma, making you seem nervous. This can also be irritating if your audience has to follow you like a tennis match.

Figure 7.10　The distracter.

The computer

Super reasonable, depersonalises language. Prefers to say things like *It could be seen as . . .* , *One can understand . . .* , *People are likely to . . .* , *The management system is in need of . . .* Uses nominalisations. Liable to stand with one arm across the body, with the other hand on the chin. Flat monotone voice.

This is a useful posture when inviting questions – without the flat tone!

Figure 7.11　The computer.

Figure 7.12   The leveller.

The leveller

The 'straight' person who occurs frequently in the business context. Typically talks about 'bottom line' and 'end result'. Posture tends to be symmetrical, with the palms of the hands in a downward position or gesture. Low tones, calm, measured tempo.

Use this gesture to create calm and to emphasise congruence in your recommendations.

Experiment

Have some fun with a group of friends. Tell them about these postures and then go round telling jokes using only one of the postures. Notice what happens to the joke – which postures enhance and which destroy the joke?

Handling questions

Honesty is the only policy when presenting. However, blatantly admitting 'I don't know' in response to a direct question from an audience member can be disastrous.

'Can you tell me the fieldwork dates?'
'Errr, no I can't.'

This just sounds lame and incompetent. 'I'll check and let you have them by email' sounds more in control, though the basic knowledge level is still the same!

The solution is to be honest and maintain credibility at the same time. No-one can know the answer to every question. It's how the inevitable situation is handled that separates great presenters from amateurs.

Here are seven strategies to help you field even the toughest questions with confidence.

Reflection and summary

Repeat the question and pass it back to your audience, 'Does anyone here have any experience with that?' Allowing the audience to help you is a strategy that can pay dividends, they will save you without ever realising it. In fact, often, the audience will revere you, because adults love to be involved and share their knowledge and opinions. After you have fielded all of the contributions, make sure you summarise the key points and then add your own ideas. Summarising at the end and repeating questions before answering will help you to retain control and authority.

Defer to the expert

This is a more sophisticated version of the reflection technique. Sometimes a question is legitimately outside of your area of expertise. You may be a marketing expert and someone asks a question about the engineering aspects of a product. This is a question that requires an engineer. If there is an engineer in the room, you could say, 'Sally, you're an engineer. Do you have any insights into that?' If there are no engineers in the room, state that you will confer with an engineer *and get back to them*. Notice I have just combined two techniques.

I'll come back to you

This works well if you do three things. First, write the question down. Be conspicuous. Make sure everyone knows you are writing the question down. I go so far as to tell the audience, 'I am writing this question down.' Second, tell the questioner exactly when you will get back to them. Be honest. Then do it. Can you get back to them by the end of the day? Can you get back to them after lunch? Third, be sure to get the questioner's contact information if you don't have it. All of these things make this strategy very powerful. It is not smoke and mirrors. It is an opportunity to go the extra mile, expand your knowledge and impress your audience and clients.

Compliment the questioner

For this to be effective, the compliment must be sincere. Sometimes I get lulled into thinking I have seen and heard it all on a particular topic. However, someone invariably comes out of left field with a question I have never thought of, and I say, 'That's a great question. I've never thought about it that way. *Does anyone here have any ideas on that?*' (I have just combined two techniques). When I use this strategy, it is usually not a conscious decision. It's a reaction. That's how sincere it needs to sound. It always works when it's sincere because audiences love to be complimented. I might also combine this technique with I'll come back to you.

Answer a question with a question

Sometimes questions are too narrow or too general to answer. Reserve the right, as the expert, to open a question up or close it down by asking a question in response.

Parallel answer

If you don't know the bull's eye answer to a question, offer what you do know quickly, to demonstrate some credibility, and then combine with a previous technique. When I was a software trainer, I used to be an expert in the Lotus spreadsheet package. However, Microsoft's Excel began to gain popularity, and I had to learn it so I could teach it. In the beginning, I was on a learning curve. Sometimes I would be asked a question about Excel that I didn't know the answer to, however I did know the answer in Lotus. Quickly, I would say, 'I know that is possible in Lotus. I'm not sure if that is available in Excel. *I'm writing this question down. I'll research it at the break and get back to you.'* Refrain from droning on and on about your parallel knowledge. Brevity is the key to this technique.

Set the rules

You can avoid many difficult questions simply by setting rules for questions in the beginning. Whenever you present to a group, you are the leader. You are accountable for everything, so lead. My experience is that if you set rules and follow them, the audience respects you. If you make rules up as you go along, you lose credibility.

The number of rules you set will vary depending on the topic. When I taught technical subjects, I set lots of rules because I knew the questions would be many and varied. I would start a software seminar by saying, 'I welcome general questions at any time about anything on the agenda. If you have a specific question about a project you are working on or a subject outside of the agenda, please see me at a break for a private consultation. Because we have limited time together, I reserve the right to stop taking questions and comments. This is not personal. It is to make certain we cover every topic today.'

Specific verbal interventions

Boomerang

This involves returning a question to the person who asked it, or to the group, so that the leader or facilitator does not take responsibility for all the questions.

Group member: 'I don't like the tack we're taking here.'
Leader: 'What do you think we should be doing?'

Maintain/regain focus

Make sure everyone is working on the same content, using the same process, at the same time.

'Let's stay together on identifying problems. Are we all together?'
'Just a moment, one person at a time. Joe, you were first, then Don.'

Say what's going on

Name something that isn't working, i.e. get it out in the open so the group can deal with it.

'It's very quiet in here. What questions do you have about . . . ?'

Avoid process battles

Prevent lengthy arguments about which is the 'right' way to proceed. Point out that a number of approaches will work, and get agreement on one to use to start.

'Can we agree to cover both issues in the remaining time? OK, which one do you want to start with?'

Enforce process agreements

Remind the group of a previous agreement.

'We agreed to brainstorm; you're starting to evaluate ideas. Would you hold on to that idea for now?'

Accept/legitimise/deal with or defer

This is a positive method for dealing with difficult people or situations that might get a meeting off track. Accept the idea without agreeing or disagreeing. Legitimise it by writing it on the group memory. Then decide, as a group, if the issue/idea is more appropriately dealt with here or deferred to another time. Record ideas or issues that are deferred and agree on when they will be addressed.

'You're not convinced we're getting anywhere? That's OK, you may be right. Would you be willing to hang on for ten more minutes and see what happens?'

'Thanks for raising this issue that wasn't on the agenda. Do we need to address that now or should we put it on the issues list for our next meeting?'

Don't be defensive

Arguing when criticised will only provoke more argument. Accept negative comments and boomerang the issue back to the individual or group.

'I cut you off? I'm sorry, please continue.'
'You think I'm pushing too hard? (Lots of nods) Thank you for telling me. How would you like to proceed from here?'

Use body language

Reinforce words with congruent body language. For example, ask for ideas with your palms open; regain focus by standing up and moving to the middle of the room.

Use humour

Make a joke to relieve tension. Be sensitive and do not joke at someone else's expense.

Protect others from personal attack

Intervene to stop someone verbally attacking another.

'Brian, you've interrupted Barbara several times in the last few minutes. I'd like to hear what she has to say as well as hearing your view.'

Dealing with difficult people

Basic approach

Accept/legitimise/deal with or defer – this intervention is a major strategy in difficult situations. By accepting and legitimising an objection or concern, negativism can be diffused and the individual can be relieved of the need to be resistant. The group can decide whether to deal with or defer the issue.

Escalating levels of intervention (see below) is another major strategy. Always start with the most subtle and least threatening intervention. Then, if the behaviour continues, gradually escalate the interventions. This strategy gives people an opportunity to let go of difficult behaviours gracefully.

Escalating levels of intervention

Try prevention first, for example, meet with the 'difficult people' prior to the meeting and build rapport before you start. Look for a win/win resolution whenever possible, i.e. is there a way to resolve their concerns/issues? Can you do this before the meeting?

Once in the meeting remain neutral and start with the most subtle intervention possible, for example, eye contact. Only escalate your intervention as you need to, and escalate slowly. Remember to work to save their 'face' using the intervention strategy of Accept/legitimise/deal with/defer.

Escalating levels of intervention may look something like this:

- Low-level interventions (win/win)
- Ignore or avoid the person
- Make eye contact
- Stand up
- Walk half-way
- Walk by them and make eye contact
- Ask, 'What do you think?'
- Touch and talk directly

- Confront the person on a break
- Confront them before the whole group
- High-level intervention (win/lose).

Challenging behaviours exhibited by meeting attendees

Doyle and Straus have proposed the following types of group meeting attendees who complicate group decision processes. They call them the 'problem people'. From an NLP perspective, it is better, from a rapport point of view, to hold the notion that these are problem behaviours and not problem people. Dealing with the behaviours can then be done in a way that maintains connection and rapport.

The latecomers

Invariably late, they lose the thrust of the meeting, especially in task-oriented sessions where the factual information is presented early. They miss the data input necessary for good decision-making. Worse, the latecomers usually talk the most – about things that have already been covered during the early part of the meeting.

Doyle and Straus advise us not to confront the latecomer before the group. They recommend waiting until after the meeting and then merely asking the latecomer why he or she is so frequently late. Don't lecture! Ask the chronic latecomer what can be done to make the meetings more important, so that he or she will want to be on time. As a last resort, ask the latecomer to perform some important function at the beginning of the next meeting.

The early leavers

While not as distracting as the latecomer, the early leaver 'drains the energy of the meeting by leaving before the meeting ends'. Again, Doyle and Straus argue against confrontation in front of the group, and recommend that inquiry be made as to the cause of this disruptive behaviour. Are the meetings too long? Too boring? Not conducted properly? Is there more than one early leaver (like the latecomer disease, it's sometimes catching)? Perhaps it would be a good idea to discover if all agree they are going to stay through to the end. This is a near-necessity for any decision-making group. Wandering in and out is simply too destructive.

The broken records

This is the person who keeps bringing up the same point over and over again. Use the group memory to acknowledge that the point is important to the individual and it has been recorded previously. If the individual is worked up over the issue and looks as if they need the opportunity to talk it out, an appropriate intervention might be, 'Why don't we take three minutes now to hear what you have to say, so you can let go of it. We want you to free your mind so you can move along with the rest of us through the class/meeting.'

The doubting Thomases

'While it is healthy to have a sceptic in any group, aggressive negativism is a damper on creative effort,' Doyle and Straus believe. They suggest a counter-strategy – get the group to agree not to evaluate any idea until all the evidence is in. When a doubting Thomas interrupts with a negative objection, call him or her to task on it as a violation of the ground rules established by the group.

The headshakers

They sit near the front of the room and shake their head, yawn, look bored or disgusted, cross their legs, take furious notes (which no-one ever gets to see or hear) and drive the meeting leader nuts. But the headshaker may be totally unaware of the activity. In such cases, a gentle question is in order. Ask if the headshaker is disturbed by the process; perhaps he or she can verbalise it. This may make them more conscious of their body language. Of course, there is always the chance that there is a legitimate gripe.

The dropouts

These characters sit and doodle, stare at the ceiling or out of the window, yawn, check airline schedules, even read the paper while the meeting is in progress. Ask a question on a difficult point of current debate and allow some time to lapse by turning to someone else before asking the dropout. The group may be surprised to discover the reason for the dropout dropping out.

The whisperers

These people can destroy the decision-making process because no-one knows what they are whispering about. It should not be tolerated. If they have something to say to each other, they can say it publicly or not at all.

The loudmouths

These people are very sensitive to deal with. Often they are the most senior person or decision-maker, making it a little more difficult for the facilitator. The most subtle technique for coping with them involves physical position in relation to the person. Moving closer and closer to them while they are talking, and maintaining eye contact, can have an effect. The physical presence of the facilitator – standing – and the individual – sitting – will often make them aware of their behaviour and they will stop talking. When they do, shift the focus immediately by calling on someone else. Otherwise, deal with loudmouths outside the meeting. If nothing else works, direct confrontation may be required.

The attackers

These people couch criticism in a personal vein, disregarding the facts and logic. The trick is to redirect the attack away from the person toward the subject. And a gentle reminder that the meeting room is not the place for personal attacks may get some results. The worst that can happen is for someone to respond in kind – the meeting can only deteriorate from there. The best response is no response at all.

The assistants

These are the self-appointed translators who are trying to 'help'. Having few ideas of their own, they participate by verbalising what they assume was not verbalised by the last speaker. They can be stopped by the simple expedient of asking the original speaker whether the interpretation was correct or not.

The gossipers

A gossiper is dangerous because he/she is loaded with half-truths without adequate supporting resources. A remedy is to stop the meeting and verify the information immediately. After a few checks prove the information to be wrong or only half-right or not applicable, there will be a halt to this tactic.

The know-it-alls

These people use credentials, age, length of service or professional status to argue a point. Acknowledge the know-it-all's expertise once, but emphasise why this issue is being discussed by the group. Such a response might be, 'Yes, we all recognise and respect your experience in this area, but the decision has to be made by the group as a whole after weighing all the alternatives . . . Will you indulge us for a while, even though some of the suggestions may seem crazy to you?' Or try, 'That's your opinion, but there may be other equally valid points of view.'

The backseat driver

A backseat driver keeps telling the facilitator what he or she should be doing. Ask them to suggest a process or procedure and check it out with the group. If the group concurs, react immediately. If it does not concur, the argument will usually be diffused. Point out that there are different styles and many ways to solve a problem, and ask them to stay on course with you.

The busybodies

The busybody is usually the person who conducts the meeting and takes phone calls at the same time. A solution is to adopt ground rules. When a meeting is interrupted, simply stop all discussions and cost the time lost. Take all the salaries and any other costs, such as transportation, accommodation, etc., add it all up and present the busybody with the cost of his or her busyness. Another solution is to teach the members of the decision-making group the difficulties of retaining in memory more than a few interactions at a time, and convince them that continuity is the essence of good decision-making – that a two-minute phone call might mean a bad decision that could be expensive.

The interrupters

An interrupter starts talking before others are finished. Often, the interrupter doesn't mean to be rude, but becomes impatient and overly excited. Deal with interrupters immediately. In a meeting, this should be a first test of the facilitator's neutrality, as people will be watching to see if they will be supported/protected. An intervention might be similar to, 'Hold on Herb, let Becky finish what she was saying.' Be impartial and fair by not playing favourite in terms of making interventions.

VIDEOCONFERENCING

The keys to making successful presentations using videoconferencing systems are planning and knowledge. Videoconferencing requires some specific thoughts and actions in order to get the best results and for you to be able to shine in this area. We will tackle this in five segments, remembering that all the notions and concepts that precede this section still count.

Logistics

'Know your audience' is a principle we have already discussed, and it is even more critical in a situation where personal contact is minimised, as with videoconferencing. Obtain as much information as you can about the participants – be sure to find out names, job titles, status and location. Other information about their interests and their experience relative to the content you are going to present, will help you be precise and succinct with your delivery. The more you know about them, the more personal and the more targeted you can make your presentation. These are two important videoconference presentation skills/principles:

- make it personalised (e.g. address participarts by name);
- make it targeted.

Arrange for a facilitator at the remote site(s)

Here are several things a facilitator/coordinator at a remote site can do to assist the smooth running of the conference:

- take roll or record who is present for documentation purposes;
- control the keypad functions, such as keeping the mute button on until someone is ready to speak;
- encourage participants to ask or answer questions;
- repeat participant questions to ensure clarity.

Send materials out to the remote site(s) in advance

This is critical! If participants at the near site (the originating site with the live audience) receive the presenter's handouts but the participants at the remote sites do not, they will naturally feel left out. Experience tells us that this will also cause participants at the remote site to disengage from the material. Therefore, it is critical to send handouts to the remote sites well ahead of time. Ensure that the material will reproduce well and be readable – a faxed copy sent at the last minute may cause problems.

Plan, don't panic

Videoconferencing, like many other technologies, has the potential to go wrong. After you send the handouts, call to be sure they have arrived and confirm they will get to the participants in good time for the meeting. Meetings run smoother if the participants are able to pre-read the materials rather than have them two minutes before the meeting starts.

It is important for you to arrive at the originating site at least 30 minutes early, to make sure the sites are connected and to give you a chance to connect up your computer, try out your visuals, etc. Actually, one hour early is better.

Testing your visuals in advance is a critical planning step. If your visuals can't be seen clearly by the participants, they will be frustrated and they will disengage. If you use presentation software, it is important to realise that what looks good on your screen, or what looks good projected, may look terrible on a TV monitor.

Advance preparation tips

During a videoconference you cannot present as much information in the same amount of time as you would in a normal face-to-face presentation. This is because you need to take more time to interact with the audience to maintain rapport using this technology. You will need to repeat information and so you need to have a simple structure. The Why, What, How, What Else grid can help edit superfluous information, and the use of frames

(Chapter 1) will help keep things on track – use the backtrack frame to summarise the information and reactions as you go.

You must plan for interaction. For example, have some specific questions you plan to ask of the participants and remember to plan to spread the questions around to the various remote sites, so that everyone feels involved.

Getting off to a good start

The first few minutes of your presentation are very important. This is the time to establish a rapport with your audience. Welcome all the sites collectively and say hello to each site one by one. As you do this, ask them to do something like raise their hands to let you know the visual system is working properly. Ask someone at each site to say something, so that you know you can hear them. Remember to smile and to let participants know you would appreciate their participation.

During a videoconference it is more difficult to follow a presentation, therefore it is critical that content is presented in a logical sequence. Arrange the information in chunks if possible. If you work from a content outline, identifying those chunks of information will be easier.

The presentation

Avoid a situation in which you show one slide after another, without the audience seeing you some of the time on the monitor. Alternate between speaking and using your visuals. To make it easier, unless are skilled at using the keypad, you may want to enlist someone to help you run the presentation, so that you can concentrate on maintaining rapport and taking questions.

Speaking too fast, combined with the delay between the audio and your moving lips, will cause you to appear out of sync and make your points more difficult to understand. Use pauses and practise a speed of speech that keeps you closer in sync.

The way to make eye contact with your remote audiences is to look directly into the camera. Eye contact personalises the interaction; lack of eye contact makes participants feel you are not really talking to them. If you find working with cameras uncomfortable, practise in noncritical situations until you become comfortable with the technology.

For participants to remain engaged, get them to respond to something periodically. A question to an individual at a site is one way to do this, or you may elicit a response from several participants by stimulating a discussion on specific areas of the presentation as it moves through its sequence, rather than waiting until the end, which is more appropriate to a face-to-face presentation.

Visuals

A poor set of visuals is the number one problem with presentations by videoconferencing systems. People want to use the same type of slides they would use if they were projecting in a lecture hall using a slide projector. This simply will not work. Television will not handle thin lines. Therefore, serif fonts, such as Times, do not display well, because parts of the letters in Times are thin. Sans serif fonts, such as Arial or Helvetica, work well, because all parts of the letters are relatively thick.

When using a computer presentation package to display slides on the videoconferencing system, letters are much easier

Top Tip – Using colours

Use contrasting colours. Blue backgrounds with white and/or yellow letters work nicely. Avoid reds and pinks!!

to read if they are 36 point or larger. This presents a dilemma, because we tend to want to cram a lot of information onto each slide, but with videoconferencing, you just cannot do this and get readability. So, it becomes even more important to send pre-meeting material – even copies of the slides can be helpful – you can then be sure that your participants can follow along, even if the visual technology goes on the blink.

CHAPTER 8

ETHICS, ECOLOGY AND CODES OF PRACTICE

WHAT'S IN THIS CHAPTER?

- What do we mean by ecology?
- Manipulation
- Ethics and qualifications
- Professional codes of practice and quality standards

WHAT DO WE MEAN BY ECOLOGY?

In NLP, the concept of *ecology* is very important. Here, it signifies that an NLP-generated change in yourself fits into the wider context, that it all 'hangs together', and, equally, when applied, does not impact negatively on others.

Within the research context generally, and the qualitative interview context especially (including ethnographic and observation work), the notion of ecology has wider implications, and brings us into touching distance of research ethics and the range of industry codes of practice.

MANIPULATION

We may as well admit this, up front. There are people around who see NLP as a manipulative system. It smacks, they will tell you, of spin, of unethical sales training techniques on how to make people do things they really don't want to do. They will point to some stage hypnotist and explain that NLP uses the same approaches, to get you on stage and barking like a dog without all your clothes. And so on.

You will hear some people tell you that it is just new age hippydom, reinvented for the new millennium. You will also hear tales of unscrupulous people misusing it more generally, and this may or may not include some insinuations about researchers' usage of the approach in questioning or in analysis. All we can say is, if you ever find evidence of misuse, report the practitioner to INLPTA, ESOMAR or a local market research industry body. They are not doing this under any genuine guise, and should be stopped, forthwith. It is an absolute tenet of NLP that it be used responsibly and professionally, and certainly Roger's training and certification, which Neil and many others have taken, requires this agreement before practitioner status is conferred. *There are no circumstances when or where misuse is permissible.*

That said, what are these complaints about? Often, they refer to our attempt to get people to reveal parts of themselves by a questioning or projective technique, or an attempt to better understand them by seeking more input about their values, beliefs or behaviour. This sounds very much like most/all qualitative research, and indeed most/all psychoanalysis or counselling therapy!

Be wary, therefore, of casting NLP in a particular light. Amongst those doing so, maybe we should be seeking more information about their own motives or presuppositions. I have met quite a few critics, and the root cause in many seems to be that they are not themselves qualified to use the approach, do not have the taught skills or the training, and as such do not support any club of which they are not members! The other brigade are often those with scientific training. Sadly, this often includes those with psychology degrees. Here, so much is scientific and so much of the mainstream is locked in a rationalist mode of development, that some of the softer new sciences can seem threatening and hard to understand. In fairness, they are frequently singing from the same songbook as our clients and colleagues, for whom a rational, linear thinking approach has been, and is, the norm and the received collective belief in the business world.

Our offer here is to encourage you to make up your own mind about the less cognitive context of research activity and consumer (people) decision-making, and to assess how and where our additional thinking fits in.

One thing we will never do is to suggest that you misuse, in any way, shape or form, the skills that you have learnt here.

ECOLOGY: NLP STYLE

Within NLP, we have to consider both internal (self) ecology and external (others') reference points. When we make a change to our outlooks, to our behaviours or attitudes, we ensure that, internally, we are comfortable with the change.

Imagine that we go on a strict diet to lose weight for a wedding or other special event. We want to look our best, get into that special outfit, etc., but our internal system does not respond well to a crash diet, and we become thin and not very well.

So, too, with less mechanical changes, and it is wise to ensure that all parts are in harmony here. From an external viewpoint, too, our crash diet may impact on other family members, enforcing on them some new eating regime to fit with ours, a new cooking requirement to cater for our new diet or some negative reaction to our weight-loss ('You look too thin!'). This is the 'ripple in the pond' notion − anything we do may have unexpected and/or more obvious implications and effects on others further out in the pond.

In the research context, we are asking that you take onboard quite a few new lessons and approaches that we have outlined in the book. It makes sense, does it not, as you sit reading this, to consider how the changes you will be considering will impact on both yourself and on others? Well, let's look at some of these.

We, the authors, encourage you to look around at how and what you will do in the future, and think about how it differs from the past. For example, when you undertake interviews using some of the specific skills and tools we have outlined, you will find that you are more involved in the respondents' world than hitherto. That is the point of this book.

So, how might it affect your world? You may develop:

- greater involvement with the respondent/s;
- higher personal satisfaction and skill levels;
- more specialist knowledge and role in research;
- wider personal horizons;
- an interest in learning/qualifying at higher and higher NLP level.

We cannot guarantee that these will happen automatically, but they are at your disposal. Equally, though, there may be some consequences that you should be aware of:

- learning to manage your own perceptions;
- your level of engagement;
- more detailed data and analysis;
- a need to influence more sceptical clients and colleagues;
- more commitment to self-development.

These are all potential effects of moving down this road. Your own internal check will help you decide if this is for you or not.

But be aware that using such techniques and concepts can change your life, and once you learn something, it is difficult, if not impossible, to unlearn it. It is likely that you will seek more learning, both within and outside the context of NLP, and this can lead you in many directions. Equally, it will have an influence on close friends and family. We hope you will be happy with the results, and that they, too, will see the development and change that you are able to bring about.

Just . . . be aware!

ETHICS AND QUALIFICATIONS

Market research in general, and qualitative research in particular, seeks to offer (and uphold) respondents' wellbeing throughout the course of the research contact (the interview) and beyond, and we seek to legislate in our codes that no adverse results follow the research contact. This is right and proper and as it should be.

However, there is no formal qualification required for entry into market research in any speciality. While we are controlled, we are only loosely, if at all, regulated in any real sense. Members of the respondent community can complain to our employers or to a professional body, and the resultant censure, if applied, would be embarrassing and a little damaging to our reputations but ultimately would, in no way, prevent us from trading. All we would do is resign from the relevant professional body and start again. Indeed, there is no real need to join any professional body to gain entry to the profession. Just start the business and away we go. This poses a couple of questions. Is this right? What about the use of NLP?

Is this right? Well, Neil has been a researcher for 35 years and thinks that some more structured certified/licensed status is urgently needed. This is not the forum in which to review this at length, but the debate has been aired in various forums, not least of all

ESOMAR. The key point is that with the increasing difficulty of establishing for our clients a real information advantage, greater and greater skills and newer techniques are inevitable if this demand is to be satisfied. This involves greater training, such as we have been implying throughout, and this, in turn, gives rise to greater risks of untrained people doing more demanding work. Currently, there is no requirement for qualitative researchers to have any kind of specific training or educational background.

If we go to a counsellor, there is at least a body, which, if membership is awarded, can show that its members have some degree of professional knowledge and skills, are authorised to practice and are monitored by professional and qualified observers. If you go to a doctor or a solicitor, they are specifically qualified and approved to practice and can have their livelihoods withdrawn. In market research, we have none of this.

Our duties to respondents require increasingly that we have such professional status, and qualifying as an NLP Practitioner is at least one step towards doing this through the INLPTA and ANLP codes of practice.

It should be the case that for a qualitative researcher to work, he or she should be formally trained in specific aspects of the craft, including, if appropriate, in NLP, and that without this, he or she should not be able to practice. I look forward to howls of rage and disagreement from many folk out there!

I believe that we owe this duty of care to our respondents, and that this forms part of our professional ethics set. We ask much of them, and this is the least they can expect from us.

I (Neil) was recently told by a client that market research is now seen as 'one of the marketing or administrative services: it's pretty much a commodity which we have to buy'. The distinction between qualities in researchers was largely ignored. In place was a simple cost equation, linked with a simple 'these are the questions we want you to ask' (i.e. read out). It is hardly surprising that clients are frequently disappointed with results if this is the way it is commissioned.

I would go further and seek client sign-up to this concept, as too often I have witnessed what can best be described as a somewhat self-centred perspective by clients towards the respondents.

'I have to get a flight to (wherever) by 3 pm' says the client during groups or attendance at an observation session, 'can't you get them to have breakfast again so I can see it before I go?

'I don't like those respondents: they are ugly and spotty!' (this really happened!).

'Quite a few of those doctors (in London) did not come from the UK. Can we have English-only ones?'

We all have such horror stories, but that itself is not the real point. It is that we are custodians of the respondents' welfare, and professional status is part of this care duty.

CODES OF PRACTICE

ESOMAR, on behalf of the world research community, and individual country-specific bodies, such as the MRS in the UK, give us a range of professional codes, with which we are obliged to comply. These certainly feature critical issues, such as respondents being protected from adverse effects as a result of the research process and anonymity and confidentiality of details/ responses. At a wider level, of course, we also have the Data Protection legislation requirements. With none of these do we have any qualms at all.

We also have a set of performance standards, usually known as quality standards. Again, this is not the place to indulge in a lengthy review of these, but it is significant that none of these have much, if any, space allocated to professional competence. We are told how to label tapes, get client approval for the topic guide, get signatures for incentives, and so on, but there is little, if any, mention of our responsibilities to clients due to our professional competence. With this, we do have some problems.

We feel that the need for professional qualifications is critical, and needs to be built in to the professional codes and quality standards systems. This is part of a broader responsibility to our respondents and to the concept of 'NLP ecology'. We have to consider the effects and impact on ourselves, our sample and our colleagues/clients of what we do, not just in a commercial sense, but in a wider sense of responsible actions.

In particular, the issue of personal self-care is one which occupies (or should do) the qualitative research community. We are often asked to work at an increasingly rapid pace. Have this project in the field by Monday; start the interviews on Thursday; interview for eight hours a day and have the transcripts/debrief ready for Tuesday; drive four hours there and back and still turn up at 8 am in the morning to work. We visit respondents in their homes, we spend time with people who are patients (in pharma studies), we encounter real people with real day-to-day problems and lives, and, if we do our jobs fully, we engage in some form of personal rapport with them. In short, we have to give a lot of ourselves, in order to do our jobs properly. Self-ecology means that we should be increasingly aware of ensuring that we maintain a sense of self-protection and our own necessary balance, while at the same time preserving our professional duties to our respondents and to our clients. This, too, has obvious wider implications for the researcher's family, friends and social circle. Whether this translates into an appropriate work/life balance, or whether this means a measure of barrier between ourselves and our respondents, such that we do not carry around the residual memory of the energy of all the respondents we have ever had (which is quite likely), is for the individual to assess in their own professional and personal spheres.

From an NLP standpoint, we require appropriate ecological review, or awareness, of the changes to be brought about, and the implications of the way in which we perform our research tasks and interviews.

NLP is a thoroughly 'professional' and 'ethical' set of learnings. We can, and should, incorporate the concept of ecology readily into the (qualitative) research canon: it fits really well and comfortably with our existing ethics, but also includes the sensible and sensitive approach to our own ecology.

Self and respondent responsibilities are an important feature of all we have been saying in the book, and are the bedrock of the ways in which we should act in our roles.

CHAPTER 9

CONVERSATION PIECES

Recorded during planning sessions for the book! Roger 'models' Neil.

Roger: OK, we're going to start at the beginning of the book and ask some questions around briefing meetings, Neil. What I want you to do is to think yourself back to heading into a briefing meeting, so we can have a look into what one of the most experienced qualitative market researchers does to get the results that he does. First of all, what sort of materials do you make sure that you have with you?

Neil: OK, well, that's changed over time. In days gone by, a pad of paper, a notebook would be enough. Over the last few years, we've all begun to do more by way of preparation and resources, so I would normally now take my digital recorder, so that I can record all of the content of the meeting and the discussion, because that will allow me to replay it for my own benefit, to make sure that I've understood nuances of what was said, or maybe some of the side discussions that the clients will have had between themselves, but also, so that if anyone ever turns round and says, 'I never said you should do that,' I can prove that indeed they did say that, so that's a kind of purely technical thing. I would now, automatically, before I go to a meeting do some preparatory work, and I would try and think myself into their business problem. I'd learn more about their subject matter, if I didn't know about it. I'd read some blog sites on the Internet. I would get some language that's typically used in the industry or the sector about the product, so that I don't look like a complete novice when I start.

Roger: And are there any questions that you ask as a rule, standard things that it's really good to know about a client?

Neil: Well, certainly, I would always want to know from them verbally, as well as in a written form, what it is that they actually (think they) want and what they're going to do with the information, assuming we can provide it for them. It's also vitally important to know timescales and budgets, and it's also equally important to know who's going to be at the meeting, not just by name, but by function. Experience shows that different functions have very different perspectives and perceptions of market research.

Roger: OK, and just give us some idea of the types of functions that often turn up, and are there any conflicts that might occur between those functions and how you might handle them?

Neil: OK. There are two levels – a functional level and a hierarchy level. Very often, market research is commissioned at a middle to low level by somebody who is not necessarily high up in the management hierarchy, and, therefore, is responsible and visible to their seniors, so there is an issue of them being defensive or them needing to look good in front of their contemporaries or their bosses. There is also a very different perspective on research from different functions. The sales function, for example, frequently doesn't understand the need for market, research, and doesn't understand our requirements for confidentiality and anonymity, so where they find a comment that looks like a sale or looks like a barrier to a sale, they'll want to know who said it individually and what the telephone number is, so they can ring and do whatever they think is appropriate. Marketing tends to want the answers and not too much of the detail. Research tends to want to give lots of detail, but not too many of the answers, and finance wants it to be cheap and, increasingly, procedurally compliant with whatever protocols are involved in their organisation. So they all have a different agenda when they turn up to the meeting, and, very often, that means they also have a different set of questions that they would like to ask and objectives for the study as a whole. Sometimes, too, the legal department has an involvement, and, actually, I guess this seems to be increasing.

Roger: OK. So, that leads me to the next question. In terms of thinking about NLP in the context of doing this – of conducting briefing meetings – what pieces from the NLP body of knowledge have you found particularly useful when doing briefing?

Neil: Well, I think the first thing really starts with my own personal state, and, very clearly, we're going to go into a meeting either with higher or lower levels of stress. If it's a repeat client and we know all the individuals, then those levels of stress are fairly low. It's a bit like going to visit somebody you already know quite well socially, so we don't have to do quite so much by way of getting ourselves into the right state. But for a new client and a new group of people, we've got to be in a state where we are able to not worry too much about those stress levels, where we can concentrate on asking the right questions. What do we do to achieve that? Well, certainly we can do a lot of anchoring stuff. We certainly want to have an appropriate, or at least a self-aware, dress code. We certainly want to make sure that we turn up to the right building well in advance of the right time. If there's any doubt about making train connections or motorway links or whatever, then go the day before.

What you don't need at this point, Roger, is greater stress than you've already got. It's bad enough going into a room of five or six or more people that you don't know. You really want to be in as much control of yourself as possible.

There is also the whole language, not just in a verbal form, but also in a nonverbal sense as well, about where you sit, what kind of control you try and exert over the meeting in the client's premises, or, indeed, sometimes on your own premises. It's very much a political dance at that level, to make sure that you're coming across as being reasonably authoritative, reasonably interested, reasonably in control, but not so much that you usurp their control. You need to listen. You need to listen out for words or phrases or subtexts that somehow just don't strike a true chord, so it's almost an intuitive thing, that you'll hear somebody saying, 'Yes, of course, we really don't mind about whether it's a little bit more expensive than the norm, as long as it's good quality,' and, at that point, maybe your alarm bells ring, and you know quite well that the real issue is how cheaply you can make it or how quickly it can be done, or is it just there to prove a point that they already have decided internally and just want some evidence?

Roger: Listening for subtext is critical. The extent to which you can use that briefing session to elicit from them their own personal states is quite a difficult task, because most of the time they're acting a part, and that part is their role or their function within the company, or they're acting in front of their colleagues, so it's actually quite difficult to start with, in the early part of the meeting, the relationship, to be able to decode much of what's going on because of all the other noise and pretences that are flying around, I've found.

So, let's take this back to the concept, the NLP concept of anchoring. What sorts of states do you find that you end up anchoring, in order to put yourself in the best one possible?

Neil: OK, I think one of the key things to avoid, and one of the key things that we try to defend against, is any kind of pre-judgement or arrogance or overconfidence. It's important to go in with as neutral a perspective as you possibly can. I think, also, that we need to feel, in ourselves, quite self-confident and quite cheerful, but not overly so – so a nice, relaxed, confident, open frame is really what's required at that stage.

Roger: So, three nice states that can be combined, and, if you look in the text of the book, you'll find that you can put these states together with a technique called spotlighting or circles of excellence.

And in terms of another NLP concept, rapport, in terms of how we use our own body language in relation to communicating with people, have you found that to work, and can you give us a few examples? Maybe you can give us an example of where that's worked really well, where you've been able to match and mirror and you've achieved something that, perhaps, surprised you.

Neil: Yes, I can, very easily. Rapport is very important. I find it a very good first port of call to make friends with the receptionist or the departmental secretary, and that will normally be something as simple as saying, 'Hi. How are you today? How are things going? Have you had a busy morning or is it always like this?' We're looking to create some kind of rapport. We're looking for them, typically female but not always, to relate back, to give you a good press when they talk about you internally.

But let's say we've gone through that stage. We walk into the meeting room. Either it's empty, because Fred and Joe are just coming down the corridor, or they're already there and you're last to join the meeting. Very quickly, we need to establish a good working relationship, a good rapport. These are complete strangers who we're meeting purely for business purposes, so, for that initial, physical interchange, use an open stance, pleasant smile (but not grinny), good, direct eye contact without staring (open-eyed, not squinty) and a nice, firm handshake. Allow them to dictate the seating arrangements. Then, body posture is very important. Lean forward. Ensure that you are in rapport with them.

You asked for examples, Roger. There was an occasion a little while ago in America, where the meeting was not going particularly well. We were there on one side of the table. They were there on the other, and the main guy and I were not bonding particularly well. There was no obvious reason for it, but he had his arms crossed and he was clicking his pen repeatedly. So, as a result of the

NLP learnings that I'd gained, there was the opportunity of doing some cross-matching, tapping on the pad in time to his clicking. Within literally a couple of minutes, that had worked extremely well. He was then leaning forward, elbows on the table, open palms, all of the normal signals that you would expect, and it worked extremely well. The meeting went off much better subsequently, but it really was . . . He was also tipping his chair back, so he's tipping his chair back, he's looking down his nose through his glasses, he has his arms folded, he's clicking his pen, and the basic message is, 'I'm really not enjoying this. I really wish I was somewhere else. You're not saying what I want to hear.' But the cross-matching worked extremely well within minutes.

You were just asking me about some details of the meeting there. Maybe I could go back and re-answer some of it, given what we've just been talking about. I think one of the things that contributes most to the establishment of rapport and establishing who I am is the NLP concept of cover all bases (CAB). Very often in a meeting like this, we'll have a number of individuals from different functions, maybe people that I don't know, and, certainly, that don't know me by anything other than name or by company. It's really quite helpful, I find, to make sure that I include all those people and create some kind of bridge. Covering all bases allows us to say something along the lines of, 'I know some of you have probably heard of me only by name, others will have met me before and some of you will have worked with me before.' In an instant, we've included all of the people in the group, and maybe there are other categories that we would cover, 'Some of you have come across market research before, some of you have been involved in commissioning it,' and so on.

Maybe that's a first stage that I should have mentioned. The other thing to use, maybe at this stage, is the concept of yes sets, and that's simply the idea that if we can get people to buy into a small number of obvious 'yes' answers, then we give them some kind of preemptive strike to say yes to the next one. So, we might say, 'Well, it's been a really terrible morning's weather. It's been snowing, but your company's doing pretty well, and we know that this is going to be a really important job for you,' and their brain's going, 'Yes, yes, yes,' and then we say, 'Well, of course, our company is certainly able to offer the solution to your problems,' that kind of thing, because we're also in a sales environment at that stage, and we want to create the impetus for them to be looking to buy from us as well. Maybe a little bit farther into the meeting, when we've settled down and those initial social exchanges and roles have been established, it's really up to somebody to take charge of the meeting, and maybe that's the client company or maybe it's us as the visiting researcher.

Roger: But, certainly, you can take charge of your half of the meeting.

Neil: Yes.

Roger: Because you're always going to have the opportunity to say something, and when you do that, I know that you do some interesting things in terms of setting ground rules.

Neil: Yes, using the concept of frames, you mean? Yes, that is an interesting one. Certainly, we would want to establish very clearly what the goals of the meeting were. It's very tempting, maybe, just to sit there and have a bit of a chat, and then, at the end of it, really not have a clue as to what it was we were meant to be doing.

Roger: I guess this is especially important when you've got people in different functions there, because often sales, marketing and finance will have different outcomes, different goals, and some way of bringing this out into the open and having a broad agreement on goals can help the meeting go more smoothly.

Neil: I think that's right. So, what is it we're actually going to try and achieve this afternoon, this morning, whenever it is?

Roger: We also ought to be setting outcomes both in terms of the project outcome, and we would head those as project objectives – what is the project actually trying to achieve? – and the follow-on question from that to the client is, 'Well, how will you know when the research has been effective? What kind of yardstick or standards or action points would you use to determine that this has been money well spent or not, conversely?' I guess this is particularly important because there are going to be times when you'll be sitting down with a client and they'll give you an outcome and then tell you how they're going to know they've got that outcome, and you'll know that, actually, the outcome that they've got is not going to deliver the evidence.

Neil: Yes. Yes. I think there is also, to use an analogy from a more complicated NLP concept, a parts management – that you may actually have two client groups or individuals who want completely different things, and it's really up to us to have some kind of parts negotiation between the two, to mediate, if you like, between Client A, who wants one thing, and Client B, who wants something completely different. It's not uncommon in a client meeting of four or five people to have two or three different perspectives on what the research is, even down to the level of who should be interviewed at all.

Roger: So, is it helpful in the context of the meeting to have some of these outcomes out and then put them on a flipchart, something like that?

Neil: Exactly.

Roger: So that they're quite visible to everybody and then people can agree that at least the meeting is going to go in a direction that might be useful.

Neil: Yes, but I think also, most of the time, we find the clients are very pushed in their diaries, so it's very helpful, also, to make sure that we have agreement on the timeframe, both in the short term, like, 'This meeting will finish at four o'clock. Is that all right with everybody?' And also in terms of the project, 'This project needs to be completed by . . .' whatever given date, because unless we have that, we have an open context, an open frame, into which everybody can pour their own prejudices or views or feelings or anticipations or expectations. So it's very important that those goals and those structures are clearly identified, and maybe using the TOTE (Test Operate Test Exit) concept allows us to say, 'What is it you want? How will you know when you've got it? How will you validate information or findings or whatever?' If that's the scenario, then fine. We know we've accomplished what it is we set out to accomplish.

I know that we could probably have this discussion under almost every section in our book, but one of the big challenges that we find most frequently is that the individual client's written brief or the clients' collective view is made up of individual questions, and what they're really not very helpful at doing sometimes is giving us the big picture, so one of the challenges during a meeting is to push them up the chunk chain to make sure that where we end up is really the objective. It may be something that is voiced in terms of purely tactical execution, that, actually, when we talk about it, the list of 18 questions that they've written down has never really been codified into an objective. It's never about understanding what makes the consumer tick. It's about individual questions that they think the consumer should be asked. So, I think that's a really important one, and one of the learnings that we have during that, is if we're struggling to get them up the chunk chain, then we can move sideways into some kind of metaphor. So, I think that's a very important additional point, which means that I've completely forgotten the question area that you . . .

Roger: We were going to talk about how you might use one of the frames. The as if frame is particularly useful for meetings that get stuck, where you get a group of people that actually can't quite find the way forward because there are too many disparate points of view, so one of the things you can do is just put everything to one side and pretend, behave as if you could do exactly what you needed to do. It's often a really good way of breaking blocks.

Neil: And, of course, we can use that technique when interviewing respondents as well, in group discussions or in
depth interviews.

Roger: OK, and there's more information about that in the
book. So, we've covered a little bit about how you use
anchoring, something about cover all bases...

Neil: Yes, and it's worth mentioning on anchoring, because we
do talk about this later on in the book, it's worth pointing out that the physical firing of an anchor – pressure
on the elbow, scratching your ear or whatever is being
used – is such an easy route to re-establishing that comfort
zone in which you wish to be – the most appropriate
comfort zone – and you'll find that you want to modify
it in the light of the client type. For example, a very hi-
tech client company will require a very different kind of
anchor frame than would be the case for an advertising
agency, and with that goes lots of dress codes and style
and so on. Many times, I've gone into a client company
in the old days, wearing a suit and a tie, and discovered,
while sitting in their reception area, that there isn't a
single tie to be seen, so one hurriedly rips off one's tie
and looks terribly casual with an open-necked shirt, or
even throws the jacket back in the car very quickly, so
these things are possible to modify, but each client type
probably requires at least conscious thought of that framework, that zone of comfort, in which you wish to operate.
What's the best day for that client? Sometimes you might
want a less relaxed and more energised client rather than
a totally laid back one. And it could well be, as you'll
notice from normal training work, Roger, that maybe
half-way through a meeting, you need to adopt a different persona. You need to get into a different state to

change the dynamic of the meeting. Maybe it's gone very flat, and you need to put on your exciting, dynamic, full of energy hat rather than your much more laid-back, passive one.

Roger: So, we can create a number of these states that we can call on tap there, prepared beforehand with the instructions that you can find in the book.

Neil: OK. Shall we move on to teleconferences?

Roger: Let's move on to teleconferences.

Neil: Because I think they're now becoming a really important part of a researcher's armoury.

Maybe I can just turn the tables on you slightly, Roger, because from a training point of view, from a theoretical knowledge base point of view, what would you say were the differences between a videoconference and an audio conference?

Roger: Let me think about that for a moment.

Neil: Now, while the technology is relatively poor at the moment, certainly with a peer-to-peer, person-to-person video cam link, you're increasingly getting 680 × 480 or whatever it is pixels. You're getting some reasonable facial expressions coming back at you and vice versa. Now that's very different, I would say in NLP terms, from simply concentrating on audio, and I'll give you an example. Hopefully, by the end of the example, you'll have come up with your answer. When I'm doing a teleconference, I actually have to close my eyes so that I concentrate solely on the audio quality, because I find that, being quite a visual person, once I start looking round at the room or out the window, my attention goes, and I don't have the direct eye contact that I use all the time. That's my greatest tool, so how would you train for that, and what sort of concepts would you expect to be different?

Roger: Well, I think the first thing that springs to mind with telecoms is this coping with the delay. When we're face to face with somebody and we're operating with rapport principles, those are pretty instantaneous moves, so one has to be aware firstly of the delay that you get in teleconferences, particularly if they're transatlantic. You can get half a second or maybe even a full few seconds' delay; so that, actually, is good in some ways, because it gives one time to think, and I think you're right in terms of the auditory input. Sometimes, just turning one channel off makes it easier to concentrate on the others, and if we're having teleconferences instead of audio conferences, you're going to get the opportunity, hopefully, depending on the camera position, to create a similar sort of rapport as you would if you were face to face with a person.

Neil: And that will still work at arm's length through that medium?

Roger: It will still work at arm's length. It'll work over the camera. The critical thing to think about is timing, and you just need to adjust your timing somewhat, so having some practice doing it face to face before you go doing that sort of thing in teleconferences is going to pay off. I also think, in terms of teleconferences, the auditory component's still going to be the most important. Even if you have a jerky picture of somebody and you can see them smiling or you can see them moving, I think that you should still pay more attention to the voice, because that's the thing you're going to get instantaneously, so some of the things that you can do are to match the speed and volume of the speech that's coming across. Those are the two easiest things to match. From there, if you want to get more sophisticated, you can start to match the voice tone, and that becomes a very powerful frame for creating rapport, so this is certainly something important in an ordinary teleconference without video. You should be concentrating on the speed at which the other person's speaking, and then the volume – adjust your own volume and speed to match theirs.

Neil: What about cultural phrases? A lot of the teleconferences I do are, almost by definition, transatlantic ones, and the speech patterns and the phraseologies are very different. For example, there's a well known discrepancy between what in Europe, certainly in the United Kingdom, is known as a bum bag, but in America is known as a fanny pack, and that's not the sort of thing that it's easy to say with a straight face, so do we use American phraseology when we're teleconferencing with the States? Do we use their slightly different (depending on what part of the country) inflections? Do we, for example, if we're doing it with Australia, use the up note at the end of a sentence? Is that going one stage too far?

Roger: I think that might be going one stage too far. I think physical rapport is more important than copying their speech patterns, and, certainly, I think they might find it a little strange if you were suddenly to use their collo-quialisms, unless we've known them for a long while and we've had a relationship built, then those things tend to merge, but at least initially, you're probably best to stay in your Englishness, and it may be one of the reasons why they like you.

Neil: Yes. I think one of the things that teleconferences particularly benefit from is tracking who everybody is and listening to voices, so, really, one of the tools that one ought to be developing is voice recognition, and that's helped a lot by having some kind of spatial diagram in front of you.

Roger: The next question to answer is how you track the conversations so that, if you, I don't know, maybe you have half a dozen people talking. Do you record them?

Neil: I would try and record them, although the audio quality on the kind of conferences that they typically have around conference tables is really not very good. By the time you've got conference quality audio at both ends, recording is a bit of a hit and miss operation, but nonetheless, what you do tend to find is that people, more often than not, introduce themselves in sequence, in line, so if they're sitting six people around a table, they will go in sequence, and that gives you the opportunity of creating a little table plan. You don't need to know if it's round or square or just a straight line. You list the names in the order in which they introduce themselves, and that gives you some kind of little template to refer back to.

Roger: OK, that's good.

Neil: And also, maybe just circle the chairperson of the meeting, so that you know when they speak, when that sound quality speaks, then it's somebody that you should be paying particular attention to.

Roger: OK, so that's a little bit about how you track conversations, a little bit about how you might use your own voice, tone and volume in order to create that sort of rapport in a teleconference. I also tend to think you have to speak just a little bit above your normal level in a teleconference, because you are at some remove from the microphone. It's not the same as having an across-the-table discussion with a person, or even a mouth-to-receiver discussion on a telephone, so there is a slight artificiality, but it's in relative tones.

Neil: And everybody's going to be doing it.

Roger: And everybody's doing the same thing, yes. Exactly.

OK, so there's a little bit about tracking conversations. Now, we know that NLP has a lot to do with language. It's Neuro-Linguistic Programming. So, I just would like you to think, for a moment, about how the knowledge of language usage in NLP has helped with these teleconferences. How does that awareness help, and what are you listening for that maybe you weren't listening to before you took the NLP training? What sort of things are you now picking up that you weren't picking up before? Because that's the sort of thing the readers would like to know, and they're going to know. They would want to ask the question, 'Well, how's this going to help me? What skills, what things, will I hear that I'm not hearing currently?'

Neil: OK, I think there are two, maybe three, key areas that I would suggest. I think the first thing is that, to a limited extent, I am able to listen to the individual speaking now. With some of the quality of the audio, it's difficult sometimes to separate Person 1 from Person 2, or however many people there are, but there will certainly be clues as to their modality preference that you will be able to listen out for, just key words and phrases that tell you a little bit about the kind of people they are – visual, auditory or kinaesthetic. There are corporate culture words, which maybe we haven't talked about in the book at all, but there are very definitely core corporate beliefs that are identifiable, and you'll get a sense very quickly if they are, for example, numbers driven, very logical, linear, rational, maybe quite auditory, and therefore would respond to a more quantitative research presentation.

Roger: What sort of things might you hear them saying?

Neil: Well, I think that the frequency of uses of words like 'how many' and 'when', rather than the softer, kinaesthetic qualitative words like 'why' and 'feelings', really give the clues away, and, very often, people will actually use more concrete identifiers of their own corporate culture and say, 'Well, my boss needs facts,' and at that point you know that there is very little point in talking in detail about qualitative techniques. Maybe you could still do a qualitative research programme, but there is no point in talking about many of the projective and labelling techniques that we might use.

Roger: OK, so you're going to scope a conversation with some of these NLP concepts?

Neil: Yes. I think there's also just the use of power words or action words, or also associative words. It's something of a debate within the market research industry, and not much of a debate at all within the advertising industry, that the advertising fraternity always use the personal pronouns 'we' and 'I', or 'we' when they're talking about the client and their agency jointly. The market research industry tends to be a little bit more arm's length and almost dissociated.

Roger: It's a much more professional stand, so we can maybe look to use those words to create or to dispel some of the relationship elements that we either do or don't want. From your experience of seeing some market researchers working, and from sitting in many meetings and training thousands of people, how would you expect that to work? What would you be looking for if you were dropped into a market research world?

Neil: If I was dropped into a market research world, with some knowledge of NLP, there are certainly things you can pick up from your clients or from your sample group without needing to ask too many questions. You can certainly pick up some of the client's values.

Roger: Yes. Very, very easily, and an easy question of what is important in this context will pull those out. They're very important to pay attention to, and certainly to repeat back to the client. So, values would be one key place where I'd always look. I'd always be wanting to find out what their values were, not just the corporate values, but the personal values of the people round the table that I'm going to end up working for, because I want to make sure that I fulfil those values, so I'd certainly be asking questions like, 'What's important to you in the context of this project? What's important to the business in terms of the success of this project?' This will give me some idea of the values that are coming forward. And it may be that one of the values is that this project produces lots of facts. On the other side of the coin, it might be that this project allows us to feel exactly how we need to put the adverts or whatever it is through for the consumers. So, values are the first step I would be looking for. Apart from listening to the visuals, the kin-aesthetic information, this is often there. Sometimes you might want to listen for that in the side conversations rather than the direct conversations, because sometimes what people have been doing will appear in the casual conversations you have over a cup of coffee, especially if they're somebody you've met a couple of times. Then I'd definitely look at values, what are their values? Then, in NLP, there's something called attention filters. Attention filters are really useful, because they tell us what we are paying attention to. What people are paying attention to. So, a simple one here would be to think of an attention argument, is your attention on the things you want, the things you're going towards, or is your attention on things that you don't want? And this is a really easy one to listen for in a client situation. Are you taking a brief from a client who's telling you all the things they don't want to happen? And then you have to find some way of including that. Or are they telling you what they do want? Very simple, and the big mistake is to take somebody that's telling you what they don't want and offer them lots of what they do wants, because they may not be ready or in the right place to take this. Then you run into the concept of pacing and leading, so we may need to pace the client in their don't wants, because they may not have focused on what it is they really want.

Neil: It occurs to me also that when we were talking about taking the brief, we didn't go on, but we probably will do, about writing our proposal, writing our response to what we think to be their problem. We also ought maybe to be asking them about sameness or difference. What are they looking for in terms of the research agency that they choose? Do they want somebody that stands out with a brand new solution or, indeed, somebody who simply can come in cheaper than the standard one?

Roger: Certainly. Certainly. One of the other questions that you could ask in terms of that is whether they have had any other projects like this completed before. Do they want something the same or are they looking for a different approach? This is going to be very, very important, because, if, in the back of their minds, they've had something that's the same and you have listed that, you offer them the sameness approach, which they may not want, and vice versa, so it's a pretty important category to investigate. What is in the back of their minds? They are comparing what you're bringing to the table with what they've already seen, experienced, paid for, etc. What is that?

Neil: I can give you quite an interesting case history on that one as well. A little while ago, I was asked to do some work for one of the major pharmaceutical companies. One of their brands had been a leading brand in major countries across Europe and the States, but had been losing ground to the major competitor brand, though without any obvious reason for it. They had done three different pieces of qualitative research and some quantitative – all based on rational interviews, including rationally-based interviews with physicians. The brands were performing to identical levels of efficacy, so there was no reason to drop a brand. They came to us because they wanted something different in a research approach, and we adopted a route of not using rational questioning. We used a lot of personality analogies. We used a lot of projective and enabling techniques. We invented a couple of techniques for use in this particular project, and the answer to their problem was that the brand identity, the brand imagery, was very different between their brand and the competitor brand, and what they had failed to do on previous research projects was ask different enough questions. They had sought sameness in their recruitment of an agency and their design of the project questionnaire, the topic guide, and what they actually required. We provided a different approach, and that was the one which actually produced the goods in the end.

Roger: Excellent. That's a good example. So, we went slightly off course in terms of the teleconferences. Are there any other NLP tools that you find really useful in the tele-conference area?

Neil: I must say that of all of the meeting frameworks I've encountered over the years, I find audio teleconferences the most challenging and the most difficult. Because it's so different to my own personal preference framework, I find it really hard to do as good a job on a teleconference as I would on a face-to-face meeting or even a video-conference. I find that very challenging, so I think one of the key things I would bring into it is a slightly different state, whereas on a personal meeting or even a videoconference, I would look to be slightly extrovert, certainly very confident, certainly quite ebullient and open, on a teleconference, I find that I need to focus very much on internal qualities, that I need to focus down, that I need almost a chunk down in a physical sense, so that there is nothing, there is no other extraneous noise except their voices and my voice. So, as I say, very often, apart from when I'm checking my notes or writing down who said what, I will actually close my eyes.

Roger: That's a good one. OK, good. We're progressing through the process of doing a piece of research. We've talked about a briefing meeting. We've talked about teleconferences as other ways that you're going to get the work coming through, and the briefs for the work and some of the things that you can do from the NLP model that will help you create the best state. Let's go to choosing a sample. We'll come back later to the proposal. So, now you're faced with choosing a sample, has NLP helped you with the prospect of going out and finding the right sample to get the best research you can, rather than just picking a random man or woman walking down the street?

Neil: I think the simple answer is that it has not yet helped us in market research in a qualitative research sense. I think there is every suggestion that it very well could do, but what we haven't done is utilise the potential of it yet. To the very best of my knowledge, there has only been one written paper about this, by a friend of mine, who wrote a conference paper three or four years ago, suggesting that we might usefully seek to recruit our respondents in qualitative group discussions on the basis of their submodality preferences, on the basis that they would be likely to respond differently to different types of questioning, different types of stimulus material and the whole dynamic of the group would be different. She ran some experiments and actually found that this did produce some differences by selecting a predominantly visual group or a predominantly auditory group or a predominantly kinaesthetic group. We did find, or she did find, that there were differences in the kinds of stimulus material in which they understood more of the detail, or about which they felt more comfortable, or many other dimensions, so the key thing really relates to stimulus material as it is presented.

There is little benefit, the argument goes, in showing a group of kinaesthetic or visual respondents lengthy, A4, text-filled stimulus material, on the basis that it's not their filter comfort zone, it is not something with which they feel at home. Whereas with an auditory group, that may very well be the format that they would put their hands up and volunteer for. If we want to communicate well on behalf of our clients, the argument goes, then maybe we should be recruiting appropriately, or at least advising the client or their advertising agency or PR company or whatever it may be, to have mixed modalities as a target audience. In a very good advert, for example, you might have some auditory material and you may also have some kinaesthetic material and some visual material, rather than simply one or the other. So, as a frame for choosing the sample and operating with that sample, you really want to be crossing all the modalities rather than trying to pick groups from one of them, because, of course, the population's not made up like that anyway, so if you pick one group, you're going to get biased results. However, this is really something for you to think about with regard to the sample, think about the stimulus material that you've provided in order to provide it in all those modalities. And also the projective and enabling techniques. You know, there will be some people who find it extremely difficult, for example, to create a visual collage. It's simply not the language in which they think, whereas another group of people may be much more comfortable using words that they've taken from magazines or newspapers rather than visual images, and, again, it's simply a little bit of a pre-think-through exercise that you need to have available to you when you start interviewing – a range of approaches or a range of analogies or a range of techniques that you use to cater for all of those different modalities that people bring to the group discussion or the depth interview.

From a purely NLP standpoint, if you were coming again and just were dropped into the middle of a discussion about how we should recruit a sample in a research company, what would you advise us?

Roger: There are a couple of approaches. First, you could test people to get an idea of where they were. Short, five-minute tests would give you a good steer as to how many of each type of person you had in that sample group. That's pretty possible. You can even do them on computer, so that might be a part of your selection process or a part of your information-gathering process. It's quite innocuous because it's not invasive. It's not a personality test as such. It's just how are people operating in the world and how do they prefer to receive their information? The second thing that I think would be pretty important, and this is something that I've observed when I've been observing focus groups, is that, very often, the stimulus material isn't provided in those three modalities. You may be taking people in and showing them big pictures, or it may be just purely text, in which case, you're not going to get the best out of the people there.

If you look at the proportions of the population, you've got pretty much 40% visual, 40% kinaesthetic and 20% auditory, so if you produce a lot of text material for a sample group, there are going to be less people there that will respond to it. You'd be better off if you're going to go one way to produce visual material plus some kinaesthetic, plus some things to do. Or some things that evoke emotions. Using text and techniques like that would probably get you a better result across the board. My favourite would be just to give people a little test, and then, over a period of time, within a sample group, you're going to build up a picture of the sort of modalities that turn up in market research, because maybe some modalities don't.

Neil: Yes. Would you go as far as maybe excluding people who have particular belief sets or value sets from undertaking qualitative research? If they're particularly antipathetic to advertising, for example.

Roger: That's the normal way of doing it. We would normally exclude people who dislike, who verbally dislike, advertising. They say, on an attitude scale, 'We dislike advertising a great deal.' You're not going to have good impact results from people like that, so I guess that's OK.

Neil: No. So the polarity responder is excluded early on.

Roger: Yes, unless you respond to them by saying, 'I don't suppose you could give us some information about this,' and they may well do so.

Neil: What about recruitment itself though? This is something that we've been debating for some time – the actual interface. Imagine you're standing on the street corner, although relatively little of it's done, or you bang on somebody's door, the normal way is to say, 'I'm doing some market research. Could you spare me some time?' And most people's answer is, 'No, I couldn't.' So, how would you advise . . . how would you train the people who actually recruit for qualitative market research to get a better response rate?

Roger: Well, I think the first thing you need to do when you knock on somebody's door is to engage their interest, so I think maybe just knocking on the door and saying, 'Hi. Can you help me with some qualitative research?' may not get you a good response. However, if you're . . . if you're involved in something, in some sort of product, it might be useful to put the product up front and say . . . (Let me say it's a shampoo) 'Good morning. My name's so-and-so. I'm running a project at the moment looking at the effectiveness of XYZ shampoo. Would you be interested in spending a couple of moments with this research I'm doing?' and I want to be inclusive, so I'd say, 'Would you like to be included in . . .?' 'Would you like to be part of . . .?' 'Would you be prepared to be part of . . .?' 'Would you be prepared to be included in the research by spending a few moments and answering a few questions?' The first few questions you might ask might be the visual or kinaesthetic ones, just to get a steer on where their representational systems, their modalities, are seated at that particular time, because they're all contextual, so at least you've got an idea of how that person's processing as you're asking the questions. I think that's much friendlier. I think I might be prepared to say, 'OK, I'm interested in shampoo. That could be interesting,' and now I know what you're here for.

Sometimes, the market research approach might be seen as an underhand sales approach.

Neil: There is a big risk. We call it *sugging* when the research cover is used to mask a sales approach.

Roger: They might try and sell something to you, so it might be important to actually think about those frames again. You know, what are you standing there on the doorstep for? In the ten seconds you've got when they open the door, let that person know that this is what you're there for.

Neil: If I gave you an example, I'd be interested in your analysis of the differences between the original approach that we took and the subsequent one, just to see how you react and how you evaluate it. We were working, a few months ago, on a project looking at osteoarthritis in the population, and it's difficult to find people to take part in this kind of extended ethnographic study. This was going to be literally two full days per person, us following them around, which is a lot of inconvenience, and although we were offering them substantial incentives to do so, it was an uphill struggle, so we changed the . . . well, I was going to use the word frame, but I don't want to put that thought in your head. We changed the approach, so, ultimately, what we got was a group of people who, when presented with the opportunity of contributing to the understanding that big drug companies have about arthritis, then turned round and said, 'Yes, I'd like to help, because no-one listens to us,' whereas simply saying, 'Here is a certain amount of money. We'd like you to take part,' produced a very poor response. What would be your NLP version of why that change was effective?

Roger: In short, it's not necessarily money that motivates us to do something, so what you did very neatly was to hook into a value, and hook into an area where people didn't feel like they were being heard, and give them the opportunity to give feedback to a big drug company. Often, if people are taking drugs, they're in a long-term illness. It's a very useful opportunity to do, much better than saying, 'I'll give you 100 quid if you'll let me follow you around all day.' So, I think what you did there was exactly what I'm suggesting for the recruitment stuff. Actually think about the sample and think about how you might interface with their motivational patterns, which is exactly what you did. You picked something that motivated them, and then you got a much better response, so, I guess what I'm saying is, half an hour's thought about the motivational keys to a group might save you a lot of foot slogging, because then you can frame your requests for inclusion in the research in a much better way.

Neil: And what additional guidance or advice or training, indeed, would you be able to offer to a group of recruiters? These are not the people who ultimately do the interviews. They're the people who find the respondents for us. They're the ones very much at the front line, banging on doors, stopping you in the shopping centre. Any particular NLP approaches that you think might be appropriate there?

Roger: I think a fast rapport-building would be useful.

Neil: Just give me a little flavour of what that might be.

Roger: I think that's a question of when you see somebody
coming towards you, move yourself into a posture that's
quite similar to theirs; quickly moving into a posture
when they're stood in front of you that's quite like theirs
– particularly in terms of head angle, the way they have
their feet, the way they're holding their arms – not
exactly alike, but similar would be very helpful, and that
quickly sends messages to the other person that this person
stood in front of them is friendly. We always talk about
smiling, and that's a good thing to do anyway. It maybe
goes without saying they need to do that. I think, also,
some of the way you phrase your requests for assistance
could be . . . could be modified to fit people's motivational patterns more precisely. Often, we respond to a
request for help. Generally, as human beings, if somebody
asks us to help, then we don't generally refuse, and we
like to be included unless we're really too busy. So, I
think I'd look very carefully at the language and the patterns that the group was going to use relating to the
product, and how they might encourage people to come
along, both using physical rapport and some of the value
sets, and, clearly, if you're looking to do some research,
you'd be already picking the sort of people you might
want to talk to, so maybe you're going for people that
look like they're in their 40s and they've got children
rather than not. So you're harmonising the recruiter and
the respondent. You're making them look more similar.
And that's the other thing. If you want to talk to teenagers, there's not much point in going out and standing
there in a suit and tie, because then they're going to be
very nervous. They're not going to want to approach
you. You do need to do that. Because you're making
contact with people quickly, you need to do that quick
rapport thing and pay attention to how you're presenting

yourself. So you might want to wear jeans and a T-shirt, or something that might get you more of the younger people coming along. However, if you're going to be dealing with people later in life, in their 60s and 70s, it may be that they don't want to be approached by somebody in jeans and a T-shirt, and what would be better would be a more formal approach. So, I think, apart from the language and the rapport, there are some other things that you could think of in terms of how you might teach recruiters to be able to get more people through their sample.

Neil: So, are we putting these things under three basic headings, then? We're putting them under nonverbal rapport-building . . .

Roger: Nonverbal rapport-building using your physicality.

Neil: . . . we're putting them under very obvious physical dress sense and dress code, and we're putting them under phraseology, words.

Roger: Language.

Neil: Language generally.

Roger: What you say. And how you say it.

Neil: And how you say it. Exactly.

Roger: OK. I think that's probably all we need to do on choosing a sample to interview.

———————

Neil: So, Roger, appreciating that there is more information yet to come, but from a point of view of responding to a brief in writing, what key NLP learnings can we take about writing back to a client?

Roger: OK, if I was just to list, without the content of what we're going to write back, we talked about cover all bases and yes sets. Now, those can be done very elegantly in writing in a much broader form than you did them earlier on.

Neil: Just a point that our readers may not know. NLP uses the word elegant a lot. How would you define elegance in this context?

Roger: This is the ability to influence without any jarring at all, so that it makes everything very smooth and very easy for the person's brain to assimilate. What we want to do is make the client's mind absorb the information very easily and have the client's mind open at all times, so that we're not using any phraseology that will shut things down or cause big questions to arise.

Neil: And what sort of phrases or what sort of hypnosis language might be useful under these circumstances?

Roger: Well, you might well use some universals.

Neil: Give me an example.

Roger: We want to use, definitely, words that pace the client. These are words like 'as' and 'while'. 'As you read this, you can begin to consider the possibilities of da-di-da-di-da', so you're actually pacing the client. It's a different way of writing a report than the very stilted, technical way we would normally write a report. We want to pace the client, we want to keep the client's brain along with ours so that they follow us at every step of the way, so this is about creating a written report.

Neil: What about tenses? What guidance does NLP give us about that?

Roger: In terms of the tense, if you want somebody to take action, you really want these phrases stuck in the present tense. What does the brain do when it sees a proposal? It seeks to criticise and to reject. It thinks it's a proposal, so what's a proposal? Is it something you're going to do? No. So, my NLP advice is, don't write proposals. Write action plans. As a start. And then, pace your client into the action plan using cover all bases, so that you can be inclusive. Use some yes sets around the company, around the project, so that you've got at least three absolutely incontrovertible facts – and they can be a paragraph each, that's OK – before you deliver your proposal, so you've already set up in the mind of the client a very comfortable, open, yes environment, and they're much more likely to pick up your proposal than if you stamp straight into the proposal. In terms of the proposal, see if you can get the client's imagination engaged, so, rather than making it dry and bullet-pointed, see if you can get some picture, with feelings and sounds if possible, of what you're proposing to do – it need only be a few sentences or a paragraph. It's absolutely fine to do that before you go into the technical details, of (a) we'll be in this place, and (b) we'll be in that place, because it opens up the imagination and allows them to visualise exactly what they're going to be getting. Use as much sensory-based language as possible, so use a good smattering of visual, auditory and kinaesthetic language, because that will connect to people's interior world much better.

What other things can we do? Now, knowing something about meta-programs and what people pay attention to, we could be doing a project which is designed for people who avoid something, so we want to make sure that we phrase . . . that we have those phrases in the project. It may be that we'd want to tell them this research will help the client *avoid* losing millions of pounds on a product that they're not sure about. You'd have to check with the client to see. You'd be referencing that on your brief-taking, as to what the client had said beforehand. If the client's doing this because they want to avoid things, then we want to make sure we reflect that in the proposal. So, you're going to be the person that helps them get around the obstacles. On the other hand, if the client is very gung ho and very enthusiastic about the product, and they're what we might call, in NLP terms, heading towards, then we want to make sure that we use mainly that language, and we don't start flagging up the obstacles. We may very well see the obstacles, but we need to be very careful in that case how we phrase and flag them up, because if we put too much of that in, we may think that many things need to be changed. If we put too much emphasis on the obstacles, the towards person will just throw it in the bin, because it won't have matched their mindset.

So that's just it, simply done, but that's just two attention builders. The other thing we can look at is the client. Does the client like procedures? Are they a client that likes things ticked off? In which case, we need to give them a procedure. On the other hand, we may have a client that really just likes to have their options open, so that the research can go the way it needs to go. You're going to need to take an assessment of the client at the briefing as to whether they're liking procedures or whether they like to have more open ends, and then, again, you're going to phrase your proposal in those terms. You may be a person that likes procedures but, if you're working with somebody that maybe wants a more open framework, the way you structure your proposal might well put them off, and vice versa, so you're going to need to be flexible. The whole thing of NLP is it makes you flexible around what other people need.

So, we've had a couple there. We also might couch things in terms . . . there's a really useful meta-program called the primary interest filter, and this you can detect very easily from what people talk about. People may talk about the places that they've been or the places that they want to go or the places things should take place in, if that's their primary interest, or they may talk about systems. They may talk about things or they may talk about people, so it's a kind of straw poll when you're with somebody to see what they mostly refer to. So, places, systems, things, people and maybe time. You can pay attention to that, so when you're phrasing your proposal, you might want to reflect some of those things. If you don't know, it's a really good idea to reflect all five, especially if more than one person's going to read the proposal. Which would be the norm.

So, you want to make sure you cover the primary interest filters, in which case, you'll have a hit for everybody that's going to read it. You'll get a hit from the systems person, you're going to get a hit from the people that are interested in people, you're going to get a hit from the people that like things and you're also going to get a hit from the people that are really interested in the place where all this is going to take place.

Neil: How realistic is it to use chunking? In terms of reflecting the brief, do you chunk up or down to the level that the brief has given you? What would your advice be?

Roger: Chunking's really important. There are two ways of reasoning: deductive reasoning, which is where you start with the big picture and end up with the details, and inductive reasoning, which is a bit like Sherlock Holmes – you have all the details, and, finally, you put them all together and make a great picture. For the most part, in business, people do big picture into details, so it's kind of a rule of thumb, you should always start your proposal with a big picture. You should always start the proposal with some large objective that will meet the client's needs if they haven't already given you that. If they give you an objective which is in the detail stage, you may want to chunk up and find out what broad framework it fits into, and then move down into the detail. Moving down to the detail too fast can break rapport and can actually stop people reading the document. So, those are two things there.

Neil: Well, maybe we should move on briefly to the presentation, because it follows on from some of those learnings.

Roger: What I would say is, if you get your report-writing sorted like this, it's going to make your presentation much easier, because you're going to really just be pulling your presentation from your report, so you're going to be starting with the big picture. You're going to be giving some idea of where it took place, what systems were in place, and so on. You know, you can hit all those primary interest filters in your introduction.

Neil: The normal conventional teaching in market research is that you produce all the evidence and then do a QED, so you'll give them, maybe, answers to each of the questions that you asked, probably in sequence, and then you'll say, 'Well, because of all that, the answer is 42.'

Roger: Yes.

Neil: How does that work in your world?

Roger: Well, it's a good, logical way to do things. I might lead people more gently to that, though. I also might have a think before I even do my presentation as to what objections there might be, and I'd want to handle those objections right up front, so I might want to say in the presentation, 'I know some of you might have been thinking . . . ,' and you can do this with a cover all bases, which is very neat, 'Some of you might have been thinking that part of this report takes us down this route. Some of you might have been thinking about this.' I'd want to cover all those objections with a cover all bases, so that we're handling them up front and we don't get surprised by them. OK, you may have one or two things that crop up after that. If you do a good perceptual positioning, hopping into the other person's shoes, you can generally pick up what they might be going to say and handle it before. Therefore, instead of waiting to get shot down, or trying to do the defensive QED thing, where you leave people no options, if you actually handle the objections up front, this usually allows, because it's a rapport-building thing, much freer discussion. So, a cover all bases around handling the objections. A yes set before you deliver your answers will work wonders for opening and keeping the minds open, and then you need to do big chunk to small chunk, so start with the big chunk and lead into the small chunks. You'll have people in the room that like big chunks, and you'll have people in the room that don't like big chunks and want small chunks, so you need to cater for both, and you don't need to spend too long in either. So, it's really like you dive in from the diving board, you do a few strokes across the pool to give people a general idea that you can swim pretty well and then you pop out the other side and tie things up. As a metaphor.

Neil: A good metaphor. And where do you stand on where do you stand?

Roger: Where do I stand on where do I stand? I want people's attention to be on me and what I say, not necessarily on the pretty pictures that I might have put on PowerPoint. PowerPoint is a visual aid, not a visual first aid, so my preference would be to have the screen to the side and stand in the middle, because I want to make sure that I've got eye contact with everybody. I want to make sure that I've got a strong connection. I also want to dem-onstrate that I'm not scared of them, I'm quite happy to stand up, and I'd be quite happy to stand up with a flip-chart, without PowerPoint, and do it on a flipchart if necessary.

Neil: But you're using the words 'stand up'. Do you mean that literally or figuratively?

Roger: No, figuratively. Even if I was sitting down at the head of a conference, I'd want the projections somewhere off to the side.

Neil: Because I would argue that if you're presenting to an audience of three or four and it's not a discussion session, you always stand up.

Roger: Yes.

Neil: And I always do. I make a point of it. Even if it was to one or two people, I would stand up.

Roger: Standing up always gives you a position of power, because you're on your feet.

Neil: And energy.

Roger: And it's also a good way to keep you safe, because at least you can move a little bit, although there are some things around that . . . some things that we could talk about in terms of how you create presence, and one of the ways of creating presence is *not* to move around. It doesn't mean to say you can't use gestures, which you should. Pacing around is the best way to lose your presence. The best way is if you focus and distract the audience. So, there are good ways to develop charisma. There are ways to stand that will root you into the ground, which will give you a very solid, powerful presence, and which we cover in the book. In terms of posture, there are ways that you can learn to walk that will give you a lot of presence, and very, very easily – just using your physiology. So, my preference would be to stand. It works much better. I think it gives you the ability to control your state much better than sitting down, and my preference would be to have the screen to one side rather than dominating the room. However, this may not always be possible, because most rooms are set up with the screen in the middle.

Neil: I would also add that when I present, the first thing I do, apart from standing up, is to put my arms out, and if you watch a lot of politicians . . .

Roger: This is an inclusive gesture.

Neil: It is an inclusive gesture. Also, we're getting people's heads going up a little bit because they're sitting down. We want them to engage brain rather than look down and focus on the agenda or the piece of paper. We don't want them to go into themselves.

Roger: We definitely, definitely want people to be in their visual mode, not their auditory or kinaesthetic. You're quite correct, yes.

Neil: Or, I will actually do that and, at the same time, say, 'Hi. I'm Neil. I'm going to be talking to you today.' It gets attention immediately.

Roger: Some of these things are our personal style, which is great, so if you've got a personal style that you can develop, that's fine. I've got some views on environmetics that we can probably put together. One of the things that I always do when setting up a room, because my main focus is training, is to set things up symmetrically. So, what I try and create for those that are looking toward me is balance on either side of the room.

Neil: So, you are literally centred in the middle of a wall space?

Roger: If there are objects, chairs, etc., then there would be a balance across the room. What we're wanting to do, really, is to balance the left and right sides of the brain. If we have a lot of junk over one side, it pulls people's attention, so, have a balance on either side – if you have your flipchart on one side, have your projector on the other. If you've got two trainers, you have two chairs. There's some central point. So, if you're going to be interviewing, one of the suggestions I'd make is to think about what you can balance around you. Are you going to have a table or a couple of tables? If you can, find a room where you can also balance the things that are behind you – you're going to have a much better focus of attention on what you're doing. If you've got something weird or interesting in one corner, it's going to pull people's attention. So, when you go into a room, go and sit where the audience will be, and ask yourself, 'What can I balance here that will ease their brains?', because what we want to do is make it very easy. We want to have people open, so we don't want them bothered by things. It's amazing what people get bothered by. If there's something that's moving around, shift it!

Neil: One of the things that interviewing studios very often do is give you a boardroom-style table, or a couple of sofas around a coffee table. Do you have any comments or views on that side of the environment?

Roger: Depending on what you're interviewing for, I don't much like boardroom tables, because I think they hide the body language and they prevent a lot of connection that can happen – it always takes longer to build a rapport when you're sitting around a table. In terms of sofas, I think you have to take a view on those, because I don't know about you, but if you're in a room with strangers, do you really like sitting on sofas? Just watch people's reactions. Just watch the way people seat themselves if you think about a doctor's waiting room. Unless they know each other, almost certainly, there's going to be one seat in between one person and the next, so, it's about our own personal comfort. If you want people to be open and you want people to answer your questions in a way that's going to be useful for your research, you're going to need to pay attention to personal space. Certainly, you have to be careful when sitting people on sofas, and, personally, for the most part, I wouldn't do it. I'd want comfortable chairs, I think comfortable chairs rather than sofas are probably the better way to go.

Neil: The work that Hall did on proxemics years ago, I think, is valuable here, and it makes sense, so I think it's good to have something in the book about those more intimate spaces.

Roger: And, I think, the other thing is, what are you going to be asking questions about? How do you need to have people in the room for that?

Neil: And that brings us to lighting and to sound, which we've got quite a lot down about already, so we won't dwell on that. Anything else on environmetics that you would like to talk about?

Roger: If we're going to cover light and sound in other places, probably the main message is balance. Create balance before you sit, and you sit at the centre of that balance, because you're going to get a much better result that way. Then there are all the other things you can consider, such as removing any distracting influences like posters and things that move. Otherwise, it's about creating a rapport and having comfortable lighting.

I have a couple of thoughts on the actual interview process, because that's on our list of things to talk about, and I do re-emphasise that, from the normal dynamics of market research, we have either got a group of strangers coming to our building, hotel, viewing studio or whatever, or we're invading their territory, which is going to their homes or their work or their place of social activity. In all senses, as you've been saying about the environmetics thing, we want, very much, to create a feeling of comfort, relaxation, harmony and rapport in them. They're the important part. It's less important how we feel about it. We can control our state. At least we hope we can! So it is very important that the whole atmosphere and comfort zone for them is as good as it can possibly be. That being so, I think the need to create the feeling of warmth and friendliness and relaxation is contributed to hugely by welcoming them with a smile and lots of open gestures, and not creating too many problems for them.

I think the first thing you should do is let people know what's going on. There's nothing worse than sitting in a room waiting for something to happen and not knowing quite what's going on. You need to frame in people's minds what the process is going to be, how long they're going to be there, what the expected outcome is, what you might want them to do, where it's going to take place, who they're going to be with. All of those things can be done very simply in just a few minutes, and will serve to relax and take away the unknowns. The only things we tend to fear are the things we don't know about, so if you can, whatever you do, in terms of interviewing, take away the unknowns. Just mention them, so that people have an internal representation of what it's going to be like when they come from the waiting room into the studio, especially if it's a studio where people haven't been before, or maybe it's a studio that's been mocked up in a hotel or somewhere. If people know what to expect, it's going to make things much easier for you.

Neil: They're in there, visually. If their mind is still wondering what they're going to be doing when they're sitting down and you're asking them questions, you've already lost rapport.

Roger: Indeed, and just as we would do in a meeting or a presentation, cover all bases, not least of all as a starting point. 'Some of you know what market research is about. Some of you are really unsure. Some of you have maybe heard of it by name.' Then go into a big picture of what's going on, and then you can move into, maybe, a few questions that might elicit their visual, auditory or kinaesthetic preferences for your benefit. Then ease into the detailed questioning of what you need to know, and you may, with the right framework, be able to dispense with the topic guides, so that you can actually observe the body language whenever somebody's asking a question or answering a question you've asked. You might want to be able to move slightly into rapport with that person so that you keep the connection, or at least make a connection with that person. We're never very forthcoming as human beings if we haven't made a connection with the person that's asking us a question.

Neil: And I would suggest that one of the first things we do is give a little bit of information about ourselves, so I always tell people who I am. 'I've got two kids and a Labrador; I work in Bristol,' whatever.

Roger: Personal reveal is always important in terms of people coming to know the person rather than the robot – the functional person sitting in front of you.

Neil: We maybe should talk about perceptual positions. Maybe from what you know of market research, you could just give us a little flavour of perceptual positions in interviewing.

Roger: There are a couple of things about perceptual positions. Well, let's talk about body position anyway. One of the things that people often do is get stuck if they're sitting in one place for too long. If you find the answers to your questions are drying up or you're not getting the things that you need, one of the things that you might think about doing is having a strategy to move people around a little bit – give them a two-minute break, have them stretch and walk around – simply changing the physiology can bring them back or bring their brains back on line with the process. This is probably the quickest and best way to do that, so you might have your stimulus material sited around the room, so that people actually have to get up and move to it, rather than by your chair, where you simply hold it up and everybody sits in the same positions.

So, that's about position and how to use people's bodies to keep their mental processes running, and, you know, think about it yourself, if you sit down for two hours, eventually, the brain gets tired, so getting up and moving around is a really good thing. As part of the interview process, we would suggest from our knowledge of NLP that, in order to keep things flowing and keep people's minds working effectively, you have some sort of strategy for moving people around in the hour that they're with you – find at least three spaces for people to get up. If you have them stitched in one place for an hour, by the time they're half an hour in, their brains won't be delivering, so, every 20 minutes, a little bit of another activity works wonders – you'll get fresh brains back every time, and you'll get much better quality research. In terms of perceptual positions, sometimes you might want to have people give their own views of the product or the service. Sometimes it might be useful to stimulate them to step into somebody else's shoes and imagine what somebody else might think about it. Yet again, a third place to go is to step them out and have them take a view of an observer. These three views can be very important.

There's a chap called Gregory Bateson, who says there's no inherent wisdom in one point of view, and, after all, what you're trying to do in qualitative research is to get multiple points of view from different people. Each individual can also have their own multiple points of view, which may be useful for you to access, so you can work this as a group exercise or you can work it as an individual thing. There are more details in the book of how you might do that. So, that would be just an idea of how to use perceptual positions.

Neil: Also, I use archetypes in a spatial tense – getting people to stand on large sheets of paper with different archetype assistance.

Roger: You mean, 'What would King Kong think of this organic shampoo?'

Neil: Yes, or what would Richard Branson do as opposed to Tony Blair, as opposed to George Bush, as opposed to whoever else you may wish to be on your 'help team'.

Roger: That's really taking second position in specific characters, so, again, it's using perceptual positions in quite an interesting way.

Neil: Yes, and also, it has a function of getting them to move physically, which is great for breaking any locked-in state that they may have.

Roger: Indeed it is, yes. Pretty good.

Neil: Well, you've also asked the question, 'How do you get a group of respondents to talk to you?' I think the answer to that is really about all of the rapport-building and the frame-setting and about the environmetics that we've described. And the other way is how you allow your questions to flow.

Roger: Yes. People don't naturally, necessarily think in the small details that you want straight away, and sometimes a jump from walking along the street thinking about what they're going to cook for tea tonight to answering detailed questions on the number of currants in a chocolate bar might need a little pacing, so one of the suggestions that I would make is that you start again with the big picture, so that people have a context. So, often, in order to make judgements and decisions and opinions, we need a context. Without a context, you'll find that the questions and the quality of the answers to your questions will be poor. That's the big picture. Then we can move into the detail.

GLOSSARY

Accessing Cues	Subtle behaviours that will help to trigger and indicate which representational system a person is using to think with. Typical accessing cues include eye movements, voice tone, tempo, body posture, gestures and breathing patterns. People also use accessing cues to 'read' another person's behaviours. We can use this information to develop rapport by matching the person's behaviour.
Affiliating	The need of human beings to affiliate with each other. One of the metaprograms which indicates what motivates a person.
Ambiguity	The use of language that is vague or ambiguous. Language that is ambiguous is also abstract (as opposed to specific). Ambiguous language can be used in therapy as a form of mild hypnosis (or

in hypnotherapy per se), during the sales or meeting processes to make your ideas more easily understood.

Analogue
Having shades of meaning, as opposed to digital, which has discrete (on/off) meaning. As in an analogue watch (a watch with minute and hour hands).

Anchor
The process of associating an internal response with some external trigger (similar to classical conditioning), so that the response may be quickly, and sometimes covertly, reaccessed. Anchoring can be visual (as with specific hand gestures), auditory (by using specific words and voice tone) and kinaesthetic (as when touching an arm or laying a hand on someone's shoulder). Criteria for anchoring: (a) intensity or purity of experience; (b) timing – at peak of experience; (c) accuracy of replication of anchor.

Associated
As in a memory, looking through your own eyes, hearing what you heard and feeling the feelings as if you were actually there. This is called the associated state.

Attitude
A collection of values and beliefs around a certain subject.

Auditory
Relating to hearing or the sense of hearing.

Away From
A meta-program – when a person's preference is to move in the opposite direction from what they don't want,

as opposed to towards what they do want. 'I don't want a 9 to 5 job.'

Behaviour
The specific physical actions and re-actions through which we interact with the people and environment around us.

Behavioural Flexibility
The ability to vary one's own behaviour in order to elicit or secure a response from another person. Behavioural flexibility can refer to the development of an entire range of responses to any given stimulus as opposed to having habitual, and therefore limiting, responses, which would inhibit performance potential.

Beliefs
The generalisations we make about ourselves, others and the world, and our operating principles in it. Beliefs act as self-fulfilling prophecies that influence all our behaviours. Richard Bandler and John Grinder state: 'Behaviour is organised around beliefs. As long as you can fit a behaviour into some-one's belief system, you can get him to do anything, or stop him from doing anything. A belief tends to be much more universal and categorical than an understanding. When you already have a belief, there's no room for a new one unless you weaken the old belief first.'

Break State
When someone 'breaks state', they are suddenly interrupting their current state and moving into a different one. Typi-cally, a break state is used to pull

someone out of an unresourceful state into a neutral one, so that they are more easily able to do what is required to achieve their outcome.

Calibration
The process of learning to read another person's unconscious, nonverbal responses in an ongoing interaction by pairing observable behavioural cues with a specific internal response. A very important first step in most NLP processes is to calibrate the problem state. That is, how is your client's body posture, where do the eyes go, how is the breathing, skin colour, voice tone etc? Knowing how the problem state looks, you have a reference point for measuring the success of your intervention.

Capability
Mastery over an entire group of behaviours. Capabilities form the development of a mental map, allowing us to select and organise groups of individual behaviours. In NLP, these mental maps take the form of cognitive strategies and meta-programs.

Chunking
Organising or breaking down some experience into bigger or smaller pieces. Chunking up involves moving to a larger, more abstract level of information. Chunking down involves moving to a more specific and concrete level of information. Chunking laterally involves finding other examples at the same level of information.

Congruence	When all of a person's internal beliefs, strategies and behaviours are fully in agreement and oriented towards securing a desired outcome. Words, voice and body language give the same message.
Conscious Competence	The third stage of the learning cycle, in which full conscious attention is still on carrying out an activity. The skill is not yet fully integrated and habitual.
Conscious Incompetence	The second stage of the learning cycle, in which conscious attention is on the task and the results are variable. This is the stage when the learning rate is the greatest.
Cross-Over Mirroring/ Matching	Matching a person's body language with a different type of movement, e.g. tapping your foot in time to their speech rhythm.
Deep Structure	The sensory maps (both conscious and unconscious) that people use to organise and guide their behaviour.
Deletion	One of the three universals of human modelling. The process by which selected portions of the world are excluded from the representation created by the person. Within language systems, deletion is a transformational process in which portions of the deep structure are removed and, therefore, do not appear in the surface structure representation.
Desired Outcome	This is the end result or goal that the person is trying to bring about at any

particular time. It could be a large, long-range goal ('rule the world'), or a smaller, short-term one ('have a five-minute relaxing break').

Digital
Having a discrete (on/off) meaning, as opposed to analogue, which has shades of meaning.

Dissociation
As in a memory, for example, looking at your body in the picture from the outside, so that you do not have the feelings you would have if you were actually there.

Distortion
One of the three universals of human modelling. The process by which the relationships that hold among the parts of the model are represented differently from the relationships they are supposed to represent. One of the most common examples of distortion in modelling is the representation of a process by an event. Within language systems, this is called normalisation.

Dovetailing Outcomes
The process of fitting together different outcomes, optimising solutions. The basis of win–win negotiations.

Down-Time
As in having all sensory input channels turned inward, so that there are no chunks of attention available for outward attention.

Ecology
The study of the consequences and effects of individual actions on the larger system. In an individual, the study of the consequences and effects

of individual components of change-work on the bigger picture of the whole individual. In all NLP processes, an ecology check is incorporated, assuring harmony.

Elicitation The act of discovery and detection of certain internal processes.

Epistemology The study of how we know what we know.

Eye Accessing Cues Movements of the eyes in certain directions which indicate visual, auditory or kinaesthetic thinking. Please note, there is individual variance, and readily available information is not accessed, thus there is no detectable eye movement.

Frame A context or way of perceiving something, as in outcome frame, rapport frame, backtrack frame, out frame, etc.

Future Pacing The process of mentally rehearsing and anchoring changes in oneself in a future situation, in order to help ensure that the desired behaviour will occur naturally and automatically.

Generalisation One of the three universals of human modelling. The process by which a specific experience comes to represent the entire category of which it is a member.

Gestalt A collection of memories, where the memories are linked together or grouped together around a certain subject.

Gustatory Relating to the sense of taste.

Hierarchy	An organisation of things or ideas where the more important ideas are given a ranking based upon their importance.
Identity	Our sense of who we are. Our sense of identity organises our beliefs, capabilities and behaviours into a single system.
Impasse	A smoke screen. When a person draws a blank or gets confused as you are working on an issue with them.
Incongruence	The state of having reservations, not being totally committed to an outcome. The internal conflict will be expressed in the person's behaviour.
Installation	The process of facilitating the acquisition of a new strategy or behaviour. A new strategy may be installed through any of the NLP skills or techniques and/or a combination thereof (e.g. anchoring, accessing cues, metaphor and future pacing).
Intention	The purpose or desired outcome of any behaviour.
Interjects	Subconscious rules that control behaviour.
Internal Representation	Patterns of information we create and store in our minds in combinations of images, sounds, feelings, smells and tastes. The way we store and encode our memories in representational systems and their submodalities.
Intuition	Consistent judgements made by people (typically, without an explanation of how these judgements are made).

Within language systems, the ability of native speakers to make consistent judgements about the well-formedness of sentences in their language.

Kinaesthetic Relating to body sensations. In NLP, the term kinaesthetic is used to encompass all kinds of feelings, including tactile, visceral and psychomotor.

Leading Changing your own behaviours with enough rapport for the other person to follow. Pacing and leading is an important part of NLP. You should enter the client's world and lead them to reach the appropriate conclusions themselves for achieving the changes desired.

Lead System The preferred representational system (visual, auditory, kinaesthetic) that finds stored information to input into consciousness.

Learning The process of getting knowledge, skills, experience or values by study, experience or training.

Learning Cycle Stages of learning to build habitual skills –
1. Unconscious incompetence.
2. Conscious incompetence.
3. Conscious competence.
4. Unconscious competence.

Learning Strategies Sequences of images, sounds and feelings that lead to learning.

Learning Styles There are many different ways of assessing learning styles. We may prefer to learn via our visual, auditory or kinaesthetic sense or a combination. Kolb identified four types of learners in the population – 35% are Divergers (why?), 22% are Assimilators (what?), 18% are Convergers (how?) and 25% Accommodators (what if?). Each type is driven to access information differently by answering the question in brackets. If these questions are not answered, effective learning does not take place.

Logical Levels

An internal hierarchy in which each level is progressively more psychologically encompassing and impactful.

Loop

The inappropriate, usually compulsive, repetition of a unit of behaviour.

Map of Reality

Each person's unique representation of the world, built from his or her individual perceptions and experiences. Also called the model of the world.

Matching

Adopting parts of another person's behaviour for the purpose of enhancing rapport.

Meta

Derived from Greek, meaning over or beyond.

Meta-cognition

Knowing about knowing: having a skill and the knowledge about it to explain how you do it.

Meta-message

A message about a message. Your non-verbal behaviour is constantly giving people meta-messages about you and the information you are providing. A meta-message is a higher level message about:

1. The type of message being sent.
2. The state/status of the messenger.
3. The state/status of the receiver.
4. The context in which the message is being sent.

Meta-model   A model developed by John Grinder and Richard Bandler that identifies categories of language patterns that can be problematic or ambiguous.

Metaphor   The process of thinking about one situation or phenomenon as something else, i.e. stories, parables and analogies. Metaphors are often used to complement the changes that a person is going through during personal development. A metaphor can also make an idea more easily understood.

Meta-position   The process of separating yourself from a system in order to gain information – 'The fly on the wall'.

Meta-program   A level of mental programming that determines how we sort, orient to and chunk our experiences. A process by which one sorts through multiple generalisations simultaneously. As such, meta-programs control how and when a person will engage in any set of strategies in a given context.

Milton Model   The inverse of the meta-model, using artfully vague language patterns to pace another person's experience and access unconscious resources. Based on the language used by Milton H. Erickson MD.

Mind-Reading	In NLP terms, this refers not to the idea of telepathy, but to the assumptions that one sometimes makes about other people's thoughts or opinions, without the other person specifying them. Typically, an individual might say 'I know my boss doesn't like me, because . . .'
Mirroring	Matching portions of another person's behaviour in order to gain rapport. It is an effect that occurs naturally in everyday communication, and can be used to increase the level of rapport felt between people.
Mismatching	Adopting different patterns of behaviour to another person, breaking rapport for the purpose of redirecting, interrupting or terminating a meeting or conversation.
Modal Operator	This is a term from the net model, which refers to those words (in English) that speak of possibility or necessity, e.g. can, should, would, will and their negatives.
Model	A practical description of how something works, the purpose of which is to be useful.
Model of the World	A person's internal representation about the condition of the world.
Modelling	The act of creating a calculus which describes a given system. The process of observing and mapping the successful behaviours of other people. In NLP, this involves profiling behaviours/physiology, beliefs and values, internal states and strategies.

Multiple Description	The process of describing the same thing from different viewpoints.
Neuro-Linguistic Programming (NLP)	The study of the structure of subjective experience and what can be calculated from that. A behavioural model and set of explicit skills and techniques founded by John Grinder and Richard Bandler in 1975. Defined as the study of the structure of subjective experience. NLP studies the patterns or 'programming' created by the interactions among the brain (neuro), language (linguistic) and the body that produce both effective and ineffective behaviour. The skills and techniques were derived by observing the patterns of excellence in experts from diverse fields of professional communication, including psychotherapy, business, hypnosis, law and education.
Neuro-Logical Levels	This is a model put forward by Robert Dilts for organising the elements that make up human psychology. The levels are:

1. Spiritual
2. Identity
3. Beliefs and values
4. Capabilities
5. Behaviour
6. Environment.

Nonverbal	Without words. Usually referring to the analogue portion of our behaviour, such as tone of voice or other external behaviour.

Olfactory	Relating to smell or the sense of smell.
Open Frame	An opportunity for anyone to raise any comments or questions about anything.
Outcomes	Goals or desired states that a person or organisation aspires to achieve.
Out Framing	Setting a frame that excludes one or more areas, e.g. possible objections. 'I will answer any question, except questions about the seating arrangements.' This is a very important concept in meetings and presentations.
Overlap	Using one representational system to gain access to another; for example, picturing a scene and then hearing the sounds in it.
Pacing	A method used by communicators to quickly establish rapport by matching certain aspects of their behaviour and/ or experience to those of the person with whom they are communicating – matching or mirroring of behaviour.
Perceptual Filters	Our unique combinations of values, beliefs, meta-programs, senses and language that shape our model of the world.
Perceptual Position	A particular perspective or point of view. In NLP, there are three basic positions one can take in perceiving a particular experience. First position involves experiencing something through our own eyes associated in a first person point of view. Second position

involves experiencing something as if we were in another person's shoes. Third position involves standing back and perceiving the relationship between ourselves and others from a dissociated perspective. Along with the idea of perceptual positions is the idea that we learn more when we are able to consider the same situation from different positions.

Physiology   To do with the physical part of a person.

Polarity   The mind compares sensory information to stored models or ideas of how reality has been experienced and organised previously. Upon receiving a sensory impression, the mind matches the impression to the stored images. If the individual initially notices the aspects that match the image, this is called a positive responder. If the person notices a mismatch initially, this is called a negative or polarity response. (There is also the possibility of a neutral response if the stimulus has no kinaesthetic value to the person.) Polarity responders tend to be called reactive, argumentative or negative personalities if the predominant pattern is to initially notice what is wrong in comparison to their ideal images. These three patterns are learned and can be changed from any one of the three to another mode, according to the desired effect.

Predicates	Process words (like verbs, adverbs and adjectives) that a person selects to describe a subject. Predicates are used in NLP to identify which representational system a person is using to process information (e.g. 'I see what you mean', 'That rings a bell').
Preferred (Primary) System	The representational system that an individual typically uses most to think consciously and organise his or her experience.
Presupposition	A basic underlying assumption which is necessary for a representation to make sense. Within language systems, a sentence which must be true for some other sentence to make sense. Mastery of presuppositions is one of the keys to NLP excellence.
Process and Content	Content is what is done, whereas process is about how it is done. What you say is content and how you say it is process. For example, the swish pattern works with smoking, over-eating, nail-biting and a host of other habits, because it works not with the behaviour itself but with the way in which an individual is compelled to do the behaviour.
Rapport	The presence of trust, harmony and cooperation in a relationship. A relationship or state of having trust and mutual responsiveness with others. Rapport happens naturally, and one of the benefits of NLP is learning how to

develop it with consciousness and deliberation, quickly and easily. Breaking rapport can also be useful in some circumstances. Rapport can be easily seen when two people's behaviours match each other – this is often accompanied by an internal sense of mutual liking and sympathy/understanding.

Reframing   A process used in NLP through which a problematic behaviour is separated from the positive intention of the internal program or 'part' that is responsible for the behaviour. New choices or behaviour are established that satisfy the same positive intention but don't have the problematic byproducts.

Representational Systems   The five senses: seeing, hearing, touching (feeling), smelling and tasting.

Representational System Primacy   The systematic use of one sense over the others to process and organise in a given context. The primary representational system will determine many personality traits as well as learning capabilities.

Requisite Variety   Flexibility of thought and behaviour. An ability to make changes on the way to an outcome/goal. This term originates from the Law of Requisite Variety, which originated in cybernetics and systems thinking. In summary, it means that whomever has the greatest flexibility in behaviour will have the greatest influence over any situation they are in.

Resourceful State	The total neurological and physiological experience when a person feels resourceful.
Resources	Any means that can be brought to bear to achieve an outcome: physiology, states, thought, strategies, experiences, people, events or possessions.
Secondary Gain	Where some seemingly negative or problematic behaviour actually carries out some positive function at some other level. For example, smoking may help a person to relax or help them fit a particular self-image. Not purely an NLP term, this refers to the situation where some apparently negative or problematic behaviour results in some positive end result in some way. This makes the problematic behaviour more likely to continue.
Second Position	Seeing the world from another person's point of view and so understanding their reality.
Sensory Acuity	The process of learning to make finer and more useful distinctions about the sense information we get from the world. One of the benefits that come from studying NLP is the realisation that so much more is going on out there than we are normally aware of.
Sensory-based Description	Information that is directly observable and verifiable by the senses. It is the difference between 'The lips are pulled taut, some parts of her teeth are showing and the edges of her mouth are higher

than the main line of her mouth' and 'She's happy' – which is an interpretation.

Softeners

Lessen the impact of a direct question by softening voice tone or preamble, such as 'Would you be willing to tell me . . . ?'

Spatial Anchoring

This is a term referring to the use of physical location as an anchor. For example, an individual might associate a particular state with a particular location. Later, when they want instantly to access that state, they can make it much easier and more effective by stepping into that location. Spatial anchoring is often used to separate different states cleanly, so that the individual can more effectively deal with each state as a distinct entity. Also called psychogeography.

State

The total ongoing mental and physical conditions from which a person is acting. The state we are in affects our capabilities and interpretation of experience. The individual will respond to stimuli differently, depending upon the state they are in at a particular time. Also, the information that the person receives from the outside world will be filtered according to the state they are in, resulting in a different perception of what is happening. This difference can be empowering or disempowering.

Stimulus–Response	An association between an experience and a subsequent so-called reaction; the natural learning process Ivan P. Pavlov demonstrated when he correlated the ringing of a bell to the secretion of saliva in dogs.
Strategy	A set of explicit mental and behavioural steps used to achieve a specific outcome. In NLP, the most important aspect of a strategy is the representational systems used to carry out the specific steps.
Submodalities	The special sensory qualities perceived by each of the five senses. For example, visual submodalities include colour, shape, movement, brightness, depth, etc., auditory submodalities include volume, pitch, tempo, etc., and kinaesthetic submodalities include pressure, temperature, texture, location, etc. Submodalities are used in a large number of techniques in NLP – by changing the submodalities of a memory or thought, we can change the effect it has on us.
Surface Structure	An utterance. The words or language used to describe or stand for the actual primary sensory representations stored in the brain.
Swish Pattern	A generative NLP submodality process that programs your brain to go in a new direction. It is very effective in changing habits or unwanted behaviours into new constructive ones.
Synesthesia	The process of overlap between representational systems, characterised by

phenomena like see–feel circuits, in which a person derives feelings from what they see, and hear–feel circuits, in which a person gets feelings from what they hear.

Systemic   To do with systems, looking at relationships and consequences over time and space rather than linear cause and effect.

Third Position   When you observe yourself and others.

Timeline   The way we store pictures, sounds and feelings of our past, present and future. This refers to the unconscious method we have for storing our memories and our plans or goals for the future. The assumption is made that if we can differentiate between today, last Thursday and our next birthday, then we must have some way of sorting time in our minds; the only question is how?

Trance   An altered state with an inward focus of attention on a few stimuli.

Transderivational Search   The act of locating meaning(s) which may not be explicit or implicit in a surface structure. When a person is asked to 'go inside and think of a time when . . .', they will typically do a transderivational search, i.e. search their memories/beliefs/wishes, etc. for an event which matches the meaning of that phrase.

Translating   Connecting the meaning of one representation to the same meaning in another representation.

Up–Time	This is the opposite of down–time, and is where the individual is paying attention to what is going on external to them, in their environment, and not to their internal processes.
Utilisation	A technique or approach in which a person's specific strategy or pattern of behaviour is paced or matched in order to influence the person's response.
Values	Values are the things that are important to you – not objects or people, but experiences and feelings, such as learning, health, wisdom, respect. They are nonphysical qualities that we seek to have more of in our lives.
Visual	Relating to sight or the sense of sight.
Well–formed Conditions	In NLP, a particular outcome is well-formed when it is:

1. Stated in positives
2. Initiated and maintained by the individual
3. Ecological – maintains the quality of all rapport systems
4. Testable in experience – sensorybased.

Well–formed Outcome	A well-formed outcome is an outcome which meets the following criteria:

1. *Positive* – ensure that the goal is what you want, not what you don't want.
2. *Own-Part* – ensure that the goal can be achieved and maintained by you, without any necessary intervention by others or by luck.

3. *Specific* – ensure goal is as specific as possible. What? Where? How? When?

4. *Evidence* – define how you will know when you have achieved your goal, in terms of what you will see, hear, feel, smell or taste when it is completed.

5. *Ecology* – ensure that the goal will maintain the positive byproducts of your current situation, and will not create any unwanted byproducts.

REFERENCES

Hoskin, F. (2003) *Do We Really Understand How People Think?* Paper presented at the QRCA/AQR conference, Lisbon.

Mehrabian, A. (1971) *Silent Messages*. Wadsworth, Belmont, California.

Mehrabian, A. (1972) *Nonverbal Communication*. Aldine-Atherton, Chicago, Illinois.

Miller, G. (1956) 'The Magical Number Seven Plus or Minus Two: Some Limits on Our Capacity to Process Information', *Psychological Review*, **63**, 81–97.

Rossi, E.L. (1986) *Psychobiology of Mind–Body Healing*. W.W. Norton, New York.

Russell, B. (1902) *The Principles of Mathematics*.

INDEX

Index compiled by Terry Halliday